OPINIONS OF
OLIVER ALLSTON

VAN WYCK BROOKS
HAS WRITTEN:

ON LITERATURE TODAY
NEW ENGLAND: INDIAN SUMMER
THE FLOWERING OF NEW ENGLAND
THE LIFE OF EMERSON
THE ORDEAL OF MARK TWAIN
THE PILGRIMAGE OF HENRY JAMES
EMERSON AND OTHERS
THREE ESSAYS ON AMERICA
AMERICA'S COMING-OF-AGE
LETTERS AND LEADERSHIP
THE LITERARY LIFE IN AMERICA
SKETCHES IN CRITICISM

Published by
E. P. DUTTON & CO., INC.

OPINIONS OF OLIVER ALLSTON

BY

VAN WYCK BROOKS

1941
NEW YORK
E. P. DUTTON & CO., INC.

Portions of this book have appeared in *The New Republic,* copyright 1941 by Editorial Publications, Inc., New York, N. Y., and *The Yale Review,* copyright 1941 by The Yale University Press, Inc.

AMERICAN BOOK–STRATFORD PRESS, INC., NEW YORK

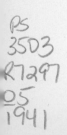

To
EDWARD SHELDON

CONTENTS

CONTENTS

OPINIONS OF
OLIVER ALLSTON

CHAPTER I

ALLSTON AND HIS JOURNALS

M Y FRIEND Oliver Allston, who died last
year in his early fifties, was a literary man of
some distinction. A few of my readers, at least, will
remember his name. He had published half a dozen
books, collections of critical essays, which had a certain point of view in common, and I am not alone
among his friends in feeling that, if he had lived a
little longer, he might have made some impression
on the mind of his time. Apparently, this was not to
be, although I doubt if Allston would have cared
very much. He used to quote a phrase from the
Bhagavad-Gita, "Let the motive for action be in the
action itself and not in the event." That a man's
opinions might have consequences, that literature itself had consequences of a very important kind, was
almost the first of his convictions, but he also felt
that a writer should disregard them. Thus he agreed
with Renan's paradox, "To be able to think freely,
one must feel that what one writes will have no consequences." Allston liked to think, as he liked to
write, and he felt that, in so far as he told the truth,
his writings would have effects, and good effects, not
because they were his but because they were true. In
this he was impersonal and fatalistic. He probably

did not care a button whether he impressed his age or not.

The reader may suppose that, in saying this, I am making exalted claims for Allston. I do not profess to have understood him, nor can I say with assurance that he understood himself. Of this I am certain, however,—Allston did not feel he was unique. He followed the lines of a well-known type, which has had countless exemplars. This type is composed of those who enjoy the use of their minds, and he said there was no pleasure in thinking or writing if one had ulterior motives. "Those who think 'for effect,' or who write to 'score,'" he notes in one of his journals, "do not know what they are missing." In saying this, he expressed a commonplace of writers and artists; and, in fact, there was nothing out of the way about him except that he was fortunate and happy. So, at least, he felt, as he also felt that his happy fortune was wholly the result of circumstances. He quoted more than once a sentence from the Koran, "Paradise lies in the shadow of swords;" and he underscored, in his copy of Melville's *Pierre,* the phrase, "Deprived of joy, I feel I should find cause for deadly feuds with things invisible." That he was happy in any sense seemed to him uncommon, and he felt that his position had its perils in an age that was unfortunate and unhappy. That all the happy men are Pharisees was a fixed idea with his contemporaries, and it sometimes seemed to Allston that the sinners had almost a monopoly of virtue. That, as a happy man, he must be pharisaical seemed to be the logic of the situation.

When Allston died, he left me his books and pa-

pers. Among the latter were a set of journals, a
dozen volumes bound in stout grey canvas. In these
he had formed the habit of writing down the thoughts
or impressions of the moment which he said he had
"caught by wing or tail." Forster relates that Dickens
began to keep a notebook at forty-three. So it was
with Allston, who had made sporadic attempts at
journalizing during his earlier life. He acquired the
habit at forty-five. That it sharpened his consciousness of the world about him was evident from the
first; but he said he wished to understand himself,
and he found that keeping a journal was good for
this. He followed an old American custom, for
Washington Irving and all the Adamses, Hawthorne, Thoreau and Emerson were inveterate
journalizers. He noted what D. H. Lawrence said
about these classic American writers, that they had
reached a pitch of consciousness beyond the "furthest
frenzies" of the French. Lawrence did not like this
"verge," much as it surprised him; but Allston disliked the opposite even more. He had no love of the
self-conscious, and he believed in the unconscious;
but, having what he called a daylight mind, he could
not like Lawrence's "nocturnal." How could one
have enough objective observation? And why was
there a necessary conflict between the conscious mind
and the unconscious? As long as the conscious mind
remained objective, the unconscious flourished all
the better. So it seemed to Allston, and, in journalizing, his motives were the same as Thoreau's and
Hawthorne's. They were the classical motives of
knowing oneself and knowing the world about one.
Allston liked to study himself, when more exciting

subjects were not at hand, and sometimes to see himself correctly struck him as far from easy. Thus he remarks, in one of the volumes, "It is said to be courageous to be frank about oneself. On the contrary, it only requires talent, but it requires talent of a high order."

When his journal was not available, he sometimes jotted his thoughts on scraps of paper. That he often did so in a state of excitement, I gather from this remark, "It is related of Mendelssohn that one of his pupils used to get him up in the morning by seating himself at the piano, in the room under Mendelssohn's bedroom, and playing an unresolved chord, with his foot on the loud pedal. This was too much for Mendelssohn, who liked to batten under the counterpane. He had to jump out of bed and run downstairs, to resolve the chord. My mind works the same way. I had a beautiful chord to resolve this morning." I have found several envelopes filled with these notes, apparently unrelated to one another, and, glancing them over, with his journals, together with some of his letters, and the pencillings on the margins of his books, I have wondered if they might not interest others. Allston liked to read short essays, letters, maxims, *pensées*. He notes a remark of Francis Grierson, whom he had known in London, "It is impossible for an essay to be too short;" and perhaps there are other readers who share this taste. In printing the present selection, my aim has been to arrange the notes to give Allston's point of view in outline. He had scarcely made this clear in his books. I think he had in mind a longer work in which he hoped to do so, but there are few evidences among his papers that he had taken this in hand. Perhaps he felt as Gibbon felt, about the *Decline and Fall,* six years after he had begun to plan it, when he still contemplated it "at an awful distance." His habits of note-taking and procrastination seem to have won the day.

Let me add a few remarks of a personal nature. Allston had travelled in his youth. He had lived for about five years, at various times, in England, France, Germany and elsewhere. In later years, he had taken long journeys through the United States. He was a New Yorker, if not by birth, at least by long inheritance. Both of his grandfathers were Vermonters, but both of them had married New York women. It was an axiom with him that American mothers are always more potent as parents than American fathers; and he instanced this by saying once that the New Englandism of his two grandfathers had been wholly sunk and subjugated in the New Yorkism of his two grandmothers. Born in a suburb of New York, he had continued to live in the metropolitan area, although on one of its remotest fringes. He had spent some years in the city itself, the birthplace of his father, and he wished not to lose his connection with it; but the life he chose was a village life, and he had vehement opinions on the subject of city-living and country-living. "I am full of prejudices," he said, "but they are all made of paper, and anyone can jump through them as easily as a dog jumps through a paper ring at the circus." He flattered his reasonableness in this remark, for he detested the city. "Every day," he writes, "I grow more and more to think of city-people as cheese-mites, as mere infusoria. One cannot know what respect is unless one learns it in the country." He speaks of "literary cocktail-parties for the bolstering of invalid reputations" as the chief preoccupation of the New York writers; and his dislike of "bigness" in all its forms expresses itself in the following note: "I hope to see all the skyscrapers filled with bats. I wish a cloud of demons would fly through the air and gather about the Empire State Building and pluck it out of the ground and carry it off and drop it in the Atlantic near the spot where the Titanic lies. I suggest a possible use for the Normandie and all the other super-ships, to carry off the skyscrapers to anyone who wants them in Europe. I should think Mussolini might find them handy for a bigger and better Venice." Allston did not write in a whimsical spirit. He thought the world would never know peace until it repudiated the power-feelings and all the power-philosophies. "You don't like noise and bloodshed," he writes to a friend. "No, but you like or admire everything that produces noise and bloodshed. If you worship 'big' things, you will worship 'big' men, who want bigger armies to get bigger nations. The admiration of super-ships, Zeppelins and skyscrapers,—that is where the war-business starts. Or shall we say the war-scuffle that has begun already in every mind that likes competitive football on the mass-production scale." Allston thought Americans loved this material grandeur because human grandeur was lacking in their minds. For the rest, he had New York in mind in writing, "There is such a thing as dying from over-stimulation. Whatever is worth discovering in my own mind only comes to the surface among quiet conditions, in which one thought grows beside another and I have time to compare and reflect."

As a matter of fact, as Allston grew older, he felt that it mattered little where one lived, so long as one kept in touch with certain conditions. This latter feeling determined his other feeling about the "regional" movements, and also about "expatriation," in the special case of Americans, as I shall show. He liked to be alone much of the time, but he knew that most critics had thriven in cities, and he seems to have set this down as a personal trait. Or was it a trait that he thought Americans ought to cultivate, perhaps much more than other people? That they did not know how to be alone was one of his frequent complaints; and he said that, with Americans, solitude too often meant neurosis,—"the devil that lies in wait for the improperly employed." As for himself, he remarks, "I like to see a great many people, nor would I be human if I did not like the *digito monstrari*. I like both these things, but I do not love them. What I love is what the mole loves, who carries on his enthralling toils in the dark hallways of a narrow house. Give the mole wings, let him become a bat, and he would still rejoice in the cover of darkness and in the midnight cave." This is a little rhetorical, for he liked a verbal flourish now and then. He said he worked best on dark and rainy days; but, in point of fact, he loved the sunlight and always got up early in the morning. As for country living and country habits, they suited his nervous temperament, for he could not stand late hours or exciting parties, and he found the bourgeois regi-

men the best for work. Concerning one of these
habits, he quoted Professor Fortinbras, "My evening
visitors, if they cannot see the clock, should find the
time in my face. As soon as it is nine, I begin to
curse them with internal execrations that are minute-
guns." And yet he agreed with the professor, "The
devil take half-hospitalities." Allston, I must add,
quoted so much that I said to him once, impatiently,
"Your philosophy is entirely made up of quotations."
(He had a special notebook in which he kept them.)
He answered, "You are right. So it is; and it's a
juvenile trait. But let me give you another. I should
like to have cut on my tombstone Pope's phrase
about Dryden, 'He was not a very genteel man, he
was intimate with none but poetical men.'" And this,
in fact, well described Allston's place among his
fellow-beings.

A word about Allston's appearance, which corre-
sponded to his occupation. He was "of middle
height, inclined to stoutness," which he said was the
recipe for critics; for, if one read the lives of the
critics, from Lessing to Sainte-Beuve, or from
Brandes to Croce, or, for the matter of that, from
Lowell to Mencken, to Paul Rosenfeld and Edmund
Wilson, one almost always found they were shortish
and stocky. In a panic fear of growing fat,—as on
one occasion when he discovered that his waist was
two inches larger than Daniel Webster's,—he sometimes indulged in an orgy of dieting. Once he pinned
up on his study wall, as a counsel of perfection, the
well-known Athenian menu, "Three or four olives,
a bit of garlic and the head of a fish." However, he
found that his figure, reduced as it might be to the

utmost thinness, always reassumed the stocky shape, and he came to look on this as an act of fate. He felt that it expressed an intention of nature, that he had been born to be a critic,—he had never wished to be anything else,—and that to fight too much with his stoutness and shortness was to quarrel with his destiny in other respects. Shall I speak of his complexion and his features, his whims and his crotchets, sartorial and tonsorial, for example? His love of the "forsythia" moustache, in which he would have liked to follow Nietzsche, if it had not proved to be anti-social? His liking for the "Polish aviator" haircut? His preference for petunias and zinnias in the matter of flowers? It is enough to say that Allston had his share of the usual absurdities of writers.

If I do not dwell on these traits, if I leave the picture somewhat vague, it is because Allston would have preferred it. That he enjoyed his obscurity will be apparent to those who read his notes. I think he looked upon this as a personal foible, but one that was characteristic of his countrypeople. He often said that Americans, who were supposed to love publicity, were actually, in their love of privacy, unique among the peoples of the world. He did not justify this national trait, and he even thought it led to many abuses, but he said that, because of this trait, foreigners never saw America. All that was real in the country was so hidden and inward, as in Emily Dickinson's poems and Ryder's pictures, that the privacy of the Spaniards in their houses, over which the travellers marvelled,—those who thought they saw the American scene,—was almost a circus beside it. I therefore leave Allston in his "cover of darkness," except in so far as he reveals himself. I must, however, add a word of warning. "I like 'bleak thinking,'" he said, quoting a phrase of his friend Henry Longan Stuart, "I like bleak thinking, as I like austerity in religion, bare, cold churches, where one feels 'alone with the Alone.' I do not like cozy sociable churches, neither do I like cozy thinking. I like the kind of thought that cuts to the bone." If he had not achieved this kind of thinking, it was towards this that he was aiming, and he sometimes achieved it in a measure. I cannot ask anyone to read him who does not share this taste.

CHAPTER II

THE LITERARY LIFE

"**I** WAS a predestined writer," Allston says, "and all the events of literary history were stamped on my mind when I was young. Well I remember the death of Ruskin, which occurred when I was fourteen. I can still see the spot where I picked up the paper announcing his death, the four o'clock in the afternoon sunlight streaming over the empty schoolroom. I can see the cracks in the floor-boards where the sunlight fell, and the woodcuts on the wall of Aldrich and Kipling. I have similar associations with the death of Swinburne. I saw it announced in *The Evening Sun,* which I bought at a newsstand at the corner of Forty-second Street and Broadway, and I see myself diving into the subway to read it. That remembered moment of excitement brings back to me the picture of all Times Square, the Knickerbocker Hotel and the faces on the corner. It is like a flash of lightning recalled from the past. At about that time,—I think it was 1910,—I was absorbed for three days in the story of Tolstoy's flight from home. It was all on the front page of *The Evening Post,* which I read in the old Hofbräu Haus on Broadway. I followed it as I later followed the Battle of the Marne to the moment when Tolstoy was taken from the railway-station. All these events occurred thirty years ago or more, and they are as vividly present to me as the pen that I hold in my hand."

It is true, this seems to indicate a sort of predestination; and Allston, in fact, could scarcely remember a time when he had not meant to be a writer. His intention was fully formed long years before he went to college; and his first act, on leaving college, was to call upon William Dean Howells, to whom he had obtained a letter of introduction. He told me that he had not read Howells's novels,—indeed, at that time, he had little interest in novels,—but he said that he almost died of fear at the thought of meeting this famous writer. I find this note about the meeting:

> It was in 1907. I wished to put to him the preposterous question, how should one set about being a writer. He was living at a hotel in New York, I do not remember which, and he received me in a little anteroom. He had heard this question put hundreds of times, and he knew as well as I that there was no answer. But I remember asking if he thought I should work on a newspaper, the fashionable notion in those days at Harvard. I certainly had no intention of working on a newspaper, unless I could write "editorials;" and this was the way I put the question to Howells. He replied that this was like joining the army with the expectation of being a general at the outset.

Allston never forgot Howells's good sense and kindness, although many years passed before he read Howells's novels. He was forty-five before he knew

how good they were. But, as for the question of
working on a newspaper, this was settled then and
there. It was not for him, and he felt it was not too
good for other writers, as I shall presently show.
Then could he do reviewing? One of his professors,
Irving Babbitt, had kindly given him another letter.
This was to Paul Elmer More, who was editing *The
Nation,* and who gave him one or two books for
brief reviews. But, all this time, he had another
plan in mind, and, without a second thought, he
acted on it. He jumped on a ship and went to London, sailing in the steerage. He gave me an amusing
account of this voyage, during which he had read
Tom Jones, sitting on a coil of rope on the deck,
for there were no chairs in the steerage. He was full
of notions about Grub Street, and he could not wait
to get to London, where he lived more or less in the
slums for a year and a half, in a street off the Strand,
in Pimlico, in Old Compton Street,—over a Soho
restaurant,—and in King's Road, Chelsea. For a
while he rented an old abandoned studio that did
not have a stick of furniture in it. There was nothing
but a model's stand, which he used for a bed, and a
moth-eaten bearskin that served him as a blanket.
He lived for one whole summer on buns and tea, and
once he was so hungry that he fainted. But he said
he had as much fun as an arctic explorer. ("I asked
Commander Stanhouse," Allston writes, "what was
the real motive of arctic explorers. 'Fun, just fun,'
he said. 'They will give you all sorts of other reasons,
but their only real reason is that it's fun.'") Allston
had a job in a literary agency, for which he received
a pound a week, and, when this was raised to thirty

shillings, he thought he was in clover. He also wrote a few articles for magazines and newspapers, and he contrived to write a book. This was his first book. It was published in London, but he wrote it in the country, in a hamlet in Sussex. He lived in a stone farmhouse that had once been a priory, in a big sunny room with casement windows.

I was there five months (he says), in the spring and summer. I dined with Farmer Adams and his wife. Every Sunday we had a boiled leg of mutton, a dish of greens and boiled potatoes and a roll of suet pudding with blackberries in it. On Monday, Tuesday, Wednesday, ditto, ditto. Then on Thursday we had a new boiled leg of mutton, a new dish of greens and a new suet pudding. On Friday and Saturday, ditto, ditto. But, O yes, I should add, it was hot on Sunday and Thursday, and cold on the other five days, and sometimes, instead of blackberries, we had currants.

Allston often spoke to me about these days in England. Later he went back there to teach, though only for a year, 1913–1914. (He was examined for his license by Graham Wallas.) But I am not writing his life; I have set out to record his opinions, and I cannot dwell on these merely personal matters. He returned to New York in the fall of 1908; and, although for two years he taught in California, this remained his centre for the rest of his life. He worked for a while on a dictionary, he worked on an encyclopædia, he edited handbooks and magazines, he made many translations. He was a publisher's reader and a general factotum,—he knew the inside of the many mansions that constitute the writer's hell or heaven. "I was an 'industrious apprentice,'" he says in a note. "I only differed from the classic type in that I did not wish to marry the master's daughter." As for his own work, he adds, "I was over forty before I was focussed, except for this or that special task. The great question for a writer is to find his focus, and to keep himself focussed. When he is out of focus he is in hell." Let me give one further observation on his earlier days in New York:

> I shared E. A. Robinson's cult of failure,—poverty, shabbiness and failure,—and at the same moment in New York. I liked mean streets and faded houses; I rejoiced in holes in the seat of my breeches and holes in the soles of my shoes. I had a horror of the appearance of success, which I still have, for that matter. If I were "successful," I should wish to wear a hair-shirt.
>
> What always worried me was not the danger of being poor, of which one hears so much,—and I have certainly had small means. I could almost have drawn the map that Robinson said he could draw, showing every free-lunch counter in the city. What has always worried me was the danger of being rich, and this haunts me still. For one can never tell,—riches may come as well as poverty, and I fear this possibility. I feel as Elinor Wylie felt, although in quite another sense,—
>
>> Down to the Puritan marrow of my bones
>> There's something in this richness that I hate.
>
> There was nothing I feared more as a young man than making money. My only motive in offices was not to be promoted, not to have a salary that involved responsibilities, not to become entangled in

the machinery of business. I wished to be an underling, and in this ambition one always succeeds. I realized how important it was that my sense of responsibility should only be engaged in routine tasks, in which I could honestly give my money's worth. Granting that I could pay my way, my major responsibilities all lay elsewhere.

He adds, by way of parenthesis:

I saw this clearly because I wished to be a writer. But I should be sorry if everyone felt as I did. Some people are born to live lavishly, and, under whatever social system, they should be allowed to do so. By these I mean the real artists in living for whom material resources are instruments of their art. There should be many boxes of precious ointment, and they should often be broken. Naturally magnificent people have their rights also. They will always give more than they take.

Allston developed late, as I have suggested, although he had begun so early. He did not regret this, though he sometimes regretted that he had begun so early. He was impressed by a passage in Havelock Ellis's autobiography that seemed to hit the nail on the head for him: "I was still firmly convinced"—at twenty-five—"that when one is young one is always liable to outgrow one's work, and was determined that I, at all events, should not fall into the error of neglecting this natural development and putting forth in a permanent form work that I might subsequently wish to disavow. I cannot remember at what age it was that I resolved not to publish a book until I was thirty, but I was never tempted to move from that resolution and never had occasion to regret it." On this Allston comments as follows:

> I was not so wise, and especially not so tranquil and confident. Perhaps no American could have been so at that moment. As all we Americans did, I conducted my education in public, and, although I do not think it matters much, I have had to pay in consequence. My early writings won a few adherents, who were less mature even than I was, and they still say and write that I have gone back on myself when I have only gone back on my ignorance and brashness.

He remarks again, apropos of his slow development:

> If my letters were ever published,—which heaven forbid,—it would be seen that I have always been a most injudicious letter-writer. I have always been too impulsive,—J. B. Yeats called me the "most impulsive of men," and he did not say it in praise. My way has always been to say Yes, and then think it over; and, thinking, I often found that I was wrong. I had said not what my nature necessitated, but what first came into my mind, because I was touched or pleased or flattered. I must often have appeared superficial without being so. I usually had the right perception, but my impulses came too rapidly for me to express it, and I was too flattered or too touched. Only now, after fifty, do I say at the first encounter (and not always even now) what, after thinking, I find that I feel and believe.

(Referring to this I find a note *On writing dishonest letters of praise:* "I gave him soothing-syrup to keep him quiet, only two or three drops. Now he comes back for more,—he wants a spoonful.") He certainly never regretted that he was not earlier known,—he rejoiced in the long obscurity that favoured his growth. Regarding this he said:

"I have been meditating on the great importance it is to a literary man to remain unknown till he gets his work fairly done. It can hardly be overstated." Thus Longfellow, in his journal, and how right he is. If we cannot afford to take this Olympian line, if we have to seek publicity, at least let us know what we are doing. I do not envy the successful authors about whom the publicity men and reporters flock, like sharks about a raft, which, when the provisions are gone, breaks up and leaves these authors at their mercy.

He adds:

When a writer begins to be successful, when he begins to soar, outwardly but especially inwardly, then, to save him from infatuation, he needs to be pelted with bitter apples.

Let me conclude this chapter with a few brief notes of a more or less personal kind. Allston liked to collect quotations that defined his own feelings. Thus he says:

I am like the historian of whom Horace Walpole said that he "never understood anything until he had written about it."

Dr. Johnson's friend Bennet Langton said he "had a queerness of constitution which seemed to leave him at his lowest ebb every afternoon about two of the clock, forgetful, weary, confused, and without an idea in his head." I feel the same way at this hour.

I feel about my work as Turgenev said he felt

about his: "When I reread my work or hear it mentioned, I have a complicated feeling, the chief elements of which are shame and the fear that people are laughing at me."

The following notes are purely personal:

I have not lost one of my "illusions." I have the same expectations of life that I had when I was a boy.

Once when I was in London, I saw a copy of my first book in the sixpenny box at a second-hand bookseller's. I passed this box many times and saw the rain falling on it, while the binding of the book grew dimmer and dimmer. Finally it reached the penny box. I felt so sorry for myself that I bought the book.

Young H. has just been here, telling me his enthusiasms. I felt like Pater's Mona Lisa, older than the rocks among which she sits. when he told me what a poet ought to be.

The following are more general:

Nine-tenths of the things that are most important to us, in our own personal lives, the things that absorb our energy and give our life meaning, not only have no interest for other people but have no traceable connection with those elements of our life that concern the world. Yet these things form the invisible soil from which our achievements grow.

"Life is a comedy to those who think." Yes, and let us keep it so. If I were to live in my feelings, without a constant activity of the mind, my face would soon be as lined with furrows as a bed of lava.

Nothing good can come from writers who are at ease in their Zion. We should all live like Israelites at the Feast of Passover.

CHAPTER III

A WRITER'S HABITS

AS ONE might expect, Allston's journals are filled with casual jottings on a writer's life. Thus he remarks: "Speaking of the Battle of the Books, in the last twenty years I have had six dictionaries killed under me, three French dictionaries and three English dictionaries, all of them worn to rags and tatters. And the four stout volumes of my Littré have been wounded severely." That the battle often went against him, one gathers from such entries as these:

> No work this morning. My brain feels like an old sponge, battered by the waves and rocks of a dozen winters.
>
> In thirty years of writing, I have not gained an ounce of confidence. I begin each new book (as I have probably always begun, although I never remember it) with a sense of impotence, chaos and desperation that cannot be overstated. I always feel that I am foredoomed to failure.
>
> Every day I begin my work with the same old feeling, that I am on trial for my life and will probably not be acquitted.

After one of these entries, as if to relieve his depression, he adds a remark of Bunyan's: "I care not at all for that profession which begins not in heaviness of mind. The first string that the musician usu-

ally touches is the bass, when he intends to put all
in tune."

That Allston enjoyed his work, however,—sometimes, if not often,—one gathers from other entries.
"What a pleasure it is to think," he writes. "Well I
understand at times the poetic rapture of the mathematician, as Bertrand Russell describes it." But I
doubt if these occasions were very frequent. If his
writing had often gone well, would he have recorded
so many shifts for getting into the right state of
mind? Thus, for instance, he says:

A little fetishism sometimes helps. Handel and
Machiavelli always composed in court dress. Buffon
did the same thing. They wooed the grand style by
dressing in it.

I also like Emerson's statement that he wrote his
essay on Michael Angelo in a coat he had had made
in Florence.

I never used to throw away any of my own old
suits until I had finished another book. When I set
to work on ———, I was wearing a grey tweed suit of
which I was particularly fond; and, before I had finished the second chapter, the suit and the book had
somehow grown together in my mind. I should not
have dreamed of sitting down to write in any other
coat or trousers. That was the book in the middle of
which I had a serious breakdown. I went on wearing
the suit, hoping it would bring back my luck; and
when I was able to work again the suit was in tatters. But "let back and sides go bare, go bare," would
I have thrown away that suit? Not for all the treas-
ure on Cocos Island. I kept the suit and finished the
book, and I always felt that my old grey coat had
turned the trick for me.

I find another note on fetishism:

> If I build a house, let me have a fetish-chamber,—
> which others may well regard as a chamber of hor-
> rors,—as befits a fetish-worshipper like myself.
> There I shall assemble the family pictures, the por-
> traits of old houses with which I have associations,
> the relics, possibly hideous in the eyes of others, that
> mean much to me. Fetishes are fortifying, and I be-
> lieve that one cannot have too many fortifications.
> The Romans had their lares and penates, which they
> kept in the penetralia of their houses and which were
> always in their minds on the field of battle. Writers,
> who also fight battles, must also have their fetishes,
> such as pictures, books and other objects, meaning-
> less to others, that recall the deep realities of their
> craft. Victories are bred from victories and all that
> suggests the victorious. If I owned an old shoe that
> Walt Whitman wore, I should keep it within five feet
> of my writing-table, and I should owe many a fine
> page that would otherwise not have been written to
> the presence of this object. But, no doubt, the effect
> would be all the greater if I kept the shoe locked up
> in a cupboard. There is something in us that feeds
> upon mystery and magic and that withers and dies
> with exposure.

Allston was fertile in these devices for gaining the
ear of the muse. The following observation refers
to another. As he mentions two authors to whom he
has just referred,—no doubt, he was reading them
at the moment,—I gather that this note was written
at the same time. He seems to have been spending
a month in the woods, for he speaks of the braided
music of a little brook that was tinkling in his ears

as he wrote. It must have been in August, for he also speaks of a locust winding off its wiry coil of sound:

How to dispose of one's tin cans. When one is writing in the morning, this is the sort of problem that provides one's afternoons with a proper focus.

Bertrand Russell is right in saying that one who wishes to do good work must expect to be bored much of the time. A state of dull vacuity is the best mental state in which to suspend one's hours of composition. When the conscious mind is over-stimulated, the unconscious mind refuses to open its door. So, at least, it is with me.

I noticed in Emerson's journal that, when he was at Saint Augustine, he spent hours along the beach driving an orange with his walking-stick. Day after day, at Saint Augustine, when I was writing there, my only object was to find another coquina-shell, washed up by the tide, to take home and use for baking fish in.

Closely connected with this is another note:

As against having beautiful workshops, studies, etc., one writes best in the cellar on a rainy day. I found that a rainy day in Florida,—and in California also,—wonderfully prospered the act of mental concentration. That is one reason why Ireland, England and Norway are so good for writers.

I always felt that the California sunshine had an ill effect on people's minds there. My friend M. W. gave me a case in point. The superior of the Catholic seminary at San Mateo complained that he could not get his students to work. Impossible to induce a vocation! The students were always "sitting about in the sun." That is why the Spaniards and Italians, who have lived in these warm sunny climates, and who have cared greatly for the inner life, have cultivated gloomy depths of darkness. They have known how to adjust themselves to this semi-tropical milieu. They have broken up the monotony of heat and sunshine by creating contrasts,—high and heavy walls, damp stonework, enclosures of deep shade, thickets of shrubbery, etc. Not California bungalows and Florida verandahs, but bare, stony cells, houses like Michael Angelo's at Florence,—these enable the mind to find its focus.

Allston liked Michael Angelo's phrase, which he said was also true of him,—"It is only well with me when I have a chisel in my hand." In two or three notes he refers to his methods:

I always begin my writing day by copying all the work of the day before, making a few slight changes. This warms me up and gives me momentum. It is like winding a top. Sometimes, nowadays, when I have finished my copying, the top begins to spin of itself.

I copy all my notes out by hand, and it often takes me as long as to read the book. But I think this drudgery counts in the end; for every note represents a moment of excitement, and I hive away the excitement by copying the note. All the care I take in forcing myself to be accurate serves, I think, to drive the excitement in. Thus my notes are all deposits of feeling, and this feeling returns when I take up my notes in the course of my work. May heaven save me from typing notes and dictating to secretaries. It is this that produces the chalk-like style of most historical writers. Good writing is felt writing, and this effect is cheaply bought at any extravagant expenditure of time and effort.

After this he adds:

> As much as Hemingway dislikes being called a
> writer,—as I gather from *The Sun Also Rises,*—I
> dislike being called a scholar. I love the phrase "man
> of letters," but for me the word scholar has repulsive
> associations. I connect it with the grind, the man
> who studies in cold blood. There are great scholars,
> who are a kind of artists, such as Edward Kennard
> Rand and Sir Herbert Grierson. But I never worked
> in this way, and that is why school and college meant
> so little to me. I could never apply myself to any-
> thing unless my blood was up. I regard accuracy,
> carefulness and thoroughness as part of the equip-
> ment of a writer, and whatever scholarly traits I pos-
> sess are incidentals of this character.

The following notes are more or less related:

> *The Artful Dodger.* Get the reputation of being a
> recluse. Spread it about that you are a chronic in-
> valid. Tell them you have leprosy or rabies. You
> must be
>> instinctively thorough
>> About your crevice and burrow,

like Robert Frost and his Drumlin Woodchuck.

Havelock Ellis says that he never really had ambition, and that this was merely a matter of temperament. He had only a certain dogged persistence in
keeping on his own path and working out his own
nature, and this, and this alone, had brought him
whatever success he had achieved.

This is almost true of me, and I do not forget Stendhal's remark, "How many precautions are necessary
to prevent oneself from lying." Until my work was
violently stopped by a neurosis, I was too deeply ab-

sorbed in it to think of advancing myself. Then, it is
true, I became an egomaniac. I have generally viewed
honours and positions with only one question in mind,
—how much of my time and energy were they going
to waste? This seems to me the normal professional
attitude. Vanity is the abnormal attitude.

Regarding another passage, I must add a word or
two. Allston seems to have planned to build a house.
I remember he said to me once that he thought it
was quite natural for every man to build one house
in his lifetime, but apparently he viewed this plan
with misgivings:

I received this morning a warranty deed entitling
me to a piece of land that I have long desired and am
glad to own. Yet, strangely, when I saw my name in-
scribed upon this deed, I felt a tremor in my bones.
This deed was full of a kind of poetry. I became a
grantee, with "assigns forever." The land was mine,
for my "own proper use and behoof." With the "en-
sealing of these presents," I was "well seized of the
premises." My estate was indefeasible "in fee simple." I was henceforth entitled to privileges, appur-
tenances and all manner of other high and mighty
rights in regard to bargaining and selling, and the
grantor was bound to defend me. I felt solemnly
proud to associate my name with these admirable
phrases, this poetry of the law that carries me back
directly to the lives of my Saxon forbears in their
mud-huts and manors,—for, like everyone of my
name, I had forbears in both. Well I know what all
these phrases represented in terms of toil and sweat
and self-respect for untold generations of these forbears, what struggles and triumphs they stood for
and what a large portion of history in this country

and England. And yet I felt a tremor in my bones.

My instinct does not claim property, however I may rejoice in it. I have another kind of estate to which it is inimical. All men are tamed nomads, born to wander after adventure, and this is especially true in the case of writers. They are, and must be, so-journers on this earth, and they dread the trap of property, the trap of possessions. "Sell all thou hast" is their motto. True writers in their hearts are like Arabs and soldiers. Tolstoy stood for them all when he ran away at the end of his life, preferring to die in a railway-station. How well I understand my friend the sailor-novelist, who cannot bear to see a garden planted round his house. He sees every shoot as a nail that holds him in place. His rolling fields re-mind him of the waves, and he longs to be off again.

Here are two or three scattered remarks:

"Whenever I feel the need of exercise, I sit still until the impulse passes." Thus my friend Hendrik van Loon.

When I quoted this to B. Z., he said that it was not properly Hendrik's. He was sure that it came from some other writer, some old writer of good vintage. Perhaps, I say; but what of it? Hendrik pullulates with these sayings, some his own, some bor-rowed or stolen, others borrowed and improved upon. But they all become his when he says them. A mind of such astonishing richness is not to be looked in the mouth, so to speak. Its rays all take their value from the sun behind them.

Well I understand the painter Rothenstein's say-ing, "It is in the atmosphere of poetry and among men of large vision and magnanimous natures that I have been most happy and comfortable." How delightful is the company of generous people, who over-look trifles and keep their minds instinctively fixed on whatever is good and positive in the world about them. People of small calibre are always carping. How affected so-and-so is! Don't you think he is silly? He was certainly quite mistaken about this or that. They are bent on showing their own superiority, their knowledge or their prowess or good breeding. But magnanimous people have no vanity, they have no jealousy, they have no reserves, and they feed on the true and the solid wherever they find it. And, what is more, they find it everywhere.

I feel about my work now as President Eliot felt about Harvard: "Things seem to be going fairly well, now that a spirit of pessimism prevails in all departments."

CHAPTER IV

A WRITER'S IRRITATIONS

I HAVE said that Allston often dwelt on the value of being bored, but he also enjoyed his irritations. In fact, he seems to have felt that the state of irritation is altogether wholesome for a writer. Thus he quotes Renan, "Well-being produces only inertia. Discomfort is the principle of movement." He continues, apropos of George Gissing:

> Gissing was one of the writers who thrive on their irritations. "Every man," he says somewhere, "has his intellectual desire; mine is to escape life as I know it, and dream myself back into that old world which was the imaginative delight of my boyhood." It was this world, the Mediterranean world of the past, that gave him a scale by which to measure the scenes that surrounded him in London; and in the last years of his life he set out to seek the traces of it in the Magna Græcia of which he wrote in *By the Ionian Sea*. What was it then that kept him for so many years confined in his City of Dreadful Night?—for he felt about London much as James Thomson felt. Not poverty alone. He hated London, with all the instincts of the born recluse. He was offended by crowds, he shrank from casual encounters, he disliked the "tongue of Whitechapel" and the "blaring lust of life." "Every

day," he said, "gives me a deeper loathing of city life. If I cannot escape from it to die amid green fields, my end will be wretched indeed." Yet virtually his whole life was passed in cities; even when he came to America, he made no effort to seek the countryside,—he spent all his time in Chicago and Boston,—and, of his twenty-two novels, twenty-one deal, at least largely, with London. Thus we can see that his instinct of artistic self-preservation was constantly at war with all his normal tastes.

Is it not a fact that novelists usually thrive best on their irritations? Hawthorne throve in the dust and wind of Salem. Flaubert, Stendhal, Sinclair Lewis, Dreiser are other cases in point; and do not Henry James's early novels show that this was also true for him? As long as he dealt with native Americans, who irritated him all the time, everything went well with James. England was too pleasant for him, and hence so much of his later fatuity. Perhaps the less we satisfy our tastes, the more they serve to give us a scale and a measure.

This may explain why Allston, unlike Gissing, chose to live in the country. "Thinking over my Boston visit," he writes, "I do not complain of my village. Everything that irritates me here stabs me into life. The half-formed thoughts I meet stir me to complete them. The half-formed demands stir me to respond to them. Here one feels one has a part to play. In Boston, one feels superfluous; this is restful, but, if I stayed there too much, I should die of too much rest. I should be killed with kindness. Boston is as soothing to me as London was for Henry James, and this soothing is very bad for a thinking man. I like a few nails in my bed."

Later he repeats:

What I like about my village. Plenty of good solitude, and plenty of the kind of interruptions that do
not soothe the social man but challenge all his pre-
possessions.

In New York, I should die of stimulus.

In Boston, I should be soothed to death.

Yes, I know what would happen. I should go the
way of all the gadflies,—like our well-known Z., the
satirist, when, in the simplicity of his heart, he took
to playing billiards every evening with his jolly neigh-
bours on Long Island. The sting of his talent atrophied. How could he find fault with all those good
fellows? He ceased to be able to find fault with all
the abuses they stood for.

That he often visited Boston, I gather from other
entries. He seems to have found it pleasant, perhaps
too pleasant, for he says: "I feel about Boston as
Lessing felt about Brunswick,—'It is not that I do
not like Brunswick, but because nothing good comes
of being long in a place one likes.'" Elsewhere he
quotes Emerson, "The things of a man for which we
visit him were done in the dark and the cold."

He may have had Boston in mind in saying, "People who are too good and cultivated lull one insensibly into a kind of fatuity. One gets into a fools'
paradise. Except in very small doses, 'good society'
is not good for writers. This is because they need to
be misunderstood, they require something harsh in
the atmosphere about them." He develops this point
in a later passage:

Children and writers feel the need of grit and
sand, of something harsh in the moral atmosphere,

that causes them to define themselves and their aims, as one needs salt in one's diet, as the teeth require both alkali and acids.

As much as to understanding, children are entitled to misunderstanding. Not the brutal variety, but the bland variety. After the primitive needs have received attention, they need to be confronted with a blank wall of incomprehension. It is by reacting against this that they define themselves, become aware of themselves and their intentions.

The same thing is true of writers and artists, and this is one reason why England has been so fertile in geniuses. The stolid egoism of the English household is the milieu for poets. Americans are too sympathetic to provide a good medium for the development of individuality. They are always talking about and trying to meet its problems, and by this very process they inhibit its growth. The process merely produces self-conscious hobbledehoys, the geniuses of the family circle who never come to anything.

Everyone, in fact, needs incomprehension, and even oceans of it. This is especially true of writers and artists. It is only when we are misunderstood by others that we really understand ourselves.

The infallible way to produce uniformity is to cultivate individuality, which, in its proper growth, is always a by-product. The age of the American geniuses, the generation before the Civil War,—certainly not yet equalled in this respect by any succeeding generation,—was an age of rigid social discipline. Michelet said he grew up like a blade of grass between two paving-stones. So did Thoreau, Emerson and Hawthorne. So did Emily Dickinson and Winslow Homer. It is true that Poe and Melville encountered too much incomprehension. The last straw breaks the camel's back, but at least a large proportion of the other straws serve to develop its muscles.

I have said that Allston enjoyed his irritations. At least, they suggested many thoughts,—I choose the following as examples:

Gibbon observes that the ancient Germans, when they were summoned to a public meeting, would lag behind the appointed time in order to show their independence. This trait was still more marked, according to Parkman, among the American Indians of Pontiac's time.

Similarly, my friend X. and other editorial potentates rattle their papers on their desks for ten or twenty minutes, before they admit their supplicants, in order to show how important and busy they are. Henceforth, I shall think of editors as ancient Germans.

My friend, the professor, lays down the law. In my next book, I must not do this, I must not do that. It makes no difference to him that Balzac did it, or Taine, Thoreau or Tolstoy. All the authors who ever lived may have done just this,—nevertheless, this is not done,—and my friend the professor would say it to Tolstoy with as much sangfroid as he says it to me. Just so the herring might say to the whale, "My dear whale, you must not blow any longer. It really isn't done. We herrings never think of blowing. No creature ever blew in Boston harbour."

(It is in connection with this that he quotes Brunetière, in *Nouvelles questions de critique:* "Knowledge or conscientiousness, delicacy of taste, tact, the art of selection and composition, feeling for style, felicity of expression, art or grace, eloquence or strength, all that formerly went under the name of talent or even genius,—do any of these qualities really count in the eyes of a decipherer of texts or an editor of unpublished documents? And public opinion, which they have already more than half corrupted, seems likely soon to side with them.")

Today I receive another of those questionnaires that are sent out to Tom, Dick and Harry, asking for my views on socialism and communism and "how the American author ought to stand" regarding this, that and the other matter. I fully agree that authors should "take sides," and I always do so; but I ignore or decline these invitations to develop my views at length. It is not that I have not strong feelings on all these subjects; but may heaven preserve me from expressing them beyond the point of a Yes or No until the spirit calls me to do so in the normal course of my writing. Well said Nietzsche, "How happy are we, we finders of knowledge, provided that we know how to keep silent long enough." If there is anything "the American author ought" to do, it is to keep the steam in his own boiler. If, storing away their opinions, writers allowed them to roll up interest in their minds, their legitimate writings would have a weight which they sadly lack at present.

A young man is writing a book on the future of society. What steps should we take to make the world better? He wants a few lines from "thinkers of the older generation." Would I send him a paragraph about it? I reply that to write a paragraph is harder than to write a book, for one has to have written the book mentally, explored the corners of one's mind, before one can reduce one's thoughts to a handful of words.

This seems to me self-evident. But what interests

me is this holding people up for their opinions, asking them what they think at the point of a pistol. It is a prevalent method in our world of gunmen. What are these opinions worth, these "I.Q." verdicts that abound in our advertising and our popular sociological literature? They cannot come from the depths of the mind. They can only come from the mental pockets in which we carry our small change, or the folders in which we keep our greenbacks,—in order to be ready in case the gunman happens to be heavily armed and makes an incontrovertible demand upon us. No doubt, there are men, such as Einstein, who have explored their minds to the outermost limit, who know on every subject what they think, and who can reduce it to a sentence or a paragraph and hand it out to a customer as a druggist hands out a bottle of pills. These men possess their "world-view" as others possess their old boots, in which they move about with ease and trust; and nothing is more stirring than the paragraphs and sentences in which these grand old thinkers discharge their minds. The sentences drop from them as apples drop from the tree of life, as naturally as other apples in their season. To force this fruit is like forcing any other fruit, which is sure to be green in essence if not in appearance. When my mind is forced, it emits every kind of untruth; and I refuse to "step lively" and talk in advance of my years and wisdom for the purpose of "throwing light" on these difficult problems. I am quite aware of these problems. They are my problems, and the business of my life is to solve them. In the meantime, I do not propose to hand out unripe fruit, and I deplore these bunches of green bananas.

I use about a quart of ink a year. I like black ink. It appears, however, that most Americans like blue ink, which, as the salesman says, is so much better "because it turns black in six months." No doubt, the leisurely business men who patronize this ink can wait six months for their effects; but time, with me, as a writer, presses. When I make tracks on paper, I wish to see them, and black ink is very hard to get. Every time I try to get it I go through the same procedure and end by accepting a compromise that leaves me in doubt, for black has turned to "coal black," or "coal" black to "koal" black,—the last form it assumed was "midnight" black. All these words protest too much, arousing in me a painful scepticism. Is "coal" black as black as black? Is it blacker or less black if the word is spelled with a k? And is not "midnight" really purple? The more this ink protests it is black, the more I am driven to doubt it, and it does not reassure me to be told that, having used as a basis an aniline dye, the makers now use a kind of nut. As in everything else in our country, we cannot let well enough alone, but must have something new at any price. The baser explanation of this is that the manufacturers are always trying to get ahead of their rivals, who might spring something new on the world and capture all their trade if they did not spring the new thing first. A nobler explanation, which the manufacturers favour, is that it represents a thirst for perfection. From this point of view, "midnight" black stands for one of the phases of a toilsome progress. The next phase may well be the black of "just before dawn," while mere "black" will remain as a primitive taste of a prehistoric race that knew no better. It is the law of life in a business world that nothing shall continue in one stay; but, while the improvers affirm that the bad gets better, it is obvious to me that the good gets worse. *Verweile doch! Du bist so schön!* goes for ink as for everything else in a world in which business motives are too good to be true.

The next note expresses a vicarious irritation:

I sympathize with my youthful neighbour, who is struggling to inject a little order, a little taste and style,—a little readability, in short,—into a mass of manuscript that is supposed to be a book. A great lawyer thinks he has written this book, and he proposes to sign it. These legal luminaries, these magnates, these presidents of corporations, these very important men who are always pressing buttons have notions of their own in regard to writing. They imagine that all they have to do, to commit their thoughts to immortality, is to command a squadron of secretaries to look this, that and the other up, and then, in some hour of ease, with their spoils assembled about them, and a box of the best cigars on the desk before them, dictate to Miss Daphne or Miss Hebe. And they are always surprised to find that no one will read their writings. So many *whereases* and *wherefores* have crept into their manuscript that, although Miss Daphne strives to conceal the fact, she would rather walk home to Brooklyn in a March blizzard than read a page of the great man's lucubrations. Then the same result always follows. The great man turns for help to some youthful writer and offers him a chauffeur's wages if he will take the manuscript in hand and make it worthy of his signature.

These very important men do not know that literature is a learned profession, ten times more difficult than law. They do not know that there are some problems which cannot be solved by pressing a button, that literary taste and skill are the reward of years of humble effort. And in this they resemble certain writers who are also very important, if one judges them by a similar standard,—the degrees and decorations they have received and the confidence with which they address the public in their interviews and radio-speeches. One knows of authors who hire young men and women to do their drudgery for them. But God is not mocked in regard to them, nor is the critic deceived. This was not the way that Gibbon worked, or Prescott or Parkman, who used the secretarial crutch only because they were halt and blind. A real writer feels about his work as a healthy mother feels about her baby. His instinct revolts against the incubator and every mechanical substitute for brooding. The writer who does not brood, in every sense of the word, the writer who is not his own drudge, who does not earn his notes by loving investigation, pays a heavy forfeit. His prose lacks depth, tone and texture, and nothing can compensate for this.

I add a few notes on minor irritations:

Formerly, when I said, I am old, or I am going to be old, or I am going to die, my kind friends always replied, Nonsense, you are not old, you are not going to be old, and you are not going to die. Now such remarks are greeted with an ominous silence. The fact is out, and there is no blinking it.

The radio. In a moment of inadvertence, the radio was permitted to carry on by itself. Eternal vigilance is the price of freedom from the natural habits of this invention.

The better I write, the more my teeth hurt at the dentist's. At least, I think they are going to hurt more, and that is the main trouble at the dentist's. My dentist has noted and told me that I have grown

more and more nervous, while my style has certainly
grown better and better. As one advances in style,
one's nervous system grows tenser and tenser, and all
one's feelings grow more acute. Of course, one is
more susceptible and apprehensive. Tell me how a
writer feels at the dentist's, and I will tell you how
he writes.

I end with a phrase of Pindar:

"A man doing fit things forgets Hades."

CHAPTER V

NOTES ON PAINTERS

ALLSTON, so far as I know, never tried to paint, nor did he ever attempt to write about painting. But he had many friends who were painters. He told me that, as a boy, before he became interested in books and writing, pictures were his first enthusiasm, and that, during a winter in Dresden, when he was twelve, he went to the Zwinger every day, for five or six months, and spent the morning there. Thirty years later, he could close his eyes and see almost every picture on almost every one of the walls. He had gone through the galleries in Italy with a drawing-pad in his hand, and I found among his papers a niggling little pencil-sketch he had made of a Fra Angelico Crucifixion. The second composition he remembered writing, when he was about thirteen, was a paper on Paolo Uccello; and later he caught lead-poisoning, or thought he had caught it, from sleeping among the wet canvases of a young Polish painter whom he had known in Paris. ("Whatever became," he asks, "of Karol Ferencz-Winzer? If I were properly posted, I should probably find he was famous.") One of his earliest memories was of an afternoon in London when he was taken to Watts's studio. Watts, at that time, had a

great name,—he might have been described as the
Tennyson of painting. Allston recalled the old man,
with his long white beard, wearing the skull-cap
that appeared in his portrait, standing in a corner of
the room, beside one of his pictures,—was it not the
"Paolo and Francesca"?—discoursing about it very
sweetly.

Many years later, at Petitpas', the French *table
d'hôte* in Twenty-ninth Street, where John Butler
Yeats lived and died, he dined every evening for
months at a time. There he saw much of Sloan,
Henri and Glackens. The Prendergast brothers and
Bellows also came there. Yeats, who painted an excellent portrait of him, was full of wit and anecdote,
and Allston was always quoting Yeats, as everyone
did who knew him. Speaking of Watts, the old man
said, "Watts, ah, yes. His literature was bad,"—
which seemed to hit the nail on the head. Who could
forget his words on idleness?—"that idleness which
is so diligent, idleness, the teeming mother of the
arts." The "sacred duty of idleness," Allston said,
was Yeats's special message to the harried and hurried
Americans. It reminded him of Thoreau's saying,
"Nothing can be more useful to a man than a determination not to be hurried." Yeats, in preaching idleness, was consistent. He told Allston how his son
"Willie," the poet, had lain abed all day as a young
man. His friends and the family remonstrated: why
should Willie lie abed when he was well in his twenties and the family so poor? He ought to be up and
doing; but Yeats said No. Something perhaps was
brewing in Willie's mind; and what, as it proved, was
brewing as he lay abed all these years? Willie

was composing *The Wanderings of Oisin,*—there was a reward for a father's forbearance. Allston recalled how tenderly Yeats smiled over the phrase, in one of Darwin's letters, "A nice soft woman on a sofa." How benignly he lingered over the words, "The Emmett cradle is never empty." He had the wisdom of the heart, so rare in New York, along with the other wisdoms, if such exist. Speaking of American art and letters, he said that exacting criticism was what they needed. He explained this in some such words as these: "Criticism should be exacting, as a mother is about her daughter's party-gown. She never dreams of comparing her girl with the girl over the way; it is understood that no other woman's daughter is to be thought of with her own. But, as the girl turns this way or that, so that her frock may have the last inspection, the mother's eye is severe as no other is, watching for any infelicity in the hang of the dress and any possible way of improving it by the change of a bow or a ribbon. So it is the kindest critic that is the hardest to please."

Allston said that Yeats was the greatest teacher he had known. He had not been stirred intellectually by his teachers at Harvard. He was too young, no doubt, to know what they were talking about, although he was impressed by their goodness, when they were good. He never could forget Dean Briggs and the depths of moral wisdom that shone in his face. But Yeats's was the first intellect that really touched him, and Allston always regarded Yeats as his master, the wisest of men and the most amusing. Once Allston spoke of De Quincey, whom he adored, and Yeats began to imagine what the ladies of Manchester said about this refractory boy who had run away to London: "De Quincey! What is he! A waif and a stray. And to think that his mother moved in the best county society and had her feet planted on the Rock of Ages!" Yeats told many stories about George Moore, whom he had known for many years in Dublin. This was the Moore who, as Susan Mitchell said, did not kiss and tell but told and did not kiss. He would say, if you met him in the street, that he was on his way to buy his housekeeper a smarter pair of corsets. He would say that, at an evening party, he could go into the cloak-room and find any lady's cloak at once. He could pick it out by the smell. He told Yeats how he had shocked his pious old-maid cousins, with whom he was dining in the country. When one of them asked, "George, why have you never married?" he replied, "Because, dear Mary, I prefer adultery." Yeats always spoke of Moore as "the elderly old blackguard in Ely Place."

At Petitpas', in the room under Yeats's, another painter lived, Mr. Perry, the oldest living Academician. He too had a long white beard, like Yeats, Watts and Titian, and he also wore a black silk skull-cap. Indeed, he was so old, almost ninety, that he had been the American consul at Venice ten years before the Civil War. He was one of Howells's predecessors there. His room on the second floor was stacked and hung with his paintings, tight photographic story-pictures, "The First Vaccination," and the like. Allston sometimes joined them at lunch, for he also lived for a while at Petitpas', and the two old painters were the only lodgers who took their midday meals in the house. They faced each other most unwillingly, for Perry was deaf and a bore, in Yeats's opinion, while Perry thought Yeats, who glowered at him, a scandalous and unprofitable idler. Perry droned along through the meal, while Yeats groaned in his beard and, from time to time, gave Allston a mischievous glance. For he loved mischief "for its own dear sake," as he once remarked apropos of the Irish. But Perry also had his anecdotes. Once, in some far-away past, he had spent a summer with Winslow Homer. They had occupied a two-room cabin on one of the Long Island ocean beaches. They slept in one room and lived on oysters, and threw the shells into the other room. The shells formed a pyramid and gradually slid off into the corners until, by the end of the summer, they choked the room.

Allston, as I have said, never wrote about painters or painting. His friend Walter Pach, who did so write, explained his attitude for him. Walter Pach, who wrote about painters, said, in regard to actors and singers, Sarah Bernhardt, Yvette Guilbert and others, "I saw them only across the footlights, and it is for others to tell about them." Allston felt that he saw painters only across the footlights, but he was always drawn to them. He says, for instance:

> I like painters. They are just like writers, without the nonsense. Of course, they have their own nonsense, but I don't have to bother about that.
>
> Why do artists of every kind gravitate to painters? It is because they are apt to be simple and happy. As Virgil Thomson says, in *The State of Music,* "The Seeing Eye has no opinions" and "The painter's whole morality consists in keeping his brushes clean and getting up in the morning." Therefore painters are "a

pleasant lot, cheerful and healthy." It is natural that the rest of us, writers, musicians and what not, who are so often morbid, are drawn to painters.

He was evidently pleased and flattered when he was taken for a painter. I find this note, for instance:

> The girl in charge of the picture-gallery asked me for a cigarette. Then she said, "You're an artist, aren't you?"—"No," said I. "What made you think so?"—"Because you can't make your hair behave."

Allston said once that he knew four men without guile, and all these men were painters. "For the purest virgin crystalline goodness," he wrote in one of his letters, "give me a painter." Elsewhere he says, "I have tried several times to provoke K. A. into saying something nasty about at least one person. But it never worked." He liked to repeat what the grocer said in a village, much frequented by painters, where he sometimes spent a summer. This grocer often let his bills run, even to the extent of a thousand dollars, to help some poor devil of an artist, and he had never had a bad debt. Sometimes, five or ten years later, from Mexico or Bali or wherever, back would come the cheque. The poor devil had had a run of luck. Yet he seems to have felt that there were other kinds of painters. On one of the fly-leaves of his Vasari, I find the following notes:

> Those artists with defeated eyes and the manners of courtiers and sycophants whom one sees in fashionable circles, hovering about the lamp of the pocket-book.

> Why do I wish to avoid such men as X, who abound among artists and writers? They are the men

with a foot in each sphere, the sphere of the mind and the sphere of the mundane. They have a super-stitious regard for those who have both feet in the sphere of the mind, after which they hanker, but, if they had to make a choice, if they had to plant both feet on one side of the line, they would take the side of the mundane, not with the integrity of worldly people, but because they lack the strength for the other side. This tormented double-mindedness subtly poisons the air about them. I know how to deal with the frankly worldly, but the effort to contribute to the self-respect of people who feel they have lapsed from the other world and lack the will to recover it, or even seek it, is not good for anyone. Healthy peo-ple are those who make clear decisions. The half-artists, soft within, affect me like stretches of marsh-land. You never know, in their company, where to place your foot, for fear of hurting their feelings, and you begin to doubt your own ground. They *give* at every point, and, meeting no resistance, your mus-cles become an illusion to yourself. It does not do to linger after nightfall in swamps of this kind. One is sure to catch malaria.

Apropos of luxurious studios, I like the account of the studio of Puvis de Chavannes. A visitor who en-tered it, expecting to be impressed in the usual way, found the walls bare save for a single sketch pinned up in a corner.

Luxurious studios are all of a piece with those beautiful islands to which so many artists resort, hop-ing to find inspiration. They are usually like Teneriffe in the Canaries, where the old English lady who lived there said to Webb Waldron, "No one was ever known to have an idea on this island."

The next two passages are more general:

Most modern art-lovers are discontented modish people who seize upon art for quite extraneous reasons. The lovers of art and literature are as few as ever, and they do not include many who are always talking of art and literature,—even professional critics,—and who claim an exclusive right to do so. Real lovers are not exclusive in this fashion, though they sometimes find it difficult to include the exclusive.

The modern artist takes as axiomatic the notion, No concession to the public taste, i.e., the taste of the gross public; but the age in which he assumed this motto has been the age in which he made most concessions to the *élite* public. Conscious of the larger herd, the artist nowadays never belonged so much to a lesser herd. One hardly knows a painter who dares not to be influenced by Derain or Picasso, or Orozco, or Benton. Never was the vogue so dominant in fields where it should not be dominant, i.e., in fields other than that of dress, where fashion has a function. Our age of alleged independence shows far less independence than the Victorian age, in which originality was almost the rule. We do not even admire the original. What people admire is eccentricity, a partial deviation from convention that recognizes convention in the act of deviating from it. This is a result of urban life, which insensibly draws everyone into a herd. The desire not to be of the herd is in itself a herd-desire. It is a recognition of the herd of which the original man is incapable.

Painters feel they *ought* to paint in the manner of Picasso or Orozco, as writers feel they ought to write in the manner of Joyce or Eliot. This *ought,* entirely modern, is a mark of the spineless.

The artists formed the *élite* herd in self-defence, in order to separate from the gross herd. But just as, in the immediate past, the enemy was the gross herd, so the *élite* herd is the enemy of the artist of the future.

One reason why Allston never wrote on art was that there was so much "literature" in it. As a writer, he looked, in painting, for something different from the trade he followed, and, in fact, as different as possible. It was for sense-impressions that he turned to painting, and he wished to see it through his senses. But the artists were so afraid he would miss the "meaning" that they would not leave him alone. They were always explaining why they had no "literature," and the literature that had grown about the subject, not to speak of the literature the artists uttered in explaining their hatred of literature, was much too much for Allston. He felt that he at least should hold his peace. It follows that his notes on painters are mere whims and trifles. Most of them are anecdotes, ungarnished, and an aesthetician would find them paltry. It may have been Vasari who suggested to Allston the notion of writing these anecdotes down, for I find numbers in his journals. But I will spare the reader these, adding only two notes about Albert Ryder:

I like Ryder's saying, after he had been working for eighteen years on a landscape, "The sky is getting interesting."

We put on a good show for foreigners, with our skyscrapers, hold-ups and cocktail-parties. But these, like the display in the Tower of London, are only our paste crown jewels. Our real crown jewels never appear, for we have no coronation times. We keep them only for the tribe. They say that New York, for instance, has no secrets, but I think, if I wished to do so, I could show them a few. There is the secret, for one, behind the name of the Hotel Albert in University Place. I always encouraged people to think that this was named for Prince Albert, or, during the first world-war years, for the king of the Belgians. What the tribe knows is that "Albert" was Albert Ryder, our tribal painter. The hotel was owned by his brother, who named it after the old man. But this is not to be told in Gath, and I should not be telling it now if the secret had not leaked out through faulty gas-pipes.

Let me conclude with one anecdote, which will do no harm. "Who told me," Allston asks, "about the barber in Quebec? My friend was painting in a field, just outside a village on the Saint Lawrence, when he noticed an odd little Frenchman, with a dandified air, dressed in a long shabby swallow-tail coat, approaching him across the field. The little man took off his hat and introduced himself as a brother-artist. His name was Samuel de Champlain, and he was a descendant of the explorer, as well as the barber of the neighbouring hamlet. He invited my friend to a soirée at his house, saying he would like to show him his latest picture, the most ambitious he had ever done. My friend, who was curious, called and saw the picture. It was a life-sized whale, frescoed on the ceiling of the parlour. As the ceiling was not large enough, he had carried his design through the window and up the wall of the house, so that the tail of the whale flapped over the roof."*

* A kind correspondent, seeing this in *The New Republic,* sends me the following passage from Flaubert's *Salammbô,* chapter V,—it describes a room in the sanctuary of Tanit:

L'appartement où ils entrèrent n'avait rien qu'une peinture noire représentant une autre femme. Ses jambes montaient jusqu'au haut de la muraille. Son corps occupait le plafond tout entier. De son nombril pendait à un fil un œuf énorme, et elle retombait sur l'autre mur, la tête en bas, jusqu'au niveau des dalles, où atteignaient ses doigts pointus.

My correspondent asks, "Why a woman in Carthage and a whale in Quebec?" Echo answers, Why? I feel that some profound meaning underlies the parallel, and I pass the question on to my readers.

CHAPTER VI

NOTES ON HUMAN NATURE

LET me assemble a few observations that might be called notes on human nature. Thus, for instance, Allston says:

> One is a long time finding out how different others are from oneself, and what wildly improbable lives, from one's own point of view, can still be happy lives. I, who could be happy in a tub, or on St. Simeon's pillar, if certain other things were right with me, think all the other folks are queer. And I continue to think them queer and am only relieved to know that they like their queerness.

One of the queer things about other people, Allston seems to have thought, was that they did not share his interest in them. In connection with this he remarks:

> Our age of psychology is not an age of interest in human nature. Think of the excited wonder with which the novels of Dickens and Balzac were written, a wonder that vibrates in their pages. This is the trait that also gives life to the great portraits of Ingres, Beechey and Gilbert Stuart, as of Velasquez and Rembrandt. No matter how good our novels and portraits may be, in every other respect, they lack this relish for character which has stamped all the

enduring novels and portraits. Our novelists turn
their characters inside out, and sometimes describe
them inimitably, but can one imagine a writer of our
time laughing and weeping over his characters, living
their lives and sharing their feelings as Victor Hugo
and Thackeray lived the lives of their men and
women?

This excited wonder over human nature was one of
the marks of the Victorian age, as of all the ages
of energy. Is there a portrait-photographer living
who has an eye for character comparable to David
Octavius Hill's? Stieglitz has an eye for certain types,
but he is more interested in other matters. The aim
and the effect of most of our portrait-photographers
is to make their sitters conform to a preconceived
type,—they all emerge from the camera as captains
of industry or as pretty women, when they are not
decorative arrangements. Well spoke Emerson, writing to Carlyle, about his "thirsty eyes," his "portrait-
eating, portrait-painting eyes." All the great novelists
and portrait-painters, Carlyle and Taine among them,
have "eaten" their characters in this way. As for
modern painters,—Derain, for example,—most of
them make their subjects look like dolls.

In no respect does it appear more clearly that ours
is not an age of energy than in this indifference to
character. The seventeenth century, like the nineteenth, was an age of energy. That is why Cromwell
insisted that the artist who painted him should put
in all the warts.

Psychology is one thing, and it is the dominant
thing today. Perception and feeling are something
else, and they are dominant in the great ages.

Allston had never lost his feeling for the Victorian
age. He had always regarded it as one of the great

ages. In this he agreed with A. R. Orage, who wrote, "I am prepared to apologize if I have ever used 'Victorian' in a derogatory sense. But I know I have not." (Neither had Allston.) "My own generation has provided the soul of the world with nothing so fine." Allston agreed with every word of this. He had attacked the "Puritan," not too wisely, he later thought; but against the word "Victorian" he had never joined in the hue and cry. For what age had produced more great characters? Was not its dominant element character? So he was amused by one of T. S. Eliot's statements, in *Essays Ancient and Modern.* Eliot, speaking of Tennyson as a friend of Frederick Denison Maurice, said, "Nothing seems odder about that age than the respect which its eminent people felt for one another." Allston said, "I wonder why? Why 'odd'? The odd thing would have been if Tennyson had not respected Maurice. Nothing could have been odder, I should say, than that. Is it possible that Eliot does not know what respect means? If respect for character strikes him as odd, one can only think so." In general, Allston felt that modern people had lost all feeling for character, and this he attributed largely to the vogue of psychology. He said that psychology tended to destroy one's feeling for values: it turned one's attention to the causes of things, whereas the significance of things was what really mattered. Meanwhile, as one who was interested in biographical writing, he continued the theme of character in the following note:

> The method of psychoanalysis, in the writing of biographies, has a very limited value, and I believe that, having once passed, it will not be used again.

If one could accept for biography the dictum of
George Brandes, that, while the romantic intellect is
interested in the significance of things, the modern
intellect is interested only in their causes, then one
could say that the day of the Plutarchs has passed
and that Freud is the master of the future. In reality, what concerns the biographer, whether "romantic" or not, is always the significance of things, while
their causes are of relatively little importance. Psy-
choanalysis serves the psychologist in the biographer
by placing him in possession of certain facts which he
cannot obtain so easily by other methods. But these
facts are no more useful than other facts, and all his
facts are useless until the biographer has reconceived
them in the light of his intuitive faculty, with its feeling for reality and proportion. This is a different
mental organ from the intelligence, which actually
paralyzes its operation. It is not the causes that matter in biography, it is the character itself, which belongs to the moral and aesthetic sphere, a sphere that
is quite apart from the sphere of causation. The attempt to turn biography into a science is as futile as
it is with history.

So much for Allston's interest in character. That
others did not share it always surprised him, and in
fact their indifference disturbed him. He felt that
it did not augur well for the future of the country.
Thus he says:

What determines the value of a civilization? There
is only one criterion, according to Leopardi,—the
amount of the singularity one finds among the people
of the country. To put this in other words, character
exists when people are interested in it and tolerate it.

Character is the basis of civilization. Variety of character is the life of civilization.

There was a time when our population was full of singularity. In old New England, as in the West and the South, the nobler types were commoner than they are at present, but also, and this is to be observed, the queer fellows, the odd fish, the cracker-barrel sages and the like,—the village atheists, even the town drunkards,—had a sort of privilege, as they had in Russia. They might have been considered reprobates, but they were encouraged as amusing, if not worthy of respect. People seemed to realize that some of these men were geniuses, *in posse* if not *in esse*. Towards all such persons, in recent times, the general attitude is one of impatience, and they have almost died out, along with the Shakers and other sects that once gave such variety to the human landscape. This indicates,—to follow Leopardi,—a definite retrogression in our civilization.

Regarding these sects, he continues:

The old Shaker house at Harvard village. Interested to observe the perfection of the MS books copied by the brothers, as the monks copied MSS in the Middle Ages. One was a New Testament, written in a round clear hand in a large folio volume. It was a rule of the community that if a copyist made a blot or an error he was obliged to discard the sheet and write it over again from the beginning.

The Shakers, and their American monastic life, devoted to weaving, carving, rug-making, etc. This is only one of the patterns of which we have lost sight in the general compulsion to make money in the shortest available fashion. People's imaginations have been so dulled by industrialism that they cannot respond to these patterns any longer. A century ago, the popular mind was filled with the biblical patterns, the patterns presented by Plutarch, etc., so that all the classical modes of living were latent in people's minds and had only to be touched into action by some inspired leader. It was this preliminary work accomplished by popular custom that made possible the influence of Jefferson, Garrison and Thoreau.

What strikes me among all the relics of our older time is the vivid reality of these life-patterns that have passed utterly out of men's minds.

It goes without saying that Allston rejoiced in every American singularity. "All the old sects have not gone," he says. "Remember Pennsylvania, and thank heaven for the Amish!" He adds, "There are plenty of odd fish in the village where I live." Meanwhile, let me offer a few of his observations on persons:

The famous Dr. X, a gallant old man, cautiously gallant,—he is now eighty-five. As he addressed me in his affable manner, his eye descended over my person, taking in the cut of my clothes, the quality of my handkerchief and necktie, even the polish on my shoes —twice, the while he maintained his well-bred conversation, discreet in every gesture and every accent, but as if to reassure himself that I was "all right." So might George Ticknor have surveyed a stranger, in Boston, ninety years ago.

Poor Mrs. Y flutters in, crying for help, as usual. She always reminds me of one of those little birds, astray on the ocean, that light on a passing steamer, preen their feathers and wildly dart about, and vanish again, most certainly to perish, unless some other ship happens along.

Our dear Z, who is both practical and deaf, spends

an hour and a half good-naturedly shouting to procure the right direction for a road that only takes two hours at the worst. It would require less time to make every possible mistake, and one would be seeing new regions into the bargain. But practical people are also idealists, and they enjoy the exercise of their practicality for its own sweet sake.

"Drunk as a lord." When my friend F. M. was travelling in the Balkans with Lord B., both as war correspondents, he noticed that Lord B. always said, "As drunk as a prince."

In London once, B and I went to an Industrial Exhibition with an attaché of the Chinese embassy, the latter, with his drooping moustache, wearing the largest and roundest of spectacles and a bright red button on his cap. Said B, calling his attention to the X-ray machine, "You can see all the bones in the body." Our Chinese companion studied the photographs. "Ah," he replied, after a pause, tapping B's arm, "you can see all the bones, but you cannot see the heart." And this was all he could be induced to say about the Occidental magic of machinery.

I like Rudolph Ruzicka's story about his Boston friend who, when he comes to New York, and settles in the great New York hotel, opens his parcels and puts away in a drawer together every scrap of wrapping-paper and every fragment of string,—so they will not be "lonely" until he can take them back to Boston.

We are developing, in our circle, a Howells-James character in the person of Mrs. W, who has so many scruples and so many emotional problems, real to her yet utterly fantastic, that she makes life a problem for everyone else. Of course, as with so many of

Howells's people and James's people, these problems
are unconscious attempts to fill a sadly empty life.
They create the drama that human nature requires,
for human nature abhors a vacuum as well as the
other kind and insists upon creating drama out of
nothing if it has nothing else to feed upon. American
life is riddled with this furtive drama. I like people
who speak their minds, and I think life ought to be
thoroughly ventilated; but, if American life had been
ventilated, what would have become of Howells and
James?

I add a note on a child:

John W, aged six, was getting off the ship with his
mother when a man, standing beside him, offered him
some chewing-gum. He shook his head slowly. "Oh,
no," he said, with his innocent air, "I don't know
anything about chewing-gum."—"But perhaps your
mother knows about chewing-gum?"—"Oh, no, I
don't think my mother knows about chewing-gum."
Then, after reflection, "But my father is so wise. He
might know about chewing-gum."

By this time, the subject was exhausted, yet nobody's feelings were hurt.

All this was said with a seraphic air, yet as if suggesting depths of irony. How can one know what
children feel? Sometimes their minds are as opales-
cent as the mind of an old French critic. This would
have been the perfect answer, in tone, if not in substance, of a diplomat or a sage of seventy-five.

CHAPTER VII

MORE NOTES ON HUMAN NATURE

IN OFFERING a few more of Allston's notes on human nature, I do not insist that they are profound. But that Allston enjoyed the profundities of others, and even their mock-profundities, one gathers from the following observations:

A man who has the courage of his platitudes is always a successful man. The instructed man is ashamed to pronounce in an orphic manner what everybody knows, and from his silence people think that he is making fun of them. They like a man who expresses their own superficial thoughts in a manner that appears to be profound. This enables them to feel that they are themselves profound.

I am always impressed by people who give themselves out as persons of large importance. At least, in this regard, the serpent of doubt entered my garden only when I had reached years of discretion. Judging by the mask and gown, the beetling brow, the gesture of command, I used to imagine that I had encountered a dozen Dantes and Beethovens.

In later years, I found that genius and virtue more often clothe themselves in a mouse-like garb than in the splendid feathers of macaws and peacocks. They follow in this the law of protective coloration, which is based upon another law, that of the conservation of energy. It takes a great deal of energy to maintain an appearance of greatness, more than the really great are able to spare.

An evening with three eminent men of law. They began to speak of literature, in all amiability, and then what a pulling out of chestnuts, fossilized for ages in the legal mind, half the familiar quotations in Bartlett, chiefly from Pope, and the question rose, Who wrote Junius? It was evident that one and all were talking as they thought lawyers ought to talk, that they were following the well-known pattern of the learned judge unbending. What children are these great men, so exactly living up to the parts that conventional public opinion expects them to play.

In *Fors Clavigera,* Ruskin relents towards lawyers enough to admit them to a "dignified almshouse," because they are picturesque,—"for the sake of their wigs." I should preserve them for another reason, also one that springs from a love of the past. For as long as lawyers exist, Bartlett's familiar quotations will never be unfamiliar.

These notes apparently deal with lady-interviewers:

She makes me feel like a syringa-blossom, she being the humming-bird. I can feel her little brain revolve and vibrate, whirring at such a rate that it makes me dizzy, while the proboscis fathoms me, all to extract a drop of honey.

She has seen everything and met everybody, and she cannot understand why I do not wish to see her. She has all the latest news from behind the scenes. She has just spent an evening at the White House, and Hitler has told her all his secrets. She has such remarkable things to say, as that Hitler in his heart loves the Jews, that Mussolini has only the kindest

intentions, and that the next war is going to start
from a difference of opinion in the Andes. It is all
new and exciting, and everything is different from
what one supposed, just as reality always is. And yet
I am not consumed with a passion to meet her.

But has she really seen things, or has she perhaps
seen nothing? How these awfully knowing people
abound! The lady neglects to consider one fact, which
is that the value of reflections depends upon the quality of the mirror. A looking-glass walking down the
road was Stendhal's definition of a story-teller, and
the world at present is full of looking-glasses. Then
why is the world so unfamiliar with its own features?
It is because most of the looking-glasses come from
Mr. Woolworth's basement.

I add a longer passage about "these awfully knowing people:"

> *You do not know, I do not know.* This is the only
> attitude to assume in the presence of the "knowing"
> political prophets. I soon saw at Washington, last
> year, that most of the officials did not know what
> was going to happen, in Germany or Italy or Japan,
> and that those who really knew the most knew that
> they did not know. It was all a matter of "feeling,"
> and the people who "feel," in regard to these events,
> are very seldom those who are "in the know." The
> only invincible ignorance is knowingness, which al-
> ways deceives the simple. When, for a dozen years,
> we have watched our favourite political prophet,
> whoever he may be, predicting revolutions that do
> not occur, and failing to predict revolutions that do,
> —as I saw in the case of my own chosen prophet, a
> very knowing man, whom I took for gospel years
> ago,—we end by ceasing to read them. (I do not re-

fer to the commentators, Louis Fischer, Swing, John
Gunther, who have added a third dimension to political reporting.) The feeling life is the only life that
matters, and, when it comes to the movements of peoples, it is the old women who know, not the brilliant
publicists, with their bright and shining information.
That is why Napoleon resorted to the sooth-sayers,
as the German and Austrian emperors, in the last
war, consulted Madame Sylvia, if that was her name.

Am I attacking the intelligence? Only when it is
used improperly. Its proper use is to solve solvable
questions, on a basis of known data. But the great
questions of life can seldom be approached in this
fashion; and those who pursue life in a straight line,
as if it were a game of chess, pay a heavy price for
their nonchalance. They lose the use of their perceptions, which are chiefly active when the intelligence is
in abeyance. For the feeling men, the brooding men,
life is a tragi-comedy, not a game. Men of this type
are always guessing. The intelligent men disdain to
guess. They base their predictions on evidence. But
as the elements of the evidence are largely emotional
elements, their predictions are usually wrong, while
the guesses of the others are often right. One can be
weather-wise about human questions, as well as about
the crops and the snow-storms.

Here are three notes about young men:

J. C. tells me about the brilliant young men at
Princeton, and I remember T.'s account of the young
men of his day. They were all going to reform the
country, and now they are clipping coupons in their
fathers' offices. "These matters are delightfully un-
certain," as Hawthorne says, in *The House of the
Seven Gables*. "At almost every step in life, we meet

with young men of just about Holgrave's age, for
whom we anticipate wonderful things, but of whom,
even after much and careful enquiry, we never happen to hear another word. The effervescence of youth
and passion, and the fresh gloss of the intellect and
imagination, endow them with a false brilliancy,
which makes fools of themselves and other people.
Like certain chintzes, calicos and ginghams, they show
finely in their first newness, but cannot stand the sun
and rain, and assume a very sober aspect after wash-
ing-day."

Eugène Delacroix, in his journal, says of his young
friend Riesener, "He is lost. He is beginning to say,
'It's too late now,' like all the lazy men who have
forever been saying with assurance, 'I have plenty of
time.' "

Do not flatter yourself that by mere inertia you
can sink to the lower depths. A well-organized person has to work, to sink as well as to rise, for he has
to violate all manner of instincts which it is easier to
satisfy. The line of least resistance is to float, on the
level where one was born, like a large inexpensive
cake of soap.

The following are more general:

To "have a good time" is the sole object of life
for untold thousands of our countrypeople. I sympathize with this ideal in people who are born for it,
but I think they are rare. However, I know a few
who have a real vocation for it. Nature intended
them to have a good time, and one feels they ought
to have it; and, when they fail to have it, when circumstances turn against them, one feels a desolation
in the general air. It is just as K. says about the Negroes, who enjoy their clothes and finery so much.

When I see a young Negro in a brand new spring suit, with a bright new necktie and a flower in his buttonhole, I feel as if every one of them should have an annual dividend to carry out this obvious intention of nature. But Negroes, in this particular, are especially blest,—they outnumber other people as ten to one. In general, I believe in supporting all vocations, knowing how rare and special they are. The vocation for a "good time" is just as rare as any other.

There is nothing to which a woman will not descend if she has a blind husband, two rickety children and an ailing mother without an income. Perhaps this explains why "pulp novels" can be written in good faith. It is easy for a desperate woman to imagine that she is a burglar, a prostitute, murderer or bandit. This also explains the ruthlessness of women in business; and, if you see a woman who seems to be resolved to make a holy show of herself, you will generally find behind her an empty larder.

C. F. met at Carlsbad one of the Hollywood movie magnates. He had himself just seen a fine performance of Lessing's *Minna von Barnhelm,* and he told the great man that he should make a picture of it. They talked for a while of other matters, and then, as they were parting, the magnate said, "Now what about this fellow Lessing? When you see him, ask him how much he wants for his play."

The notion of sexual continence came from the Orient, from the most sensual regions where the sexual temptations were the strongest.

No doubt, every virtue originated at the point, in the group, where the opposite temptation was the strongest. Gluttony and acedia were the sins of the monastic life because eating and idleness were almost the only channels through which the monks could know excess.

The monastic mind was the sieve of antiquity. Through this everything was filtered that has come down to us. Thus little but the noble and the ribald has survived, the monastic mind in action and reaction. The monastic mind is the measure of ancient society as we know it.

As the English, who may well be the last of the imperial races,—for the empires rising now are of quite another order,—as the English have been certainly the handsomest of races, so every race must have been beautiful at the time when it was dominant. Think of the Romans of the great period, and the Greeks down to Alexander; for energy and vitality presuppose health and comeliness. No doubt, in their heyday the Serbians, the Syrians, the Babylonians shared for a time this personal physical splendour. The Bible gives us Judith, Ruth, Naomi as types of the classical Jewess; and one may take Colonel Hutchinson as characteristic of the classical Puritan type of the seventeenth century.

From Allston's various journals I gather these brief remarks:

There are some people who take a fierce delight in doing what they do not want to do.

Earnest people are often people who habitually look on the serious side of things that have no serious side.

Good people are often sweet, but sweet people are not so often good.

How few people are able to praise without appearing to patronize, even when they sincerely admire.

What solemn zanies are these sex-pedants, with their talk about "love-play."

Nothing is sadder than the consequences of having worldly standards without worldly means.

Suggestion for a collector,—to collect lenses ground by Spinoza.

What a strange separation of faculties is possible in a human being. X, as a man, is the soul of kindness and honour, yet intellectually,—and I speak by the book,—he is both a fool and a knave.

Cant is moral assumption without moral feeling.

There are some knots that have to be cut. When two live wires become entangled, one cannot grasp the wires to separate them without renewing the shock. It is often so in human relations. One has to cut the knot, no matter at what price of self-respect or otherwise unnecessary misunderstanding.

Nothing is so soothing to our self-esteem as to find our bad traits in our forbears. It seems to absolve us from them.

It is only the instructed soul who represents the present. The crowd is the soul of the future in the body of the past.

After one of these, Allston adds:

Epigrams are truly like coins. There are very few whose image and superscription are not obliterated if we carry them long enough in our mental pockets.

CHAPTER VIII

AMERICAN TRAITS

A GREAT number of Allston's jottings refer to American scenes and people. He had travelled widely through the country. He seems to have been seeking for what he might have called a rationale or philosophy of American life; but he could never feel that he had succeeded in getting his mind around the subject. "It is like trying to grasp," he remarks, "a planet in the making. A planet is a handful, at best; and, while the core of this planet is certainly solid, much of it is molten, and some of it is steam." He was always puzzling over it, and he liked to collect remarks about it that were uttered by discerning foreigners. He noted what Turgenev said to Hjalmar Boyesen: "Europe I often think of as a large, dimly lighted temple, richly and magnificently decorated, but with the dusk hovering beneath its arched ceilings. America presents itself to my thoughts as a vast, fertile prairie, at first sight somewhat barren, but with a glorious dawn breaking on its horizon." Elsewhere he quotes from a speech of Herbert Spencer's, delivered in New York in 1882: "Because of its size, and the heterogeneity of its components, the American nation will be a long time in evolving its ultimate form, but its ultimate form will be high."

Naturally, Allston's impressions are often conflicting, and his views are often momentary and partial. Moreover, he was touchy, or inclined to be so, when foreigners criticized the country. He quoted Edward Everett Hale's remark, "People who come from other countries and write about our affairs are apt to make mistakes." Sometimes he could not forgive them for making the sort of mistakes that his countrypeople also were prone to make. Thus, for example, he says:

Our French and English friends like to hear about the "American language," the "American rhythm," etc. They force themselves to see American traits in our writers and have no interest in them unless they can find these traits. They wish us to be as unlike themselves as possible, and I do not blame them for this; for naturally they are in search of new sensations. They would be happier still if we painted our faces red and wore feathers.

Do I mean that I wish Americans were French or English? I wish us to be what we are, whatever we are; I wish us to be the effects of our natural causes, as the first step to being something better. But I do not wish America to be a sideshow, in its own mind or in the minds of others. Our French and English friends are entitled to their impressions, and, if they enjoy the "American rhythm," that is their affair. I know what they mean by the phrase. It certainly describes an American symptom, but I think it is a very bad symptom, allied to St. Vitus's dance, and one which, I hope, is not organic. To encourage it seems to me criminal, and what I resent is not that our French and English friends enjoy it but that we perform to give them pleasure. Our "American rhythmists" remind me of the South Carolina pickaninnies who perform the Charleston along the roads because the Northern tourists throw them pennies. The real things of America have nothing in common with this rhythm, which is both superficial and psychopathic.

Other notes reveal the chip on the patriotic shoulder:

The United States is living in several stages of history at once. This is what foreign observers cannot seem to forgive. Dick Turpin and Jack Sheppard were popular heroes in England in 1750. Englishmen should understand our Pretty Boys and Dillingers. The Dayton-Tennessee case echoed round the world. But how long ago was it that the greatest university in Spain prohibited the teaching of Sir Isaac Newton's theories?

In reality, at the present time, England, France and Spain are also living in all these stages. There are gangsters and gunmen in Marseilles as there are in Chicago, as numerous and as ferocious. The people of Brittany are behind the times in the matter of Evolution. So are the shepherds of the Shetland Islands. Then why does the world expect so much of the mountaineers of Tennessee? Why is the limelight turned on the Dayton case?—as upon the American gangsters and gunmen, while the gangsters of Marseilles go unobserved? All these anachronisms are visible with us, and for a good reason. It is because Americans think they ought to be well-behaved, up-to-date and educated people, and because the world expects this of them; and the world is outraged when they are not and makes a great hue and cry about it. Who expects a Breton peasant to have correct ideas about Evolution? Who expects a Corsican bandit to behave like a civilized man? Our foreign friends who smile at us pay us a high tribute. They are judging us by our own American standard.

"America is an extraordinarily ghostless country." Thus my Irish friend,—a lover of ghosts,—who compares us with England and his country. He means that America has a great deal of exposed surface, and this is the novelty for Europeans. They are not interested in our nooks and crannies, where the ghosts abound, because these are too much like their own. They come here for new impressions, and our exposed surface gives them a dazzling array of these. Our "ghostlessness" is as striking to them as the ghostly is to Americans in Ireland and England. Nothing ever takes them to Poughkeepsie or Portsmouth or Charleston, or the pre-urban surroundings of the past generations. But Kipling found more of the ghostly in Vermont than he ever found in England because he spent three years there; and I fancy there are more ghosts in the South, between Savannah and Memphis, than there are in any similar area in Europe. From Hawthorne to Henry James, from Mary E. Wilkins to William Faulkner, our storyteller's world has been peopled with ghosts.

I distrust Santayana's "Epicurean contentment" with a world run by cardinals and engineers. For is not this the moral of Mario van der Weyer, the hero of The Last Puritan, his novel? I say the hero, for which is the hero, Oliver or this other young man to whom in his Epilogue Santayana says, "Any future worth having will spring from men like you"? Of course, Santayana never understood this country, and does not The Last Puritan tell us why? Consider this picture of Emerson's house in Concord: "To feed Oliver's idealism they stopped on their way back at Concord . . . They looked at the dreadful little house in which Emerson lived, and at his cold little sitting-room; and then they looked at each other. *Could such great things leave such mean traces?"* Not a word about the moral beauty of this habitation, not to speak of its simple grace and charm,—which left Emerson free to live in the mind. It was merely cold, little and dreadful.

Suppose one turned the tables and imagined the Italian thinkers in the Rome that Santayana likes so much. No doubt, their dwellings are of "white marble," like Santayana's talent, and one could not call these dreadful; but, in their world of cardinals and engineers, what has become of their freedom to live in the mind? Should we not be obliged to say, fifty years hence, *Could such mean things leave such great traces?*

There is nothing about Emerson's house that I do not like. But one would expect a thinker to prefer the tub of Diogenes to the Rome of Santayana.

To follow this crescendo of patriotism:

Poor little Pirandello gives out a statement, on landing in New York, defending Mussolini's Ethiopian war with the analogy of our dealings with the American Indians. Astonishing how little these continentals know about the American mind. Of all the aspects of our history, except perhaps the Mexican war, the Indian aspect is the one that makes every decent American blush. And that is the best self-defence this Italian can think of.

It was not provincial, thirty years ago, for foreigners not to know what Americans think. It is provincial now, especially when Americans, with their uncensored press,—uncensored, at least, by the government,—know more about Italy than the Italians know, and more about Germany than the Germans.

But, while Allston was often touchy when foreigners criticized his country, he loved to chastise it himself, in this resembling the French and the Eskimos alike. He enjoyed nothing more than commenting on American foibles. For instance, he says:

I usually find Englishmen refreshing,—S. D., W. M., H. L. S. and others,—because they are invariably direct, unequivocal, outspoken. Beside their conversation, too much of our American conversation is indirect, over-abounding in tact, equivocal, diplomatic, as if one were always having to consider people's feelings, always thinking twice, fearing to step on someone's toes. It is all circumlocution and beating about the bush. One would think Americans never knew where they stood. Englishmen almost always suggest veracity and courage; Americans too often suggest mendacity and fear. There is a long story behind these two attitudes. We are the victims of many circumstances which we have not mastered. One of these is the mixture of races who cannot meet without equivocation and are always putting forth tentacles to feel one another out. But it plays the devil with our minds.

Americans in general are no great shakes at conversation, and one of the reasons for this, I think, is that we are too sympathetic. All conversation among sympathetic people tends to adjust itself to the weakest link in the chain. If one person is self-conscious, they all tend to become self-conscious. If he has a woolly mind, the conversation becomes woolly. I have seen a whole table demoralized by one poor lamb whose secret wish was merely to be somewhere else.

Many men I know are so used to stupid people and bad conversation that they cannot conduct the real thing. One is always clearing out of the path of the talk the boulders of misconstruction with which the dull have been permitted to strew it. The primary meanings of words are the only meanings that no one takes for granted. Thus, when religion is mentioned one has to explain that one does not mean the Spanish Inquisition or the Baptists of Georgia. This makes good talk impossible. Too many intelligent Americans are half-consciously in reaction all the time against the narrow conditions of their childhood, a fact that also explains the small-minded bitterness of many American novels. Good writers and good talkers take it for granted that they are living on Mount Olympus.

How generally uniform are American minds.

Percival Lowell, in *Chöson,* speaks of an old Korean map-maker who left America out of his map of the world. But he mentioned some French sailors who were said to have seen it. "On reaching it, they found it to be one vast level wilderness. The only sounds of life which they heard in this great wilderness were the cries of some parrots in the distance."

I seem to remember hearing these cries myself.

I add a few other notes on American foibles:

Boston people are usually sure they are right, even when they are wrong. Western people are often afraid they are wrong, even when they are right. That is why the West owns the future.

"Keep moving, keep moving!" So the guards tell us in the subway. As if Americans needed this advice! We have done nothing but keep moving since the year 1620. We have moved from Plymouth Rock to Connecticut, from Connecticut to Ohio, from Ohio to Wisconsin, from Wisconsin to Dakota, and from Dakota to California. Is it any wonder that, arriving in California, and having nowhere else to go, our countrymen have gone up in the air?

Much of the weakness of the American mind is due to our ingrained habit of taking our bases lightly and shifting them so easily,—moving our habitations, resorting to divorce,—instead of committing ourselves for good and all to one fixed base and set of relations. Our history is a kaleidoscope of creeds and no-creeds, and the habit of pioneering and changing homesteads, —"tents of a day,"—at every obstacle or at every prospect of better fortune elsewhere, the habit of the permanently transitory,—all this has taken from us the stability of mind, the continuity of environment that one must have in order to produce great things. How familiar in my childhood was the sight of a dwelling, mounted on beams and drawn by horses, uprooted from its original situation, in process of being dragged through the streets to better its position somewhere else. Half the streets of my childhood were periodically blocked by these foolish structures, —sometimes even churches,—endeavouring thus to get up in the world. The divorce mania appeared on the scene after the moving-mania and somehow struck one as a consequence of it. The secret of living is not to shift one's base, in any respect whatever, except under a force of circumstances that amounts to a moral compulsion. Otherwise, life is bound to be a waste, shallow, trivial and unproductive.

These Daughters of the American Revolution, with faces like angry stone walls,—they will have to change their expressions if they wish to save the country.

For arrogance, look homeward, angel. For every race on the planet the vulgar American has an oppro-

brious epithet. It would take a Rabelais to exhaust
the names he showers on his fellow-beings,—wops,
dagoes, heinies, squareheads, frogs, sheenies, limies,
chinks and dirty Irish. Commonly uttered in good
humour, these names express a latent attitude which,
under pressure, may yield in social relations only the
deposit of contempt that easily turns into animosity.
As with everything else in America, we see this in
terms of fair weather. What will be the effect of a
few good storms?

Beside the Chinese, we Americans are like spoiled
children. Every now and then, for a bath of ethics and
good manners, I visit the Chinese missionaries; for so
I call the laundrymen who abound in our villages and
towns.

CHAPTER IX

MORE AMERICAN TRAITS

IN SOME of Allston's American notes, he deals
with international comparisons. I have already
given a few of these. Here are two or three more:

> Wool-gathering is the great American intellectual
> vice, stewing and day-dreaming for lack of direction.
> Few of us get under way before we are middle-aged.
> In Europe there is more of the tradition of command,
> and of self-command as both a cause and effect of
> this.

"Alas, at thirty-five to be still preparing for something!" Thus Dmitri Rudin. How many times, within
the last twenty-four hours, has this apostrophe been
addressed to the American air. It is one of the trag-
edies of our writing life that so many of our writers
begin too late, when their mental bones, so to speak,
are set in impossible patterns and they cannot find
their true orientation. Observe what Flaubert wrote
at the age of thirteen: "I see with indignation that
the censorship of the press is to be established again,
and the liberty of the press abolished . . . It is of his
conscience that the man of letters is now being robbed,
of his artist's conscience." There are few American
writers under thirty as conscious of their vocation as
this shows Flaubert to have been at the age of
Huckleberry Finn. I offer no solution of this problem,

such as that everything depends on our developing a school. We have to state problems before we can solve them.

It is largely to the aristocratic tradition that Englishmen and Frenchmen owe their superior sense of being entitled to their own souls. Aristocracies have kept open the right of way for all the rebels and artists. It is because we have no recognized aristocracy, to maintain this pattern of personal freedom, that we so seldom feel we are justified in breaking paths of our own.

Allston did not regret that we had no aristocratic tradition. He felt it was wholly contrary to the American genius, and it had proved too costly in other respects. But he felt that its absence encouraged certain American weaknesses, to one of which he refers in the following note. As we had no recognized aristocracy, everyone could claim to possess it. In this, as in other matters, the "lid" was "off." Was not the desire for social prestige almost the leading trait of Americans? Who did not wish to be one of "these distinguished people"?—if one was to believe the advertisers. Who did not wish to be a "socialite"? Thus he says:

How deeply ingrained in the American mind is the desire for social prestige. One sees it, amusingly enough, in the life of Mrs. Eddy. Her devout biographer, Sibyl Wilbur, is less at pains, one would almost say, to prove Mrs. Eddy's piety than her good breeding, her taste in dress, the quality of her rustic antecedents, her misfortune in having been dragooned into marriage with a "flamboyant" dentist, her obligation to desert the "narrow-minded artisans" who had been her first disciples when she began to form her clientele in the higher circles of Boston.

Then we have Dr. Buchman, who is always talking of "moral rearmament," and who remarked not long ago, "Thank God for Hitler!" His specialty is to seek for "key people" of social position. The Saviour's key people, when they were not fishermen, were publicans and sinners; and something like this has been the case with all the true religious cults. Is not Buchmanism the first religious cult that has ever made social prestige its bid for approval?

In regard to Buchmanism and Mrs. Eddy, I find this further note: "In all the realms of the pseudo, the improperly grounded, the money-motive plays a large part. This is true in the pseudo-artistic realm as well as in the pseudo-religious realm." Referring to Dr. Buchman's "key people," I find this copy of a letter to a Buchmanite friend: "I seem to disagree with you as regards the importance of all such people, the importance of their activities, the kind of education they stand for, the institutions they found, etc. I am disillusioned with a business world, both in action and in reaction, in its way of getting sick and getting well,—and these big bouncing bustling ignorant boys belong, to my thinking, to the Stone Age. But then I don't believe in activism and vitalism. I think they are wrecking the world, both without and within. I should like to see the world alive in the intellect and spirit and dead to all the things these people stand for." More or less in connection with this, he quotes from Francis Parkman's *Vassall Morton:*

"You're a victim of the national disease, Rosny," said Chester. "Rising in the world!—that's the idea that ruins us. It's that that makes us lean, starveling, nervous, restless, dyspeptic, hypochondriac,—the most prosperous and most uncomfortable people on earth. Sit down, man, and take of our ease. What garden will thrive if every plant in it must be dug up every day, and set out in a better place?"

Not unrelated to this is the following:

For years I was unable to interest myself in American history because of certain phrases that blocked my path. Whenever I opened Rhodes, for instance, I encountered one of these phrases that stood like sullen watch-dogs at the gate of the subject. "The resumption of specie payment" was one such phrase. What it means I know, but I did not know it in the days when I knew nothing of history, and I know that I shall not know it again in the misty days before I die. It is not that I have not *resumed,* or do not know what *specie* is, still less that I do not know the meaning of *payment.* But the effort to associate these meanings is too much for my mind. So it was when my life began, so will it be when I am old, and now that I am a man I do resent it. I do not wish to know too much about the "resumption of specie payment;" and I deprecate this phrase and the part it plays in every account of the age that preceded my own. Why this repetition of emphasis? And why, as a boy, especially, did I resent it? Because of what it seemed to symbolize. It made me feel that money-questions dominated American history, and I was in revolt against money-questions and the undue place they held in the national mind. It was largely for this reason that I could not enter American history, and I think this explains the indifference of many others.

These paragraphs deal with other American traits:

When I was in England, at the sanitarium, and we used to cut down trees,—or cut them up,—I always by preference used an axe when all the Englishmen used saws. The doctor, observing this, remarked that all his American patients had always used axes, even when the saw was more effective, and he asked me why it was. It is a hundred years,—as I am surprised to find, thinking it over,—since any of my forbears has really lived in the country; and it is more than a hundred years since any of them used an axe, as a means of livelihood, or in the building of a homestead, or for any essential purpose. And yet is this not plainly a case of inherited aptitude? Every American of the old stock has a pioneer backwoodsman somewhere near the base of his family tree; and I was amused by a passage in Tocqueville's travel-diary (recently discovered): "The country-dwelling Americans spend half their lives cutting trees, and their children learn at an early age to use the axe against the trees, their enemies." We Americans are axemen by instinct. We all have a Leather-Stocking under our skins. We even invented the axe.

Thinking over the difference between the Civil War and the first world-war, as also between the North and the South, I compare Charles Francis Adams and Walter Page as ambassadors to England. Adams was the statesman, Page was not. What do I mean by this, and what was the reason? Adams was the public man by instinct, the impersonal spokesman of his country. Page was always the private man, swayed by his personal feelings, as modern men are apt to be and as Southern men are apt to be. (Of course, the old Southerners were quite different, and for a very good reason. They were statesmen in grain, more than the Northerners were.) Imagine Adams governed by an affection for Lord John Russell, as Page was governed by his affection for Sir Edward Grey! And yet undoubtedly Adams knew Russell better than Page knew Grey.

The tough New England strain. I predict that on the last day of this planet, when the sun hangs cold in the sky, only two men will be left to face it. One will be a Chinaman, and if you ask the other he will say, "O yes, I was born at Cohasset."

The American voice of legend is rapidly changing for the better. Yet there are still enough voices to justify Howells's question, "Who can defend the American accent, which is not so much an accent as a whiffle, a snuffle, a twang?"

In the presence of an ugly voice, all my Christian feelings instantly vanish. I am willing to believe that a person with an ugly voice may have intellect and all the virtues, but I have to struggle with myself to maintain my composure when I am confronted with such a voice.

Yet there are worse voices than ugly voices. Who was it said that, at the University of Chicago, they teach all kinds of voices, as a regular part of the curriculum? You choose the sort of accent you wish to have and emerge with an Oxford voice or a Harvard voice or any other voice that takes your fancy. No doubt, the provocation for this is great, and I well understand the desire to escape from the shocking flatness of most of our voices; but, to me, the synthetic voice is far worse. I prefer the worst voice in its native state to the mellifluous notes of the radio-announcers. How sorry is the voice that is a simulacrum only,—one runs at the sound of such a farce. The curse of our civilization is the assumption of these external effects, with no sharing of their underlying causes. Let us have voices of character, even if the character is undeveloped, until the developing cause produces the developed effect.

Newcomers in this country, of the second generation, often acquire a plastered-on English voice. This is natural. A real American voice cannot be acquired. It has to be *lived into,* and this takes time. But it is easy to acquire an English voice, not of the natural type but of the mask-type,—the so-called Oxford whinny, etc.,—which always has an element of the ventriloquistic. One learns it as one learns golf or tennis.

As for the real American voice, what poetry it is capable of! I have heard President Lowell utter the words "Civil War" so that they sounded like a ballad.

Here are two notes suggested by country living:

On my afternoon walks in winter, I always receive the same impression from the effect of the sunlight on the farmhouse window-panes. It is the winter light of four or five o'clock, and it produces in me an indefinable sense of desolation,—like the whistle of the railway trains in wide empty spaces of sea-coast or prairie. I am stricken at once with a lonely feeling, as if I were abandoned in the void between the worlds. Byron must have had this feeling when he wrote some of the passages in *Cain* and *Manfred.* Charles Burchfield catches this effect of light on the window-panes of the forsaken houses that he paints in so many of his water-colours.

I find a word that describes this sensation, under the same conditions, in one of the old Vermont ballads:

Till when length he reached the cabin,
Black and desolate it stood;
Cold the hearth and windows *ralist*
In their stillest solitude.

This word, with its indescribable associations, reminds me of the Polish word "zal," of which Liszt makes so much in his life of Chopin.

Ralph Boyer has been telling me of an Indian footpath he used to see as a boy, along the Delaware river, near Trenton. It was clearly marked, although hidden by the underbrush, and the local woodsman who showed him where to find it had traced this path miles northward until it joined the old Mohawk trail. Nothing catches more at one's imagination than these ancient paths, which are apparently never obliterated, —like the path round Walden Pond in Concord, "worn by the feet of Indian hunters," as Thoreau says. In Concord, there is another path, along the ridge by the Boston road, which Hawthorne wore with his feet, during his last brooding years, 1860–1864, and which was still clearly marked three years ago. Prescott wore a similar path at Lynn, where he had a summer villa. There was a cherry-tree beside the house, and he plodded round and round this tree for hours every day. He could not, in his blindness, venture further, and the shade of the cherry-tree protected his eyes. The traces of this path remained for years.

There was a path like this in our garden in California, which had not been used for a hundred years. It was worn by the Franciscan monks of the mission, and was said to have led to a spring. In England, at various times, I have seen the traces of two disused Roman roads, one from Shooter's Hill, the other from one of the Sussex downs. They were invisible on the plain, even if one happened to walk along them, but easily seen from above, although they were covered with waving grain. Or am I mistaken in thinking that the Sussex road was a Roman road? It may have been the one that Kipling speaks of,—

> See you the dimpled track that runs
> All hollow through the wheat?
> O that was where they hauled the guns
> That smote King Philip's fleet.

However it may have been, Elizabethan or Roman, the plough, during all these hundreds of years, had stirred only the earth on the surface. The subsoil had remained so packed by the traffic of those far-off days that the grain in the ruts still grew in a different fashion from the surrounding grain. Mary Austin told me it was the same way with the pioneer trails over the Western deserts, that a road, once beaten, however long disused, was never quite blotted out.

Let me end this chapter with a few notes on well-known Americans whose paths Allston crossed at various times. Some of them are Harvard memories:

President Eliot had a personal grandeur that one might fail to find the equal of, in a long life passed in a dozen countries. It was a grandeur of bearing, voice and presence which, in its perfect simplicity, explained why republican Rome felt that it was better than the empire. But he was practical, O how practical. The only words of his that I remember, from the only speech of his that I remember,—his address to the freshman class when I was in college,—are the words "serviceable fellowship," which I think he meant us to regard as the great prize and object of college life. These words shocked me at the time, and it was because they shocked me that I recall them;

for it had never occurred to me that "fellowship" could be "serviceable," far less that one should make it so. The phrase has stuck in my mind, for thirty years, as a very strange sort of fishbone to have been inserted there by a great master of learning.

I saw Theodore Roosevelt once or twice. He came to a tea at the *Advocate* sanctum when I was in college. It was my first experience of animal magnetism raised to the proportions of the jungle, for one could feel his presence approaching down the corridor, before he came in sight, "like echoes whispering where great armies be." Another guest was there, the English author, W. H. Mallock, who had written *The New Republic*. Roosevelt, hearing his name, grasped his hand; and then, although the meeting was quite impromptu, he poured forth a flood of comment on Mallock's views and books, every one of which he seemed to have read. It was like Niagara falling on a fern. The little old man was stunned with confusion and pleasure. Since then, I have never had a doubt that Roosevelt, whatever else he was, was a portent, if not a man of genius.

I saw Mark Twain in his coffin, the only time I ever saw him. I was walking up Fifth Avenue one April day in 1910 and saw a great crowd gathered about the Brick Church. Someone said it was Mark Twain's funeral, and I crossed the street and went into the church. The funeral was over, and most of the people had gone out, so I climbed up to the gallery and went to the front; and there, just below, lay the open coffin, with the old man's white hair spread abroad and his shoulders in the famous white flannels.

Allston had no love of pragmatism, but regarding William James he said, "I am drawn to his person-

ality as helplessly as a filing to a magnet." He regretted that he had never heard any of James's lectures:

> To think that I was such a puppy as to go through
> Harvard College without once hearing or seeing Wil-
> liam James. And then, one day, in New York,—it
> must have been in 1909,—I met him face to face in
> Twenty-third Street. I can see the spot now, at the
> southeast corner of Madison Square. His face rose
> out of the crowd, hurrying beside him, shining with
> goodness and wisdom, just as I had seen it in the
> pictures, with the pepper-and-salt Norfolk jacket and
> all. I have always believed in William James's face,
> knowing that he must have been right at bottom.

Such "meetings" as these are all but spectral.
Scarcely more tangible are the human encounters
suggested by the paragraphs that follow:

> How much a simple phrase, rightly remembered,
> can mean! My dear old friend in England, S. E.,
> went to school with a son of Matthew Arnold and
> visited the Arnolds on one of his vacations. He re-
> membered how the great man entered the room, and,
> lifting his left hand, waved it in the direction of
> the awe-struck boys, saying, in a sweetly deprecating
> sing-song voice, "You may sit down." As much of
> Arnold lingers in this picture as there was of conduct
> in his theory of life, not that I disagree with the
> theory of conduct.

> There also comes back to me a phrase uttered by
> Charles Eliot Norton on one of his "Dante eve-
> nings" at Shady Hill, perhaps when the sherry was
> being passed, with the little silver basket of caraway
> cakes. It was to the effect that the picture of heaven
> in the Book of Revelation,—with its excess of precious

stones,—was such as might have been conceived "by
a New York woman." What a phrase was that for
expressing how Boston and Cambridge felt about the
gaudy New York splendours that had vulgarized their
beloved Newport.

Still a third phrase comes back, in a reminiscence
of my childhood. It evokes a house of the eighteen-
sixties, of which I used to hear much, where Horace
Greeley was lunching on one of his political journeys.
"You can be fixing me some" was the phrase, in reply to a question of his hostess, whether he would
have a little salad,—uttered no doubt with one of his
hands in the butter and his honest pumpkin face shining over all.

CHAPTER X

EXPATRIATION

LIKE most Americans, Allston had doubts about expatriation,—that is, in the case of his country-people, and especially artists and writers. It was not that he did not like to travel. He said that he was born with a Baedeker in his cradle, and he had felt, in his earlier years, that he lived ten times more intensely in any other country than his own. Later, he seems to have thought that youth was the time for travel, because one could yield oneself to pure sensation, whereas, in after years, one had to think, and travelling dislocated one's basis of thinking:

One's mind swims with the ships (he writes), and whirls and races with the trains and buses, and one is overwhelmed with surface-impressions. It is impossible to take these impressions as one used to take them, when to receive impressions was an end in itself. One has to reflect on all one sees, and, with one's judgment in solution, owing to fatigue, speed, motion, too many abrupt transitions, one realizes how little one has mastered the context of any given object. How can one look at a cathedral as one looked at it in one's early twenties? A little knowledge of architecture, a little knowledge of history is not enough. Everything one sees is charged with meanings that

carry one to the heart of the world and life; and the
logic of this fact leads one far. It leads to the conclusion of all the mystics that any room in any village is much like any other room or village, that, in
fact, the more one stays at home the better one
understands the world and life.

Allston, who was not a mystic, and who cared for
many things that mystics seldom care for, had almost
arrived at this conclusion. It was true that to know
one had to see. On the other hand, the conditions of
seeing all too often destroyed the conditions of knowing. *To have seen* was doubtless indispensable, but
that was another matter.

That the danger of all this was a certain smugness,
Allston well knew. He spoke of the Shakers, for
instance, admiring some of their communal forms,
their handicraft and model farming, but he recalled
what Emerson said about them, that they were
"peasants, with a squalid contentment." It was only
the mystic's ecstasy that justified the mystic's ex-
clusions,—if one shut out everything else for the
"Alone," and did not possess the "Alone," what a
poor thing one was bound to be! This was the law
with every quietism and every other form of self-
contained existence. It required either ecstasy or
wisdom; and Allston did not feel he was wise enough
to lay down laws for himself or others. If he had
ceased to care for foreign travel,—at least, as he had
cared in other days,—he travelled much in America;
and he felt that his indifference to foreign travel was
largely the result of his interest in this. Travelling
elsewhere for a special reason was quite another matter. If he did not care for travelling in general, it

was partly because he felt that life was short. I find
this note in one of his guide-books:

> Baffled by the multiplicity of all these doors past
> which one can see only through the key-hole. Blank
> incomprehensions of a creature "moving about in
> worlds not realized."
> For travel, I wish to see only the countries that
> I have seen before, into which I have a degree of ini-
> tiation. The rest, much as one may know about them,
> in the casual way of all modern men, can never be
> anything more than moving pictures, mere shells and
> outsides, like so many animated postcards. When I
> think how far I am from understanding even my own
> country,—it would take me a thousand years to un-
> derstand it,—I wonder what I could get from China
> or Java in a three or four weeks' visit.

And yet, "Who knows?" he adds. "I might dredge
up from my mind all manner of unexpected thoughts,
the kind of thoughts that only come to life in these
sharp and unforeseen encounters."

As for the subject of living abroad, or expatriation, much discussed in America in recent years, he
sometimes wondered if it was a subject. It was so
personal a question, so governed by individual circumstances, and, on the other hand, expatriation, in
a modern world of international interests, was often
so inevitable and so natural that to discuss it at all
seemed fatuous.

> Who am I to discuss it (he says)? I have often
> wished to live abroad, and, if I have lost this desire,
> it is mainly because America has grown so interest-
> ing, or because I have grown so interested in it; and
> many of my friends are Europeans who have come to

live in America or Americans who have gone to live
in Europe. There are obviously no laws that apply to
them all; and did not Heine and Turgenev live in
Paris? Did not Dostoievsky spend years in western
Europe? And how about Landor, Strindberg, Ibsen,
Nietzsche? They all lived for decades outside their
countries. The more I think about deracination, the
more I remember Ibsen's advice to Björnson, "Go
abroad, carissimo! Both because distance gives a
wider range of vision, and because much more value
is set upon the man who is out of sight." Ibsen said
he had never seen his home so clearly, so fully and so
minutely as from a distance and during his absence.
Was it not so with me in former times?

It had been so, in fact. The moment he left America,
in his younger days, his mind was filled with America, which he had largely taken for granted while he
was living in it. Indeed, he had written two books
about the United States during long visits in England. (He had sat, while writing one of these books,
on Captain Cook's sea-chest, for he had rented a
house, in a suburb of London, that belonged to two
of Cook's descendants. It was a battered old red
morocco trunk, bound with brass studs, and he said
that sitting on it gave him the feeling that he was
another explorer, engaged in adventurous voyages.
"But I often had to shift my seat," he added, "for
some of the brass studs were very sharp.") Allston
had always come home again at the end of eighteen
months or so, but Ibsen had lived abroad for twenty-
seven years, and he had never ceased to think of
Norway, nor had he ever ceased to understand it.
Allston also recalled what André Gide said of Mau-

rice Barrès, when the latter published *Les Dé-
racinès,* that "if he had not gone to Paris, he would
not have been able to write the book in which he
advised others to stay at home." It was true, the
deracination of which Barrès spoke was that of the
provincial who goes to the metropolis. It was not so
much a question of leaving one's country. But what
difference did this make? Obviously, with countless
mortals, it made no difference whatever.

There were obviously also other cases in which it
made a great difference. It might be an individual
and personal question, but were there not classes of
persons, groups and types, who, in the matter of
expatriation, were affected in generically different
ways?

I have often noticed (Allston writes) that the
French, both men and women, find it very difficult to
adjust themselves to what they delightedly call the
"American rhythm." Where Englishwomen tramp
about, as if the whole planet were equally theirs, and
as if they felt at home, in all conditions, I have seen
Frenchwomen in the woods, unreconcilable, as their
gestures showed, to the fact that the woods were not
Paris. On the other hand, the French adjust themselves to the ways of the South Sea islanders, which
other racial groups are unable to do. The effects of
expatriation plainly differ with types as they do with
persons, as one sees in the fact that certain races are
colonizing races and others are not; some races are
able to "hit it off" with the circumstances of other
races, while others again are antagonized or sterilized
by them.

Allston, who thought much about this question,—as

I gather from the number of comments I find in his journals,—had his own racial group in mind, and especially the *genus* artists and writers. What did expatriation mean for them? Was there any solution of the problem at which they had all arrived? Could one generalize from their experience? Allston's papers bristle with these questions. He knew how complex the problem was, and he had an extreme distrust of simplifications. On the other hand, he felt that a hundred years, or all American history since Washington Irving, had yielded such a number of examples that one really had some basis for generalization. He had arrived at a conclusion that somehow *felt* true, on the whole. It seemed to indicate an American trait that set Americans off from Englishmen, and certainly from many other races. What this was he explains in the following note:

> The literary history of England proves,—or so it seems to me,—that Englishmen can be at home in all the four quarters of the earth. They seem to lose nothing by expatriation, or, at least, very little, they can adjust themselves so easily,—adjust, if not adapt, —to so many exotic forms of living, without losing their own form, that, while their expatriation may bring nostalgia, a homesick feeling for their native ways, which, for the rest, they carry with them, it seldom brings the malaise that Americans feel,—almost always feel, sooner or later. I can think of many Englishmen, famous or obscure, sick or well, from Landor, for example, to D. H. Lawrence, who have lived for long years outside their country and whose creative life has flowered superbly, to whom, in fact, the geographical question, in this particular aspect, has scarcely ever occurred. On the other hand, with

Americans, the question of expatriation is ever
present, and they are always uneasy in foreign lands.
Henry James, for instance, could never forget it, and
he was always uneasy. Englishmen are naturalized in
America every day and continue to be Englishmen
serenely, in all but the political sense. Naturalization
for James was a spiritual crisis, and even an agoniz-
ing crisis. He had to overcome a tremendous resistance to surrender his nationality, and even then he
left secret directions to have his ashes buried in Massachusetts. What a retrospective light this threw over
the whole nature of his life in England! He felt as
apologetic as a guilty child who has been disloyal to
his mother, and this was absurd enough, but how
revealing. As for the rest, sooner or later, almost
every American feels as James felt and said on many
occasions,—in his "fierce and bitter" outburst to Amy
Lowell, recorded by Foster Damon, "I have cut myself off from America, where I belonged. Don't make
my mistake." Archibald MacLeish sums up this feeling, in his *American Letter:*

> Here we must eat our salt or our bones starve.
> Here we must live or live only as shadows.

Just why Americans felt this way when Englishmen did not, Allston often wondered. But that they
did so feel he was convinced, and it interested him to
find that Dostoievsky felt the same way about Russia.
Dostoievsky's letters were filled with bitter complaints during his years of forced expatriation. It
was not only that he felt an alien, in Dresden, Ge-
neva, Berlin, Florence, Milan,—"like a slice cut from
the loaf." He was morbidly afraid of losing touch
with Russia; he said he could not live without Russia, that he could not write without Russia and that

to "get out of touch with Russia" was to lose the power to write. His daughter, in her biography, remarks that Turgenev spent his whole life abroad and "remained eternally Russian,"—as Ibsen was eternally Norwegian,—while Dostoievsky's "Russianism" depended, or so he always felt, on his bodily presence in Russia. Why was this? Was it because, as his daughter says, he was only partly of Russian blood, because he was a "Lithuanian," a "Norman," a "German," and felt that it would be all too easy for him to be "absorbed by Europe"? However one explains it, the fact is important; and Allston felt that it threw some light, an indirect but interesting light, on the question of American expatriation. He explains this in a note on four writers, two Russians and two Americans, Turgenev and Dostoievsky, Henry James and Henry Adams:

> Aristocrats like Turgenev never lose their racial traits. However they are men of the world, they have the blood of the makers of nations in them; they are makers of their nations, and they know it, and invincibly proud of their nations, and they are indelibly stamped with the nations they make. A lifetime of expatriation cannot erase their inherited form; and this is also true of men like Ibsen, who spring from an ancient rooted unmixed stock. In the same way, Henry Adams was an American aristocrat, descended from the makers of his nation. After a long life as a man of the world, he retained his original traits, as Turgenev retained them. He never questioned these traits, nor did he fear to lose them or wish to lose them.

> It was otherwise with James and Dostoievsky, so totally different in other respects. They were alike in

this, that both were *uneasy* about their countries. The question of nationality in both these men remained the central question, and neither of them could take his country for granted. To become "more Russian" was Dostoievsky's passion; he trumpeted everything Russian and favoured the Slavophile party to realize this idea. To become "less American" was James's passion,—in short, the same medal in reverse. One of them feared to lose his nationality, the other wished to do so, and this fear or wish, as the case might be, determined the character of their work. Is it not therefore significant, in regard to both, that both belonged to "nomad" families,—I use Dostoievsky's daughter's word, and the Jameses were certainly nomads,—of mixed descent and recent immigration? For Dostoievsky's daughter is always dwelling on the "European" character of her father's childhood. And what was the character of James's childhood?

That this analogy had the widest bearings, Allston seems to have felt. He said that if communism had not come in and minimized the heart of this question,—that is, the Russianism of the Russians,—Russia would be full of Dostoievskys, as America has been full of Henry Jameses; for this was the meaning of the statement, so often made by social critics, that Russia and America are alike in being "young countries." It is not that they are not full of "old" people, like the rest of the world, but they are youthful social organisms. In other words, there are masses in both countries who have not actively shared in the past of the country, who do not know and feel its whole past. Most of the Russians are peasants, who have only known their fragment of soil, and they are attached to Russia only as an extension of their soil (for which they may well fight superbly). Thus, while their roots are deep, they have not shared in the history of their country; and that is why, in spite of its age, the Russian social organism is described as "youthful." The political sense of the masses is of recent growth. In America, the political sense is deeply planted and widely spread, more widely spread, undoubtedly, than anywhere else, and, "young" as the country still may be, it could not be called so properly if it were wholly peopled by the old stock. But in America there are untold millions who have not yet struck down their roots. They have not achieved an American form.

Did not this explain the American feeling in regard to expatriation? And did it not also explain why Americans seldom throve abroad? As there were so many of recent immigrant stock,—and Henry James was of this number,—they could not feel sure of their country. They felt that their roots were shallow, or that they had no roots,—the pioneer habit of shifting bases uprooted even the oldest stocks,—and that any sort of transplantation condemned them to a surface-existence. Hence the general prejudice against expatriation, which is felt to have a touch of "treason" in it. And why "treason"? Allston asks.

> It is because we are born parts of a still unformed organism. Our American instinct requires us to share in the forming of this organism. We all feel this organic political need. It is the recognition of our fundamental social instinct, in the peculiar circumstances to which we are born; and we instinctively feel that those who do not share it are somehow traitors.

Is it not, for that matter, because we are unformed that we have been over-borne in Europe? We have paid an exaggerated tribute to the form of others, and this is incompatible with self-respect.

Here lies the grain of truth in D. H. Lawrence's statement that America is not our "blood-homeland" but only our "spirit-homeland." Lawrence knew little about the Americans of the old and settled regions,— very few foreigners know anything about them; but there was an element of reality in this remark. It is only when America has been menaced, in these new world-wars, that we have come to feel how fully it is our blood-homeland.

Regarding American artists and writers, the effects of expatriation seemed to confirm Allston's feeling; and he said that the belief in roots, as a necessary element in the life of the artist, a belief that was almost universal, was equally well-founded. Heine, as he said, was an unwilling exile, and Victor Hugo re-entered France within twenty-four hours of the proclamation of the Third Republic. Turgenev lived in Paris very largely because Madame Viardot lived there,—he repeatedly said that otherwise he got nothing from it, and every summer he went back to Russia for a "strengthening bath." Stockholm ignored Strindberg, but Strindberg haunted Stockholm, and Nietzsche was careful never to lose touch with the Germans, who provided him with a perpetual reason for being a "good European." What instinct of self-preservation governed these men, most of whom lived more pleasantly abroad than at home? Evidently their own countries gave them something that foreign countries could not give; and

the fate of our American expatriate writers seemed
to point in the same direction,—even when their own
country gave them little, they gained still less by leaving it. That was what the Russian "wanderers" discovered in the days of Pushkin, and it was after the
wanderers discovered this that Russian literature
really came into being. Allston, who notes this, quotes
from Ibsen's *Brand,*—a villainous translation, for he
could not read Norwegian:

> To a man's feet his native haunt
> Is as unto the tree the root.
> If there his labour fills no want,
> His deeds are doomed, his music mute.

What Ibsen felt, he said, most writers feel, and they
surely would not feel it without some reason. That
Ibsen continued to feel so Norwegian, after a long
life of expatriation, might be a proof of Ibsen's greatness, or of the antiquity of the culture from which
he sprang. But he stated a law that writers feel to be
true. On this point Allston adds:

> If, at the end of his life, for Henry James, the ques-
> tion of naturalization in another country seemed such
> a dilemma, what shall one say of his earlier years?—
> the twenty years in which, against his tastes, against
> his intellectual inclinations, he hesitated to break the
> tie that held him to America. It was the question of
> the "native soil,"—specifically this question, as his
> writings show,—that accounts for James's lifelong
> hesitation, for the question crops up in his latest
> novels. And you know (Allston soliloquizes) my feel-
> ing about James. It does not seem to be a fashionable
> feeling, among the intelligentsia, at this moment, but
> I think it is well-founded, just the same. I feel that

his later novels,—after he had lost the sense of his country,—were air-plants, not earth-plants, and that really great books have always been earth-plants. James was perhaps the most magnificent air-plant in the whole history of literature. What does that matter? If one spends one's life among air-plants, the virtues of air-plants come to seem transcendent. If one lives among the earth-plants, one has another scale of values; and to me all these novels put together are not worth five chapters of *The Scarlet Letter* or *Moby Dick*. They lack the essentials and fundamentals, from my point of view. No virtuosity can make up for this, nor any exotic equivalent of a moral position.

Allston felt that all American writers who lived long abroad tended to be air-plants in this fashion. He said their vogue at the present time was due to the character of the time, in which so many people lived like air-plants,—they had lost touch with fundamental values and therefore over-esteemed the virtues of air-plants. But I shall return to this later when I assemble Allston's views on modern books and writers. Let me wind up the question of expatriation, in its American bearings. If Americans, as a rule, felt strongly about it, if, in the case of Americans, expatriation caused them to "live only as shadows," to return to the phrase of MacLeish, there must be a reason for it; and the reason must lead to a conclusion. I have given Allston's reason, the fact that many Americans have shallow roots and that consequently any transplantation tends to destroy what roots they have. And what was his conclusion but André Gide's? In the paper on Maurice Barrès that I have mentioned, Gide took issue with Barrès and said that if he had not uprooted himself he could not have written the book in which he counselled others to retain their roots. Transplantation is good for the strong, he said,—"this is the education that the strong demand." And Allston said, "No doubt, and they should have it, the Landors and Ibsens, the Turgenevs and Heines, and even good Americans like Henry Adams." These men are strong because their roots are strong; they are incapable of deracination, no matter where they go or how they live. But what does Gide say about the weak? *"Quant aux faibles: enracinez, enracinez!*—the weak should root themselves, they should root themselves." In this sense, many Americans are weak; and they will never be strong until they know it and follow out the logic of their position.

CHAPTER XI

A BUSINESS WORLD

ALLSTON was a socialist. When someone asked him what he meant by this,—was he a "parlour socialist"?—he said, "No, a kitchen socialist." To the kitchen he would have added the cellar. If he did not write on political questions, it was not because he lacked convictions. He had strong feelings and beliefs regarding public matters, but he said that feelings and beliefs did not always produce interesting thoughts. "The more one is in love," he added, "the less one has to say on the subject of love, the less, I mean, that others wish to hear." His thoughts developed most naturally in other connections, and he once said, quoting Flaubert, "Literature is an ocean large enough for me." In one of his letters, he wrote, "I agree with you about politics. They badger me all the time, both from the outside and from the inside. One gets an appeal in every mail, and my blood-pressure reaches the bursting-point every time I look at the morning paper. But what is the use for us? It is a good thing to have the emotions, but unless one checks these emotions the upper part of one's mind gets so blood-shot that one cannot see into the deeper parts.

If I refuse
My study for their politique,
The angry muse
Puts confusion in my brain.

Politics are for more impassive people." He said that he voted for Thomas Jefferson and his heirs and assigns, whom he usually found in the socialist party. For the rest, he said, "A writer should be a free-swimming creature."

He was, however, a socialist by long conviction, and every year more definitely so. He said that socialism seemed to him "fairly insipid with veracity," as the elder Henry James said of the writings of Swedenborg (and might have said of socialism also). He was not a socialist in what Wells called the "resentful phase," for he had no more reason for being resentful than Norman Thomas or Bertrand Russell. He had seen the existing system in its sunniest aspect. It had always treated him kindly. Without engaging himself in competitive business, he had shared some of the fruits of competitive business, and for this he was certainly grateful. Then why did he oppose the existing system? Partly because it jeopardized the interests of others, and partly because he thought that competitive business was bad for those who prospered by and through it. For industrialism, as such, he had little liking, greatly preferring the kind of society that Thomas Jefferson hoped for, although he well knew that the world would remain an industrial world for the present, under any economic system. But he could not see why "industry" had to be "industrial," and still less why competitive business was necessary in any case. Were not able men in business

professional men? Were they not essentially civil
servants whose place in the world would remain unaltered if they were civil servants in name, as in fact?
Their functions would remain unchanged in a socialist world, in which, having more security, they would
run fewer risks; and while, for the rest, he allowed for
the risks,—for the element of hazard and the "game"
that Americans demand, as I shall presently show,—
he felt that the rights of others called for this change.
Besides, he was convinced that, for most men, competitive business was almost the worst form that life
could assume. That it injured the self-respect of men
and too much else that gives existence value was one
of his settled convictions. I can explain his socialism
best by dwelling for a moment on this subject.

Thus, for example, he writes:

"In America, men are belittled and cramped by the
competition of business, from which women are, or
ought to be, free." So says Francis Parkman in one
of his notebooks, and I agree with him heartily. Is
not this the reason why Henry Adams said, "The
American man is a failure"? Adams was right in feeling that American women are, on the whole, superior
to American men. There is a spaciousness in certain
types of American women that has no counterpart in
the other sex;* and the whole observing world has
shared this feeling since the Civil War. Our men are
less developed than our women, precisely for the reason that Parkman gives, because competitive business
belittles and cramps them.

Allston's notes abound in similar comments. He did
not admire what Ruskin called the modern "mone-

* If Allston had read Sinclair Lewis's *Dodsworth*,—which recalled a
well-known type of American man,—he might have felt differently here.

tary asceticism, consisting in the refusal of pleasure
and knowledge for the sake of money." The proper
ends of asceticism were very different from these,
he felt; and elsewhere he says, of the passion for
money, "It is like the magnetic mountain in the
Arabian Nights that drew all the metal out of the
ships and sent them to the bottom."

It is true (he adds), we cannot live without money,
or even the passion for money, under our present system. Thoreau succeeded in doing so, and no doubt he
would have lived in the same way if he had lived in
our time. All honour to those who can follow him, as
a few can, especially if they have the luck to live
in Maine. But one has to possess a greater personal
force to live Thoreau's life in our conditions than
people had to possess in Thoreau's time. One does
not so easily command the good conversation on a
dollar a day,—or fifty cents, earned by manual labour,
—that abounded in the Concord of 1850. If one is
the true prince or princess, shut up by a cruel step-
mother, one can spin or weave into cloth of gold the
merest heap of straw. But poverty is indeed a prison-
tower for modern men of less intensity. It is a Charyb-
dis, in our conditions, and opposite lies the great
American Scylla, or, shall one say, the nymph changed
by Circe who bears the name Neurosis, a truly hor-
rible monster, bred by an industrial civilization.

I believe in the classical doctrine of poverty for
those who are able to follow it. For I agree with
William James, "We have lost the power even of
imagining what the ancient idealization of poverty
could have meant; the liberation from material attachments, the unbribed soul, the manlier indifference, the paying our way by what we are and do and

not by what we have, the right to fling away our life
at any moment irresponsibly,—the more athletic trim,
in short, the moral fighting shape." But, as we are not
dealing with classical conditions, we cannot, without
circumspection, preach the classical remedies. People
speak of the romance of poverty; and there is romance in poverty as well as in riches. They speak of
Saint Francis and his friars, they speak of the Hindu
holy men. But these Hindus, like Saint Francis, are
able to count on the faith of the population to put
rice and coppers in their bowls. In other words, they
are secure; and only when we guarantee the kind of
security they have can we know once more the romance of poverty. One cannot count on our population,—either one has money or one starves. At best,
in municipal shelters, one has no freedom. So I say
one cannot, without circumspection, preach the classical remedies; for they lead to insanity too often. But
is this to defend an order of things in which money-
making plays so large a part, and with such disastrous
consequences? Writers have no reason to defend it.
Writers are supposed to be in league with heaven
and expected to be satisfied with manna. They have
nothing to gain from a system which, for the rest,
they certainly cannot admire. If, for other men, the
effects of the system are as evil as they appear,—evil
for the victors as well as the victims,—one would expect any intelligent man to wish for and work for a
better system.

Later he seems to have reconsidered this question of
riches and poverty. Was it not still possible to "live
on a crust"? The poet E. A. Robinson had done so,
and a few others might do so; and, while this could
not be asked of any man, any successful attempt to

do so was bound to clear the air. Regarding this, he remarks:

> Well said Carlyle, "Make thy claim of wages a zero, then hast thou the world under thy feet." Let no man ask any man to make his claim of wages a zero; but, if there are any volunteers for this heroic role, now is the time for them to break the ranks.

As for writers and artists, they were naturally socialists, Allston felt. Had not Carlyle, Arnold, Renan and Dickens revolted against the coming capitalist system, the world of money-lenders and railway-magnates which they saw rising about them? Most of Allston's friends were on the "left;" they were "on the side of the heart, not on the side of the liver," and this was a matter of constitution with them. He explains it thus:

> Writers and artists are naturally socialists. How could it be otherwise? It is alien to them to work for profit, and they see human nature instinctively in their own image.
>
> Our economic order is based on a low view of human nature, and one that my experience does not bear out. It assumes that men will only work for profit, and that, with security, comes sloth. Hence the fear of a socialized industry and a universal wage. The human nature of artists disproves—for artists—these assumptions. I have never known a man whom I wished to know for whom the motive of profit was an incentive, at least in comparison with other motives or except as providing the security that a universal wage would provide as well. Nor have I known a man whom I wished to know for whom security served as anything but a stimulus, an oppor-

tunity to do the work he could not do without it. These economic views are only possible among human beings who have little experience of the higher types. And how does one know how many people are of the higher types, or would be if they had a chance to be? If the business men had security, might they not change their point of view? Numbers would, I know; and they would be more surprised than I if these numbers were great numbers.

Feeling, as he did, that to change the system was a matter of wishing to do so,—and I shall say more of this presently,—Allston felt free to express his dislike of the system. It made men dull and uniform, he thought, obliterating their personal traits, while it stunted their minds and blunted their feelings. What were its effects in the happiest cases? Allston felt that failure in a business world was sadder than other forms of failure, because men sacrificed so much that was human in their efforts to qualify for a business success. How was it when they succeeded? Was it much better? Not much, he seems to think in the following note:

An evening at H——, the paradise of the smart young business men and their often charming wives, in one of the houses that abound there, shrines of luxury and synthetic taste, synthetic in the chemical sense, in which everything represents discrimination, —that of the dealer, the buyer, the decorator,—but nothing represents the discrimination that matters, that of a culture achieved in personal lives. Such houses, and one finds them in tens of thousands, suggest a pocket-book and a clever mind. One sees the shopping-raid of the pretty young wife, who spends a week in town, with a fund of twenty thousand to draw upon, going the rounds of the best department-stores, the auction-rooms, the antique-dealers, makes a selection of their selection and hires an interior decorator to help her in the arrangement of her booty. What people of real taste spend the intervals of years achieving, adding a touch here and there to the *mise en scène* of their lives, as some new interest develops in them, or some new emphasis of an old interest, these people achieve in a fortnight, with two or three rubs of Aladdin's lamp. But how wearisome it is, like every simulacrum.

Is it not also pathetic? Of course it is. And are not these young people decidedly touching? To be sure, they are. Then why do I make fun of them? I have no such intention. But their way of living is dull, and not only to me. They will be bored themselves in two or three years, and, as likely as not, divorced. They can only endure existence now by incessantly drinking cocktails. Everything in their lives is external. They have put nothing personal into their setting. How can they draw anything personal from it? Then why should they wish to keep it? If a hundred thousand dollars will buy a chateau, furnished from Madison Avenue, and they can get the hundred thousand, why should an English manor-house please them long, when the manor-house costs only fifty thousand? These young people are touching now, as all young people are touching, but I should rather not see them twenty years hence. If business associations and business ambitions have destroyed their imagination at the age of thirty, what are they going to be like at fifty or sixty?

That the life of business made men dull was not its only defect. It was also vitally dangerous, Allston felt. He quoted the statistics of one of the life-insurance companies. The average life-expectancy of the city-dweller, typified in business-office workers, was from four to five years shorter than that of the country-dweller, while the average length of a woman's life in this country was seven years longer than the average man's. "When I was in college," he adds, "the fathers of seven of my friends were dead or dying. Most of them were killed by the business life and its morbid excitements. Thirty years later, most of their mothers are still living." He continues, apropos of Thomas Wolfe's *Of Time and the River:*

In this American novel, as in so many others, the father is a broken reed, the mother, in her way, strong and even heroic. This is the Sherwood Anderson pattern also; in fact, one might call it the all-American pattern. It is typical of this country, on all social levels. "The American man is a failure," and how often one has to repeat it, in how many connections. The mother, in our typical novel, is usually stable, the father unstable, at best. This seems to indicate, by general agreement, whether conscious or not, that our scheme of life is more propitious for women than for men.

What a world, moreover, is this world that Thomas Wolfe describes, that most of our novelists describe, —"more land, more wooden houses, more towns, hard and raw and ugly . . . ugly disorder and meanness."

I add that the moral of this novel is the moral of dozens of other American novels: "The great masculine flower of gentleness, courage and honour died in a foul tangle."

Was the answer to this more business and greater profits, for a handful of property-owners? Was all this not rather the result of the "worship of size, mass, quantity and numbers," with no regard for quality and human welfare? That the American mind was saturated with business modes of thought and trains of feeling was the theme of a number of Allston's notes. A business world, he felt, destroyed itself, because it destroyed the values that make the world worth saving.

That many young men of his acquaintance had come to this conclusion was a fact upon which he often dwells. He writes:

> They have turned against the business life, and all it represents; and, as for them America and business are almost interchangeable terms, they have turned against their country also. They are better informed than my generation was in everything that concerns the world about them. They have read such books as Josephson's *The Robber Barons* and contemplated the lives of the business heroes, Jay Cooke, Pierpont Morgan, Vanderbilt, Rogers, who represented success in a business world. They know the mottoes of these heroes: "I owe the public nothing . . . It's good fishing in troubled waters . . . Nothing is lost save honour . . . The public be damned." These young men have not cultivated "awareness" for nothing. They have gone behind the scenes of the business life, and what they have seen is not attractive. They know that Richard Croker belongs to the past, but they know that what he said to Lincoln Steffens has its timeless meaning: "Ever heard that business is business? Well, so is politics business, and reporting,— journalism, doctoring,—all professions, arts, sports,

—everything is business." Cultivated business men never talked in this fashion, and Croker was anathema to men of their type. But that this is the business mode of feeling, the feeling that prevails in a business world, that this is "business psychology" is equally plain. It is the note that President Coolidge struck when he said, "The business of America is business." That American life reflects it the world in general feels; and these young men feel it also, in turning against the life of business. And they feel that the strong, who should have been representative, have betrayed the country. That business should be abolished even from business,—that is, abolished from industry,—they have come to feel also; and, in so far as Americans defend a business world, and say it is "American" to do so, they feel they are not Americans themselves. Nor do they wish to be so. They are going over in shoals to views of life that are alien not only to business but to everything else in America as well.

Could one ignore this symptom?—considering that the young men in question were those of whom any observer would say that they represented the future? The more sensitive they were, the clearer their minds and the better trained, the more they were convinced that the business system was a bankrupt system. They left it to the economists to say that it was economically bankrupt. They felt it was morally bankrupt. A system in which success and failure alike represented vital failure, a system that belittled men and cramped them, drew the metal out of them, blunted and dulled them and killed them off like soldiers in front-line trenches was one that had to bear the burden of proof. The presumptions were all against it

in the minds of the young. Allston, who shared their
feeling, continues as follows:

I cannot forget what Ruskin said about the business system, when it was in its heyday, at its best,
when it allowed more scope for human nature than
it later came to allow, with the intensification of competition. This is what Ruskin said: "In a community
regulated only by laws of supply and demand, but
protected from open violence, the persons who become rich are, generally speaking, industrious, reso-
lute, proud, covetous, prompt, methodical, sensible,
unimaginative, insensitive and ignorant. The persons
who remain poor are the entirely foolish, the entirely
wise, the idle, the reckless, the humble, the thoughtful, the dull, the imaginative, the sensitive, the well-
informed, the improvident, the irregularly and im-
pulsively wicked, the clumsy knave, the open thief,
and the entirely merciful, just and godly person." Is
not this a realistic statement, one that expresses in
human terms the meaning of success and failure in a
business world? There has been some displacement
of these values: more of the "proud" and "industrious" men find themselves in the failure-class, and perhaps more of the "reckless" and the "well-informed"
have got into the ranks of the successful. But this
general classification still seems sound, and what does
it indicate in regard to the future? That those who
stand for the future, the "sensitive," the "imaginative," the "thoughtful," along with the clumsy knaves
and the open thieves,—in short, those who represent
variation,—are those who do not thrive in a business
world and therefore cannot believe in it and will not
support it. It may sometimes be a personal grievance
that alienates them, the fact that they, as persons, do
not thrive. But neither do their virtues thrive, and

can they disbelieve in these? What would become of society if they did so? That the best of the young, the makers of the future, can have no part or lot in a business world, except as the merest makeshift means of survival, seems to be a natural deduction. They feel as they do because they have to feel so.

In arriving at this conclusion, as it seemed to Allston, they were saying what poets and artists have always been saying, what thinking men have said since the beginning of time, what Agassiz, for instance, implied in saying, "I have no time to waste in making money." It was the greatest workers who had felt this way, and in this the greatest workers had agreed with those,—the aristocrats of the past,—who felt that there was something base in trade. These aristocrats, with scant respect for work, despised too much in trade. They despised the work *in* the trade as well as the fact that the work was done for gain. But their contempt for gain was well-founded, and Allston was convinced that the profit-motive, except as a means of security, and merely that, had never played an animating part in the work of any worker, in any field of work, without detracting somehow from the worth of the work and from the integrity of the worker. Thoreau, he said, spoke the sober truth, not as a writer alone, but as a pencil-maker and surveyor, as a gardener and carpenter and mason, when he wrote, "To have done anything by which you earned money merely is to have been truly idle."

CHAPTER XII

COMMUNISM

BUT what was one to do about it? What could be done with a business world? What was Allston's notion of socialism? I shall come to this in my next chapter. Meanwhile, I offer a few of his reflections on two other current methods of meeting this problem. For communism and fascism were equally reactions against the plutocratic scheme of things. Allston saw these movements as almost interchangeable, and he was almost equally opposed to both. But he remembered what G. A. Borgese said in his book on fascism, *Goliath:* "The equivalence of the two perils, fascism and communism,—not to speak of preferences accorded to the former,—is a half-conscious lie of the panic-stricken propertied classes. Russian communism,—now in one way or another on the wane, at least as far as the Marxist-Leninist formula is concerned,—hurt interests, maybe legitimate. It also hurt feelings, certainly sacred. But even in the obtuse-minded barrenness of its self-styled atheism, it reserved a wide place for the cult of ideas and hopes which were dear to old Plato and to young Christ alike, and which make the very substance of God. No interest has been served, no feeling has been spared by fascism; and all fine things of earth and sky have been defiled." Allston, in this, agreed with

Borgese; he had found much to admire in communism, although he had never liked its methods. But
when these movements joined hands to fight against
the ideal of freedom, he closed his ranks, he said,
and fought them both. For he agreed with Benedetto
Croce, "Socialism without liberty, or not achieved
by means of liberty, is not true socialism." But I shall
have more to say about this anon.

Specifically about fascism, Allston had not much
to say. He seems to have felt there was little to say
about it. It was pure activism. It was a denial of
thought, and the only way to oppose it was with fists
and guns. I find in Allston's journals only a few brief
notes that might be felt to have a bearing on it. Thus
he says, for instance:

> Fascism and suicide,—equally negations of life,—
> appear most frequently in those who have had "all
> the advantages."

> He takes it for granted that what is good for his
> income is also good for the country. Whenever a
> political measure is good for my income, I am in
> clined to suppose that it must be bad for other
> people's.

> The "revolt of the masses,"—yes,—but who are
> the masses? The Iroquois of Princeton, the Mo-
> hawks of Yale, the red-painted Micmacs of Harvard,
> who are so pleasant until they are threatened and
> then behave like other barbarians.

> I say that the gilded savages who swarm in the
> country clubs,—those cardboard imitations of Eng-
> lish aristocracy in its surface-aspects,—do more to
> debase standards, intellectual and moral, than the
> so-called masses have ever had a chance to do.

The mass-mind in high places, that is the thing to attack and the point at which to attack it.

But, while Allston had little to say of fascism, he had much to say of communism, which had captivated so many American minds. The core of socialism in it had won these minds, together with a disbelief in other methods that sprang from the American tradition. He often wondered why it had won these minds, and he had his own notion of this. He explained it in speaking of a friend who said he had once been a communist, but who felt that the only hope for the country now lay in a "revival of the American tradition." Of this friend he said, "He is not a communist now, but why was he a communist once? Because he saw in Soviet Russia something his country did not give him and that he is not sure it gives him at present,—else why should he speak of *reviving* the American tradition? I, too, believe in reviving the American tradition, but I am not sure that it needs to be revived. It seems to me that it needs only to be stated. But, in so far as my friend feels that it needs to be revived, he remains in part a communist even at present. He is, one might say, an unconscious communist, waiting to see *if* the American tradition, *when* it is revived, can compete with the faith which he once found in Soviet Russia; and in this he resembles an untold number of others who are waiting to see what we can do in this country. For what have they seen in Russia? They have seen, with all its failures, a valiant effort to bring about a just social order, in which no one will ever go hungry, or lack employment, where all children have good food,

good medical care, good education. With all its failures, this *was* the effort of Russia : and, if I say that a
country with millions of unemployed, with the horrors of our share-croppers and the horrors of our
factory-towns, is not in the right position to throw
stones at Russia, I am saying what these Americans
are thinking. If we are to have our American way,
we shall have to prove it to people who were not born
in Russia but were born in Missouri."

Allston had much more to say about the younger
thinking people who had gone over to communism in
tens of thousands. It was natural, he felt, that Soviet
Russia should have appealed to them.

> Young people (he says),—all people, for that
> matter,—need faith as they need hope and action.
> They need, above all, romance,—one may smile at
> the word, but this is the word I mean and I use it
> precisely. Young people are courageous, and they
> wish to be asked to use their courage. They are gal-
> lant, and they wish to be asked to fight; and you can-
> not say, Peace, peace to them, when they know there
> is no peace,—they know that life is a fight from be-
> ginning to end. All they ask is to feel that they are
> needed; and you may say if you choose that modern
> young people are not romantic. I say they are still
> more romantic for denying the word. For what is
> romance? In 1776, in this country, the romance of
> the young was revolution. In 1850, this romance was
> the cause of Abolition. Later, our romance was
> money-making; and, since every romance produces
> its heroes, who have been our heroes? The patriot
> fathers once, then Garrison and John Brown; later
> Pierpont Morgan and the builders of railroads. The
> young, in every generation, have followed these

leaders, but the romance of money-making wore away; and after the first world-war we entered an epoch in which this country seemed to have no ideals. That is not true, of course, but what is true is that our only ideals were those of the past. The ancient spirit of this country was reduced to the diet of the bear who sits in the tree, in winter, sucking its paws. Our idealism subsisted on its own fat,—and what happened to the younger people? The more they went to the devil, the more honest they were; for they could not believe in ideals that were long since played out. Well, during these years, a new romance arose in a far-away land beyond the sea; and, while a few went to Paris, more went to Moscow. It is of no importance what Lenin and Trotsky were: they became John Browns and Garrisons for our younger people, who had no Browns and Garrisons to contemplate at home. They seemed to be reliving the lives of our patriot fathers; they seemed to be translating into action the words of our Declaration of Independence. They were founding a great new civilization, just as our forbears did, that answered the needs of the world they lived in. Whether or not the Russian leaders were all they appeared to be,—this is quite beside the question; for no one whom we were producing even seemed to be great, on this heroic scale of greatness. We were producing advertising geniuses and President Harding. We Americans are the most romantic of peoples. More than any other, we need heroes; and we cannot make heroes of people who only make money. Not for long, not for a dozen years; and Russia was the world's romance for fifteen years, because the search for social justice is the romance of our time. Who can wonder that Russia evoked the gallantry of gal-

lant people and won the young by tens of thousands?
The young, whose perception is keenest, flocked to
that standard, and the problem is to win them back
to ours.

That is our real challenge,—how to make America
the land of romance that Russia has been for younger
people, in the modern sense of this term and in modern conditions, and then to make it ten times more
romantic. For things have to be romantic if they are
to capture Americans. How not to revive our tradition, but how to state it, and to make this statement
realistic; for, while we are romantic, we are realistic
also,—we are modern men as well as modern Yan-
kees. It is strange that this needs to be done when
one considers that from our Revolution sprang the
French, and that Jefferson and Paine were the fore-
runners of Russia. We have owned the future. The
future is our native land; and that is just the trouble,
I suppose. We have heard all this so many times that
these high-flying phrases have lost their edge. We
have taken the romance of justice and the future for
granted. The Athenians tired of hearing Aristides
called the Just, and we are tired of all this talk of
human rights. But Aristides remained Aristides, and
what, if we think it over, has America remained?
What has it become once more for countless dis-
affected souls who recently found their El Dorado in
Europe? What was it Thoreau said at the outbreak
of the Civil War,—"We have discovered at last that
we have a country;" and thousands who, loving Europe, have found what Europe otherwise stands for,
are finding that they have a country too. Some of us
did not feel this way during the first world-war. But
most of us feel it now, when we are fighting invisible
wars; and I think we should feel it again in a visible

war if we knew we were fighting not nations but evil itself. Paris has lost its charm, and Moscow is losing its charm with our growing sense of what Washington has come to stand for.

I must ask the reader to recall that this was written some years ago, before the second world-war broke on the world; and the rhetorical tone of the passage seems to indicate that Allston had an audience in mind. He did not naturally write on tiptoe, and I wonder if he was composing a speech. I know that he ran for the Legislature on the Socialist ticket, and this may account for a few of the oratorical touches that I find in his notes on all these matters.

Allston, like everyone else, was struck by the growth of national feeling in the years during which the fascists were rising in power. Our writers were re-dramatizing the American tradition, and they were also telling Americans the ugliest truths about themselves. "They have shown us that we can take the truth," he said. "And think of the novels, poems and plays that are turning over our soil for the crops of the future. Our tradition is more realistic than we sometimes imagine; and, if realism means some sort of economic collectivism, is economic collectivism an alien notion?" He continues:

The Declaration of Independence speaks of "all men." Is there not something collective in this conception? And have we forgotten that John Quincy Adams wished to make our economy collective? This Republican president, mark the word, hoped to develop the national wealth on a collective, not a competitive basis. He thought there was a volume of energy stored within the Union, enough for the prosperity of all, and he thought that if this could be brought into use in accordance with the laws of science it would lead the population to perfection. For this reason John Quincy Adams promoted the study of science, while he fought with all his might against the bankers, who stood for competition and disruption. I do not have to speak of Andrew Jackson. I have only to return to the Adamses, to Henry Adams, who, holding in mind his grandfather's faith, said of himself in his *Education,* "By rights, he should have been a Marxist." And why was Henry Adams not a Marxist, or, as I should have wished, a collectivist of the true American stripe? Because he cared more for money than he cared for his country,—one should read his last collection of letters if one has any doubts about this. Collectivism exists in our tradition, even our Republican tradition,—for one does not have to mention the Democrats, not to speak of the socialists in our tradition, the Brook Farmers, Bellamy, the novelist Howells. And let me mention two other well-known facts, or facts that should be well-known. In 1783, the last year of the Revolution, Benjamin Franklin wrote to Robert Morris: "All property, except the savage's temporary cabin, his bow, his match-coat and other little acquisitions, absolutely necessary for his subsistence, seems to me the creature of public convention. Hence, the public has the right of regulating descents, and all other conveyances of property, and even of limiting the quantity and the uses of it. All the property that is necessary to a man, for the conservation of the individual and the propagation of the species, is his natural right, which none may justly deprive him of; but all property superfluous to such purposes is the property of the public, who, by their laws, have created it, and who may therefore, by other laws, dispose of it, whenever the welfare of the public shall demand such disposition. He that does not like civil society on these terms, let him retire and live among savages. He can have no right to the benefits of society who will not pay his club toward the support of it." Was Franklin a collectivist, or was he not? This was the patriotism of our Revolution, and we are within our rights in supporting it now, although it is now supposed to be unpatriotic. How it became so one finds explained in *Folkways,* in which William Graham Sumner shows how in the eighteen-eighties "American ideals" became the reverse of what we thought they were. But twenty years later than the eighties, another Republican spoke in the good old strain, the author of *The Man Without a Country.* If there was ever a man who had a right to speak for patriots, Edward Everett Hale was this man. Well, Dr. Hale, in a book called *We, the People,* recommended old-age pensions and the government ownership of coal-mines; and he said, The people own the roads, the schoolhouses, the lighthouses,—why then object to the "ownership of wealth in common"? I quote Dr. Hale's words because he was not "without a country," and I say that Dr. Hale made this statement in the very year, 1903, in which he became the chaplain of the United States Senate. I do not say that Dr. Hale represented all our tradition,—but who can say that he was disloyal to it?

So much for American socialism, or economic collectivism,—did Americans have to go to Russia for it? But, as against the communists, Allston said, we have to consider something else:

No movement ever succeeds in a country, no move-

ment ever goes far, without the consent of the people
and their sympathy with it; and communism cannot
go far in this country because Americans are *naturally* free. We have a great deal more to lose than
chains. And that is why collectivism cannot be truly
achieved till the people want it. We have our prole-
tariat, if we have to use this word, and to that extent
we have failed. They are more than a drop in the
national bucket, but I think they are only the first half
pint, let us say, in the gallon; and the rest of the bucket
is filled with something else, and this something is not
money. Two-thirds of it is self-respect, the heritage
of freedom, and we will surrender our money before
we surrender that. We are not, and will not be, a nation of slaves, for we have not been trained to live
under czars and kaisers. So, in order to have our collectivism, we have to change the minds of people, and
that is bound to be a long slow process. We cannot
achieve our ends by any short-cuts, whether of the
fascist or of the communist order.

What can writers expect, I should like to ask,
since so many of our communists are writers? In a
way, we writers are a collectivity; but are we not still
more individualistic? Suppose someone said to us,
You cannot have your freedom, you cannot speak
your minds or write your thoughts. I pity the writers
of Russia almost as much as those who call themselves writers in the fascist countries. Our people allow us our freedom. Are we in a position to tell them
that they cannot be free? We are certainly free to
point out that the freedom of one may mean the
enslavement of others. We are bound to show that
freedom is not simple. What we can best show is
where the joy of living lies and point to the patriot
fathers to prove that for us. For they certainly had

a better time than we have; and one of the reasons
for this is that in the good old days the rich were a
good deal poorer, and the poor were richer. Because
the rich were poorer, they were also more adventurous,—they were not afraid of taking risks; and the
poor who were not too poor,—they were the people.
There is the story that writers can tell, and, if they
tell it early and often, I think we shall see some surprising results in this country. Our life, at the present
time, is not very amusing. We live in a world of anxi-
ety, a world of terror; and I do not think the rich enjoy their riches very much more than the poor enjoy
their chains. We should tell them how to be free
again, as Americans used to be free, when those who
had a little more than others were happy to see that
others did not have less. Those were the days that
have made us tough and stable, and that is why we
are humorous and sensible too.

It was the communist writers whom Allston had
in mind here, for in every field he was always thinking of writers. In the following chapter, I shall have
more to say about them, in connection with Allston's
point of view.

CHAPTER XIII

SOCIALISM

WHILE Allston, as I have said, had sympathized
with communism, he fully shared the American faith in freedom. Communism, he remarked, was
not "in the American grain,"—a fine phrase of William Carlos Williams; for, as he continued, "There
is an American grain, and I wish to live with it, and
I will not live against it knowingly. I believe in a socialized world and a socialized country, and so do
most American writers; and we know that this country can only be socialized in the American grain.
Psychology and anthropology and history tell us this,
even if common sense fails to do so. The communist
mind runs counter to the American grain. It is truly
alien and will remain so."

What he meant by this I can best explain by a few
scattered notes on communists and communism:

The feeling of the communists for Russia,—this
is the last American colonialism. It is the colonialism of the last wave of immigrants, who have not yet
discovered that we have a tradition too. We had the
first word in Revolution, and we can have the last
word also,—if we are willing to utter it.

How long are Americans going to play Button,
button, who's got the button?—England?—Russia?

—who?—when all the time we have the button ourselves.

The Russian lady fell into a swoon of faith as she
related how her husband, the Commissar, said, "Do
you think I ought to wish to have coffee this morning?" The dear man was so in the habit of thinking
we that he could not imagine even wishing to have
coffee unless all Soviet Russia also wished it. Not
unless they could have it, but *unless they wished it.*
That is a difference between Russians and ourselves.
I can easily imagine feeling that I should not have
coffee unless all my countrymen can have it also; but
not to be able to wish my wishes unless all the others
also wish them,—that would be the end of life for
me. Is not communism the only religion to break the
first law of progress, that we should be able to vary
in our secret thoughts?

Thank heaven, we are born recalcitrant. In Russia,
when they have a *Golden Calf,*—which affords a
faint savour to orthodoxy by offering a faint breath
of the heterodox,—they talk about it for ten years.
It is as rare as a murder in Sweden.

The American communist writers are obliged to be
still more orthodox. This is partly because their vitality is usually low, but it is mainly because they are
recent converts. It is only the old orthodox people,—
sure of their faith,—who can take liberties with it.
It is the hereditary Catholics who joke about the
saints, as Lenin joked about communism, as Karl
Marx said, "I am not a Marxist." Our owlish American communists cannot take such liberties.

One can be dogmatic only in fields that have non-
rational premises. I know that communism is a religion, but this is not enough unless they admit it.

They follow Stalin when Stalin follows Hitler, and they profess to do so in good faith. I say that opportunistic methods act like poison on writers' minds. We have to follow our beliefs and not pretend to beliefs we do not possess. Ends may justify means for people of action, but they corrupt good manners with folks like us.

His solution of all social problems is to set up a guillotine in Park Avenue and leave the rest to chance.

My youthful communist friend here. I cannot endure this wooliness of mind. A writer's first duty is to fight for his own clarity. Except as a writer, he can do nothing for political ends; and he can do nothing if he is not clear. The important thing is not, What is your party? but, How do you stand to any party? Or, rather, you must settle this question first before you settle the other.

As Allston was not a communist, so, as one sees from these notes, he was not a Marxist either. "American necks," he says, "will never be at ease in the Marxist yoke." On this he writes as follows:

I have never been a Marxist, but I have an American socialist grain that is as tough as the Marxist. Marxism controverts my instincts, or, shall I say, my primary sentiments, the structure of my personality. I am a free-willer from the outset. I am a convinced idealist who is fully convinced that idealism will remain the American way. It has been a tough way thus far, and it will be tough. The materialists will prove to be the tender-minded ones, in the United States, in my opinion. If they were not tender-minded, they would not be so confused at present. For why are they confused? Because their primary sentiments are the same as mine, and they are running counter to them. My sentiments, my instincts and my party are all of a piece; and I have lost no illusions because I have never had any. I have found human beings intelligent and decent, and I think they will have the good sense to save themselves. But controverting one's primary sentiments lands one in sophistry; and I think the result on the minds of writers of all this splitting of hairs,—the jesuitry of the communists, I mean,—is bound to prove fatal in the end. Americans will have none of it, for the American mind demands honest feeling and clear thinking and a frank repudiation of the false and the rotten.

Regarding these "primary sentiments," he continues as follows:

Of course, all socialists owe much to Marx for stiffening the movement as he did. But I repeat that Marxism over-rides our primary sentiments. The fight that Finland put up certainly showed that nationality is a primary sentiment with human beings. The family sentiment is also primary, so is the religious sentiment, so is the sentiment of free will; and these sentiments are the bone and tissue of the human psyche,—at least, they are so with Americans. How absurd to try to socialize the world by sneering our bone and tissue out of court. The communists are utterly inhuman, and socialism must be human as well as social. Can it not still be tough-minded? Ten times more so. The tough-minded thing is the realistic thing, and how can one be realistic if one denies the human constitution? Marx is good for socialists who know how to make discriminations, but I think Americans otherwise rightly feel that the Marxist psychology is purely European. Most of our radicals

do not know how strong the American line is and
how tough is our psychology as well. Why not run
with the grain instead of against it? They had better
run with the grain if they wish to run at all.

All this more or less defines Allston's view of socialism, which had made small headway in this country because it had failed to achieve its American
form. He said that a fundamental "self-possession"
was a prerequisite of all advance in any sphere of
action within the nation, and that socialism would
never win this country until the American psyche
was embodied in it; and, first of all, it must accept
idealism, for this was the Open Sesame of the American mind. I find this note in Allston's journals, reporting a conversation with a communist friend:

"You really are an idealist, aren't you? You really
believe that ideas come first?" He might have been
addressing a dodo, not with contempt but with a kind
of incredulous wonder, the wonder of a naturalist
who knew that the dodo had once existed but who
also knew that it was long extinct.

Yes, ideas come first, *after the original pressure*.
The pressure comes first, but the pressure is not
articulate. Therefore, it cannot create a programme,
and, as action is useless without a programme, I
believe in the priority of ideas. It is just as Ibsen
said, "Except as afterwards invented, the conscious
guiding principle is never present in the general
sentiment of the people."

All social movements evolve in the same way.
First there is pressure, slavery in the United States,
serfdom in Russia, abnormal misery among the
workers, persecution in a racial group. This acts first
on creative minds because they are the most sensitive.

They feel the pressure in themselves and others and set to work to form a programme for it,—abolition, socialism, a revival of racial sentiment or whatever this may be. They formulate the pressure into an idea that gives it direction. So we have Garrison, Mazzini, Marx, etc. Without this formulation, what could the mere pressure produce? Without it, those who carry the idea into action would be acting in a chaos. A generation of humanitarians, who felt the pressure of the evil, was necessary before a Marx arose; but where would the Marxists be if there had been no Marx? Where the Medici tombs would be if there had been no Michael Angelo. Who testified most to the importance of Thomas Paine in our Revolution? The active leaders of the Revolution, Washington, first of all. In the same way, poets have created nations, as any Ukrainian will tell you.

In this country, the creative intellect is weak; few believe in ideas, and socialism makes little headway. Why? Because, requiring ideas, yet not believing in ideas, it takes them over ready-made from others, whose history has been totally different from ours. How can Americans be Russians? The movement must be acclimated here; and, unless we believe in ideas, we shall not produce them. Therefore I expect for the present nothing but broken wooden heads.

Now I do not propose to present at length Allston's view of socialism. I merely offer a few suggestive thoughts. Thus he writes:

I hope for a socialized world, but I do not think it will come any quicker if we misinterpret human motives. How much of the man is the economic man? All of the man, said Marx,—which explains why Americans are not Marxists. When people have at-

tained the economic level that millions have attained
in this country, they see life not in terms of economic
necessity but in terms of a game. It is the sport of the
thing, very largely, that draws Americans into business, just as, in the eighteenth century, men were
drawn into gallantry, or, in the seventeenth, into war.
The chance, the gamble, the hazard, this is the de-
termining motive, as often as not. Don John of Aus-
tria and Casanova are more universal types in our
business world than the miser in his counting-house,
who is also playing his game with gold; and to say
that the working-man wishes to be a capitalist,—and
that he does so wish is the despair of the Marxists,—
is to say that he too wishes to share in this game.
The vast free minorities of the Western world, of
which we are the greatest residuum, are shot through
and through with this conception, the heritage of the
age of chivalry and the age of exploration; and the
fact that communism succeeds in Russia is largely the
consequence of another fact, that the Russians as a
whole do not share in this heritage of the wager.
They did not know our age of chivalry, they did not
know our age of exploration. The great objection to
Utopia, a socialized and reasonable world, in the eyes
of our *moyen homme sensuel,* is that it would be dull;
and this belief is shared by everybody who is above
the level of destitution except the small minority of
writers and artists who know that they would always
find life exciting. Security means everything to me, as
to every man of imagination; for security permits the
man of imagination to live undividedly the life he
loves. Therefore most writers are socialists by instinct. They have everything to gain from a happy
world, a world without war or competition, a world
without riches or poverty, a world without prejudice
or hatred, in which the inner life can develop freely.

But security, as it appears, for the average man, means an eternity of dullness, and only the old desire it. The poor boys long for adventure, they long for the hazard, just as much as the rich boys; and because they long for adventure, they will not fight for security. They could obtain security by the vote, without any thought of resorting to violent measures, if they could agree to do so. The poor could vote their wealth away from the rich; and they would do so if they were willing to lose the chance, the hazard of wealth for themselves. For wealth means romance, it means adventure. It is the great wager of the average man, who has no inner life, no imagination, as dreams of knight-errantry, conquest, exploration or glory were the great wagers of other times.

What do I conclude from this? That to socialize our world the socialists must abandon their doctrinaire methods and adopt a realistic point of view. What is realistic with Russians is fantastic with us. Outside the areas of exasperation, the coal-mines, the textile-mills, etc., socialism will make no headway here until it accepts the motives that govern minds. It must offer a "moral equivalent" of the modes of life which it supplants. Bread-and-butter motives will not suffice if one means to appeal to Americans; and yet we are a "capturable people," beyond all others, in the fine phrase of Waldo Frank.* And why

* "For our hope, there is the truth that we are a capturable people. It is in our blood to be captured; to be captured 'high.' Among the colonials were men who had been won by the 'new' ideas of Europe; Puritan, Calvinist, Quaker, etc., were capturable men beyond their conservative brothers . . . Often have the Americans been captured; and never remain captive! . . . Aristocracies captured the colonials, captured the Revolution (turning out the true settlers who were tories); libertarians and romantics captured the young Republic; countless sects and panaceas have for a day won fragments of this capturable people, who never remain settled. We are still volatile: still, hence, dissatisfied: still capturable. What will happen if there come a group or groups of men to capture this longing folk . . . a group who have, really, what they claim to have, and what the folk need?"—Waldo Frank, *The Rediscovery of America*.

should a socialized world *not* be made to appear as a wager, as a chance, as a hazard, as a gamble? To me it so appears already. To make the United States a magnificent country for all the American people, to fill it with beautiful dwellings, to wall in the rivers and clear the forests, to abolish poverty and poverty-bred states of mind, to take men out of the cities where they fester, to restore country life on a social basis, to replace the parasitical occupations with skilled handicraft and real production,—does not this represent adventure? It is an ironical fact that one cannot move Americans by appealing to their motives of self-interest only. For us, the great motives of life are romantic motives, and all the great realists have known it.

Let me add the following:

The socialists are always discussing ways and means, and this is as it should be; I only complain of their taking ends for granted. This is very short-sighted, for human nature does not work this way. People do not fight for what they take for granted. In fighting for a better world, one must conceive the better world; one must conceive and re-conceive it. What is it going to be like? How shall we behave when we get there? Excepting Lewis Mumford, we have scarcely any thinker, nor have we had one for a generation, who has presented a fresh conception of the world that socialists wish to see, or the ethics of socialized living. The haziness and indifference of socialists here has much to do with their general failure. Try to take love for granted with a woman and see what happens to the relation. All the life goes out of it, for the end is lost. The lack of prophetic vision and the crude ethical concepts that pervade our socialist fiction are a poor advertisement of the programme.

Everyone in America seems to be somehow bewildered, or perhaps the best word would be astray. Astray from what? The tremendous promise of our Revolution,—Jefferson, Paine, Lincoln, Whitman. We have lost the scent, but we know it is there.

Nothing good can come until one says and feels, *I* am to blame, myself, my group, my region, my nation. *I* am to blame, *we* are to blame; therefore I and we are responsible.

To say that I am to blame is the part of the thinker. To say that we are to blame is the part of the aristocrat.

But what does our dominant class say? Who is to blame from their point of view? Organized labour, or unorganized labour, the workingmen, the immigrants, the people of non-Nordic stock, the Reds, anyone and everyone but them. *They* are not the culprits, no, never; it is never they who debase our standards. Were the members of the Liberty League and the D. A. R. ever known to beat their breasts because the nation was going to the dogs? Has any one of them ever humbled himself, thereby recognizing a standard from which he has lapsed, a standard for the nation as well as himself? The "revolt of the masses" which they deplore is the revolt of the unsuccessful, measured by the standard according to which they have been successful. This is too often the standard of clever chicanery used for their own aggrandizement.

Improvement always comes from above. But the "above" in this country is only such by virtue of the force which actuates the lower in less degree. Let those who complain of the "revolt of the masses" first make sure that they are not themselves the "masses," after the definition of the phrase laid down by the author of it.

The author of this phrase is Ortega y Gasset, and I quote him further as follows: "Every present-day European knows, with a certainty much more forcible than that of all his expressed 'ideas' and 'opinions,' that the European of today *must* be a liberal ... The most reactionary of Europeans knows, in the depths of his conscience, that the effort made by Europe in the last century, under the name of liberalism, is, in the last resort, something inevitable, inexorable; something that Western man today *is*, whether he likes it or no."

Yes, and for this reason how many bad consciences there must be today in Europe. But we have not the excuses of Europe.

I note that various writers, following James Joyce and others, have taken to speaking of "the rabble." This is the time to say that there is no such thing as an American rabble. When Alexander Hamilton said, "The people is a great beast," he backed himself out of the American door. There is one categorical imperative in American life, that one must respect man as such. Whoever does not respect man as such is, in America, a traitor.

Proletarianism is alien to the American view of man. It springs from societies that have bred the slave mind. We must not lower to the slave mind, or exalt to the master mind, but raise to the classless human mind.

The proletarian mind is limited by necessitarian circumstances. Nobility, chivalry, moral grace and beauty are natural offshoots of a surplus of energy, aristocratic freedom, etc. Such is the time-worn phrase, but these traits are well exhibited by the everyday people of Maine, for instance, who have preserved in the simplest circumstances most of these aristocratic characteristics. I could give, at almost any length, chapter and verse for this statement. These values are the values of the victors of life. Society must rescue the victims, but the victors' values must prevail.

CHAPTER XIV

A PHILOSOPHICAL INTERLUDE

ALLSTON was an idealist, and he would not have denied the charge if he had been described as also romantic (however he felt this word had been compromised). He had grown up in the years before the first world-war, when the future of mankind was an exciting vista, and his values were substantially formed before it. During the years that followed, he was aware that his point of view was not the view of his contemporaries; but he saw little reason to change it. He felt that the American world was bound to return to his point of view because it was an expression of the American psyche; and was it not even a part of the psyche of Europe? Croce implied that it was when he spoke of "that romanticism which is identical with philosophical and historical idealism and spiritualism, and which therefore follows their destinies, and rises again (for it cannot help rising again) in absolute unity with them." (*History of Europe in the Nineteenth Century.*) Allston felt sure this was true of America, at least, for its mind was idealistic in grain and essence. He had much to say of this, as I shall show in a moment. The American mind was saturated with a sense of "that which has to be,"—again in Croce's words, —as opposed to "that which is."

Allston's conception of socialism followed from this. He felt that to change the system was a matter of "wishing" or "willing" to do so; and what he meant by this I shall presently explain. Meanwhile, he quoted Ortega y Gasset: "Everything is possible in history,—triumphant, indefinite progress equally with periodic retrogression. For life, individual or collective, personal or historic, is the one entity in the universe whose substance is compact of danger, of adventure. It is, in the strict sense of the word, drama." Drama implies will, and, in a sense, at least, free will, the will that creates the patterns of living; and Allston agreed with William James's statement, "The rivalry of the patterns is the history of the world." Whereupon Allston says:

What is my pattern? I should like to substitute for the business pattern, or, let us say, the industrial pattern, which dominates our life today, the pattern of the craftsman, beginning at a sufficiently humble level so that all could participate in it. Gandhi's example counts for something here. Take away from the factories and business half their present products, take away all the foolish products that stultify and dissipate the race and are made possible only by advertising and a false and preposterous standard of living. Take away from the factories all the products that can be made better by hand, and that men are happier for making. Let men develop once more the skillful hand and the cunning brain. Let us all be producers of one kind or another. For this new world of superior products an inventive society like ours could soon devise a system of distribution.

This was only one facet of Allston's view of socialism, and I shall not attempt to offer others. For he
foresees an objection even to this, which he meets in
the following words:

"You cannot turn the clock of history back." But
styles are revived every moment, in clothes, in types
of building. Forms of government have been revived,
under our very noses, the most atavistic forms, primitive despotism, for example. One can draw anything
out of the past. If Hitlerism, why not handicraft?
(He was aware, of course, of all that was new in
Hitlerism. He knew that patterns are always resumed
in terms of the new generation.)

Do we really believe that modernity expresses the
sum of wisdom? Then why has it led to the mess in
which the world exists at present? Modernity is not
all-wise, neither was antiquity entirely foolish. The
world belongs to mankind, to do with as it chooses;
and mankind has the power to impose on the world
any forms it thinks wise and good. If Hitler and
Mussolini can impose on the world, on a hundred
million men, forms derived from the past that are
plainly evil, they have at least proved two things that
modern men were forgetting; first, that the forms of
the past, whether good or evil, may still have the
force to be effective, and, secondly, that the human
will can still remove mountains. If, in the case of these
two despots, the mountains were the best that men
have raised, this does not alter the fact that they
have removed them. To turn the children of Italy
and Germany into little mechanized savages is no
small achievement; and, if these despots have destroyed the myth of an automatic progress, they have
also destroyed the myth of social determinism. And
the logic of this leads one far. If the evil forms of

the past can flourish again, why not the superior
forms? And if the human will can be so effective for
evil, can it not be equally so for the good?

I gladly grant that the will of these despots is no
mere personal will. They are the agents of history,
as Tolstoy might say. They are the resultants of all
the forces that lie behind them. They are the spear-
heads of hidden social tendencies that were scarcely
visible until these despots crystallized them. But how
do we know what other social tendencies are hidden,
waiting for other crystallizations in spear-heads of
another type? Why assume that we know history in
all its potentialities of the past and the future?—that
we know which hidden tendencies will make our future? Why take for granted an evil future because
the present is evil? Why assume that Hitlerism is
the dominant stream of tendency because it is for
the moment the dominant fact? Is there any reason
to suppose that it may not be a minor stream or
prove to be no stream at all within another decade?
Suppose another tendency comes to the front, suppose the mood of humanity suddenly changes,—as it
has changed a hundred times before,—and a Peter
the Hermit emerges instead of a Hitler? What then
will become of the wise men who prophesy doom?

Allston had been struck by a passage in one of
John Eglinton's essays that amplified his feeling in
this matter: " 'They reckon ill who leave me out,'
says Brahma in Emerson's poem; and the saying may
be applied to the 'anticipations' of sociologists like
Mr. H. G. Wells, which leave out of account the
possible effects on the whole structure of society of
the renewal in mankind of a disposition for spiritual
adventure . . . He must be very dogmatic or unim-

aginative who would affirm that man will never
weary of the whole system of things which reigns at
present . . . We never know how near we are to the
end of any phase of our experience, and often when
its seeming stability begins to pall upon us, it is a
sign that things are about to take a new turn. Man,
after all, is still man, the same being who flung himself into the wars of religion in the sixteenth and
seventeenth centuries, who departed on the Crusades,
who peopled the deserts of Egypt and the East, the
forests of Germany and the isles, with hermits; and
there is no reason, should the idea of doing so enter
his head, that he should not try some new experi-
ment." Was not this incontrovertible? Allston asked;
and, speaking broadly, he went on from this to say,
"The world can be anything that man desires, and
men can make it anything they wish."

"But who will believe a writer when he says these
things?" Allston remarks on a later page. "Statements of this kind are called 'naive' when a man of
letters expresses them. If we wish to be respected in
our main positions, we have to get a scientist to back
us up." Here I must digress for a moment. Allston
had himself the respect for science that is merely another name for common sense; but he was amused by
the superstitious awe with which men of science are
regarded. He said that American writers often expressed their contempt for writers, but seldom failed
in respect for men of science; and, while he also respected science, he was often puzzled by the scorn
that writers felt for their own trade. Max Eastman
had written a book, *The Literary Mind,* for the sole
purpose, it seemed, of expressing this scorn, while he

could not say enough in praise of science; and
Sinclair Lewis, Theodore Dreiser, Mencken had idol-
ized scientists and science. Was not a scientist, Ar-
rowsmith, the only hero that Sinclair Lewis had conceived? Allston pondered much on this,—it struck
him as a singular comment on American letters; but it
seemed more and more natural, as he thought about
it. For modern writers have been the victims of a
confusion of values,—they are not sure of their foot-
ing in their own field; while the scientists, in their
field of values, are on firm ground and therefore possess their integrity more easily than writers. They
deal with ascertained facts, and they can test these
facts by simple standards. The modern man of science
is more obviously admirable than the modern man
of letters, and indeed, in a majority of cases, is actually so; and Allston saw that unless writers took a long
view of their trade they were pretty sure to regard it
as inferior to science. The living heroes were mostly
in the opposite camp. But Allston's heroes were not
"living" heroes, or, rather, he saw writers in a time-
less light. His idols had lived in all the epochs and
seemed to him contemporaneous; and he did not see
why writers should have to go outside their trade in
order to discover men they could wholly admire. As
for this modern idol of the literary trade, he quoted
William James, who certainly knew it: "Of all insufficient authorities as to the total nature of reality, give
me the 'scientists,' from Münsterberg up, or down ...
Their only authority *at large* is for *method.*" Allston knew there were many scientists who were also
wise men, wise just as other men are, because they
have lived and thought intensely. He observed that

these wise men of science, whenever they offered reflections on general problems, offered them, not offi-
cially as men of science, but as men who had lived
and thought *through the mode of science*. In this
they were like the wise of all professions. Allston had
friends among these men,—the great Hans Zinsser,
for one,—and nothing embarrassed them more than
to be quoted not as qualified *men* but as *men of
science,*—that is to say, outside their special field.
It was not they who fancied that men of letters are
especially prone to naive or extravagant statements,
for they knew too well the faults of their own profession. They left this charge to the men of letters themselves,—whom they were quite willing to respect.
But Allston, who liked to quote them because they
were wise, sometimes quoted them also as a matter of
tactics. In making the sort of statement that people
call "naive," he often cited, in corroboration, even
when it was not called for, a phrase from some well-
known man of science. He felt that, perhaps, by this
procedure, he might convince other writers.

So I return to his remark, "The world can be any
thing that man desires, and men can make it anything they wish." He seems to have felt here that his
usual naivety passed all bounds, for he cites Alexis
Carrel at some length.

I am glad (he says) that Dr. Carrel won the Nobel
Prize. It gives him the right to speak as rashly as a
writer, for not only is he a man of science but now
"money talks" through him. He is like the village
atheist who was also the village squire. As long as
he lived in the big house, no one could gainsay him

when he said he approved of playing cards and danc-
ing on Saturday night.

Well, then, who says that we can have the sort of
world we like, regardless of all the determinisms?
Who says that "none of the dogmas of modern society are immutable"?—that monstrous factories and
inhuman cities, industrial morals, faith in mass-production are not indispensable to civilization? That
we cannot and need not adapt ourselves to a world
that has been created without respect for the laws of
our development? That we can overthrow industrial
civilization and bring in another conception of progress? That we can transform its values and organize
it with reference to our needs? The world will listen
to science, especially when there is money behind it.
Mr. Nobel has made it possible for Dr. Carrel to
say what all the poets and prophets have always said,
—when the world has never believed the poets and
the prophets.

And, after quoting one scientist, he quotes another, a
scientist who justified his latent optimism. For Allston, as an idealist who believed that men could
change all systems, approached this social problem
in a mood of hope:

It is thrilling to learn (he writes) from Breasted's
Dawn of Conscience that, while the Age of Weapons,
on this planet, is doubtless a million years old, the
Age of Conscience and Character is definitely datable
at little more than four thousand years. This, as the
author says, corroborates Emerson's intuition that
the human is literally in its dawn and that all the
greatest things are still to come. When one considers
that, within historic time, man has been "completely
unaware of conduct," how can one question the exist-

ence of a definite progress or the probabilities of the
future?

Now, Allston was at odds with many of his friends,
whose point of view, he said, was deterministic.
Much as they disliked the Spenglerian *Weltan-
schauung,* and even took exception to Spengler's
logic, they shared this author's fatalistic mood. They
merely rationalized it on other lines. Often they accepted Marx as the one and only prophet; sometimes
Henry Adams or Theodore Dreiser. Most of them
united in feeling that "free will" was played out, and
that anyone who talked this old stuff ought to go back
to the farm.

As the farm was just what Allston liked, he never
disputed this question. He believed in free will, as I
shall show, but he took small pains to defend his position. Like Barty, in *The Martian,* he did not reply
or explain himself, but "smoked many pipes and
mildly wondered." However, I find this note in one
of his journals:

Considering all we know of the origins of philosophies, I mean their temperamental origins, well
shown by Nietzsche, it is surprising what weight has
been given, objectively, to such a work as Spengler's.
I do not mean Spengler's perceptions, many of which
are enthralling and many of them true. I mean his
view of life and the world as a whole (and with it all
the other determinisms). I cannot forget the remark
of our friend, Professor E. of Munich, about the
young Germans of his son's generation,—how "utterly helpless" they felt until Hitler appeared. If
Spengler's philosophy rose from Bismarck's mood of
"blood and iron," *this* was the emotional matrix in

which its influence rose; and it appealed to the young
of all countries in so far as they shared this post-war
mood. Can we ignore this obvious fact in our view of
Spengler's philosophy? If Spengler won the day, it
would prove that this mood was universal. But it
would not prove that Spengler was objectively true.
For what would become of Spengler and Spenglerism
if and when this mood universally changes? And the
one thing we know is that all moods change.

All real philosophies have glimpses of the true,
but the true lies beyond and behind all philosophies.
A philosophy may rise from a thousand causes, defeat, unhappy personal relations, too much tobacco
smoke or too much beer, dyspepsia, low spirits, or, on
the other hand, elastic spirits, health, courageous
freedom, good red wine or the "fair water" that
Democritus loved. How can the philosophy of too
much beer appeal to the man of champagne? How
can it seem to him true, or be true for him? Thus the
universals of the Germans have never convinced the
French. We feel ourselves in conscience bound to follow every train of reason, but in the end, we find, we
think as our constitution obliges us to think.

Thus, with these emanations of "blood and iron,"
we have a right to reject them; we are even obliged
to reject them if blood-and-iron is alien to our natural
constitution. And free will exists for those who feel
that it exists. Those who do not feel free are the defeated. In an age when defeatism is the rule, those
who defend freedom are attacked as canting fools.
They do not lose the right to their position, or even
the right to rejoice in it. As freedom is the state of
healthy souls, how can they not rejoice in it? How
can they not regard it as an absolute value?—for how
can we know we are not free unless we measure our

state by the norm of freedom, as we measure defeat
by victory and sickness by health? But the business of
the free is to make good their position, and they will
find this hard enough not to crow over their freedom.
Besides, they are children of good fortune and ought
to know it. The chances are that the defeated have
encountered odds which they have been permitted to
escape. Let them therefore continue to affirm their
position, but let them sing small in doing so.

Allston had had no training in philosophy, and he
seldom wrote in this fashion; and I am only quoting
him here to explain his use of the word "wish." His
few remarks on politics would have no meaning unless I made this clear. As regards philosophy, he
rarely discussed it, and always with the utmost diffi-
dence. He quoted once from Goethe, "If I am to listen to another person's opinions, they must be expressed in plain terms. There is quite enough that is
problematical in my own mind." He quoted again
from the *Conversations with Eckermann,* "I have always kept aloof from philosophy. The standpoint of
the natural human understanding was the one I preferred." He set this down in good faith, but also, I
think, in self-justification; for he felt that a modern
man ought to know philosophy, and often, in the
presence of his friends, who were adepts in this realm
of thought, he had the uneasy air of the insufficiently
educated. Once he remarks in his journal, "Can I be
talking philosophy? Am I really moving freely in
this realm of discourse? Has it happened with me as
it happened with Prescott, who found himself talking mathematics? Prescott had scarcely been able to
add a table of figures when he began *The Conquest*

of Peru. Then he found that he had to describe the astronomy of the Incas. There was no escaping it, and, in order to do so, he set to work at mathematics, and, before he knew it, he thought like a mathematician. Has something similar happened to my bloodshot brain? Has it come to pass that I, forced to work out my astronomy, have really learned to think like a thinking man? This is too much of a miracle for 1940." Indeed, as he continued, it proved to be so. He had found, after many trials, that he made no headway with abstract thinking, and, feeling that life was short, he abandoned himself to his tastes. To justify himself again, he copied out a passage from Thoreau's Journals (Vol. V) : "It is essential that a man confine himself to pursuits,—a scholar, for instance, to studies,—which lie next to and conduce to his life, which do not go against the grain, either of his will or his imagination. The scholar finds in his experience some studies to be most fertile and radiant with light, others dry, barren and dark. If he is wise, he will not persevere in the last, as a plant in a cellar will strive towards the light . . . Dwell as near as possible to the channel in which your life flows."

Usually, then, in discussing the will,—since he had no head for metaphysics,—he followed Dr. Johnson's shorter method, "We know that we are all free, and there's an end on't." Allston qualified the doctor's dictum to describe his own inferior state: "I am free only in the morning. When I get up from lunch my will is determined." Elsewhere he adds, "But I am most myself in the morning;" and he felt that Americans in general were a "morning" people. In spite of this, few of his friends believed in freedom.

They did not believe in freedom even in the morning.

This paradox interested Allston, and he discussed it in several notes. Let me offer one or two:

> Whatever their conscious beliefs may be, Americans are instinctive free-willers. They may think they are determinists, but, when this is the case, they always turn out to be fatalists, and that is quite a different matter. William James's *Psychology* made this clear: "The fatalistic argument is really no argument for simple determinism. There runs through it the sense of a force which might make things otherwise from one moment to another, if it were only strong enough to breast the tide. A person who feels the *impotence* of free effort in this way has the acutest notion of what is meant by it, and of its possible independent power. How else could he be so conscious of its absence and of that of its effects? But genuine determinism occupies a totally different ground; not the *impotence* but the *unthinkability* of free will is what it affirms."

And Allston continues as follows:

> In this sense, I say that all American fatalism assumes and demands free will. It springs from a kind of disappointment, and this is the characteristic American mood from Mark Twain and Henry Adams to John Dos Passos and William Faulkner. Our world has not lived up to its assumptions, and the single man feels helpless before the mass. Hence these tears, or this hard-boiled denial of the right to weep. But this does not argue that free will does not exist; it merely affirms that the will is not effective. It pays the highest tribute to the will, for it says that life is meaningless and empty precisely because of this nega-

tion. How many Americans are there, living or dead, for whom the will has not been the core of life, either in its operation or in its suspension?

The only unthinkable thing, for American minds, is that the will should not exist; and that is the reason why, when it is not effective, its impotence seems to Americans so overwhelming. One could never imagine an Asiatic writing as Dos Passos and Faulkner write. It takes long generations of disappointment, hundreds and thousands of years of disillusion to produce the deterministic frame of mind. Or perhaps the true determinist is one who has never known expectations. Fatalism presupposes hope, and any child can be a fatalist. Take away his kite or his train of cars, or lock him up in a closet, and he sees life stretching before him as an endless desert or prison. We have lost so many kites and trains of cars, in our recent American history, we have had to exchange so many nurseries for closets, that we have ceased to think of ourselves as the children for whom the world was one big vacant lot.

I shall have more to say of this in the coming chapters, which will be concerned mainly with Allston's views on books and writing. I have tried to define his view of political questions and what he called the American conception of life. What was his conception of criticism?

CHAPTER XV

CRITICISM: THEORY

"I HAVE never wished to be anything but a critic," Allston writes. "When I was fourteen, my greatest man was Ruskin; and, although I wrote two stories in college and the usual number of bad poems, I meant to be a critical writer and have had no other ambition since. So the saying that a critic is one who has failed at something else has no meaning for me. Why indeed should I wish to be anything else? I even narrowed the field. I wished to be an American critic, or a critic of things American; and, narrow as this may seem to others, it seems to me an infinite field. One can get more poetry into criticism than most poets have, more character than the novelists, more thought than the philosophers. Of course one doesn't!—but one can. Style, history, art, religion, poetry and everything else can be read into this narrow field or drawn out of it."

I have already said that Allston was a predestined writer, and he adds, "I am much more a writer than I am a critic." But he had some reason for thinking that the form of his writing was also predestined. As a young man he had read the work of the great critics almost to the exclusion of everything else. He had read the "literature" of Dante before he read Dante, and he laughed as he recalled the pedantry with which he had known "all about" writers before he knew the writings of the writers themselves. He was a professional long before he had a profession, he had put the cart before the horse; and it amused him, as he glanced over his early publications, to see with what audacity he had talked of authors whom he had scarcely read at all. "Ignorance, sheer ignorance,"— in Dr. Johnson's phrase,—had lain behind some of his boldest generalizations; and he liked George Saintsbury's saying, "It is the drawback of the youthful poet or novelist that he is insufficiently provided with veracity." This was also true of critics, including himself. He had developed late, although he had begun so early, because he was so long in acquiring veracity and knowledge.

He was a critic, then, as I have said, by predestination, and he was willing to accept the impeachments that were sometimes brought against his trade. He was amused by Sibelius's remark to his "only pupil," —"Remember, a statue has never been set up to a critic." But, as a critic, what was his point of view? I have sometimes wondered if he had one. He had, of course, a personal faith, the sum of his perceptions; but, if he knew precisely what this was, he certainly never expressed it. He was an emotional type, impulsive, like most Americans, who seldom saw himself *de haut en bas*. He was always "seeing black" or "seeing red." He was irritable, excitable, unstable, easily provoked and soon exhausted. He deplored these American traits, as he always called them, for he felt that they were fruits of a youthful culture. He loved the impassivity of the deep-sea mind, with its Asiatic draught and gravity. The American mind,

he said, was a fresh-water mind, which had its own
virtues of coolness and clearness, but the ultimate
saline wisdom was usually beyond it; and, however
this may be, I doubt if Allston could ever have seen
life steadily or seen it whole. Nor could he see himself with sufficient detachment. He wrote from his
passions and instincts. But he had a certain Yankee
shrewdness, and he said he had never felt more flattered than when A. E. wrote to him, "You think
straight." He might have been still more flattered if
someone had said that his leading trait was good
sense.

I find it especially difficult to characterize his
point of view because of his dislike of theorizing.
His mind was extremely concrete, and he usually
passed from point to point without rationalizing his
ends or the steps between them. Because of this habit,
he accused himself of laziness. "I should like to be,"
he says, "a 'patriot of the Muses' country,' in Emerson's wonderful phrase, but to analyze and state the
meaning of this phrase is utterly beyond my slothful
mind." It is true, he was always striving for clarity.
He has much to say regarding this, as one may see
in the following notes:

> I like definitions. I like the firm, fresh, crystalline
> thinking of the great writers, who do not share what
> Saintsbury called "the vulgar fear of the common-
> place and obvious." I have an imperfect sympathy
> with our well-known poet who is so afraid of utter-
> ing a *cliché,* of saying something that someone has
> said before, that he never finishes a sentence. (It is
> true that to make the obvious not commonplace one
> has to be a Tolstoy.)

Always begin with elements. Restate elements.
They are the least considered in ages of sophistry
like ours. All the elements need to be restated. It is
always surprising to find how confused people are in
regard to them. Define; always give definitions, and
always insist on the primary meanings of words.

In the matter of language, I like severe correct-
ness. By this I mean a long and sound etymological
history for every word one uses. But I except collo-
quialisms. The test for these is whether they are in
use among people whose character and occupations
one respects, as farmers, sailors, etc., usually people
who are close to the elements. This is wholly different from city slang, which springs out of the gutter
and is gaudy and cheap. I also have a natural contempt for fashionable usage.

(He was referring here to the language for critics.
He delighted in the colloquial phrases used by American novelists,—for instance, the phrase "drugstore
cowboy.")

Allston was eager to clarify his mind, but his distrust
of theories was equally marked, and he has much to
say on this subject also:

Theories,—how Renoir and Degas abhorred them!
Artists should abhor them, except in regard to technical questions, and I say that critics should abhor
them too. I have no theories and wish to have none.
They are all grey, as Goethe said, and I love the
"green golden bough of life."

Nor, while I like incidental definitions, do I like
total definitions of literature, the function of criticism, etc. Neither formula nor treatise could ever
comprise so vast a subject. But I like suggestions of
definitions, such as Pater's, in *Appreciations*,—"It is

on the quality of the matter it informs or controls, its compass, its variety, its alliance to great ends, or the depth of the note of revolt, or the largeness of hope in it, that the greatness of literary art depends, as *The Divine Comedy, Paradise Lost, Les Misérables,* the English Bible are great art,"—which of course consigns Pater to the second class.

I never get anything out of abstract discussions. They never rouse my mind. Whatever they might give, I get from a novel of Balzac better. A good novel at once heats my mind and sets the source of all my perceptions flowing. A Balzac "interior" recalls all my interiors; his *ville de province,* my own; his town, my town; his types, my types,—and all the bells begin to ring in my buried city.

He continues:

I, as a groper, always used to feel at a disadvantage in dealing with theorists and dogmatists. Now I let them talk. For I observe that these dogmatists all fall sooner or later into the hands of greater dogmatists, either Hitler, Stalin or, in another field, the Pope.

This makes it additionally difficult to define Allston's point of view, especially when one considers the following note:

As a critic, one should be wary of terms that end in *ism,* Classicism, Romanticism, Naturalism and the like. All these terms must go back to the buttonmoulder, for they are played out. A critic in our time must mint new coins. If he cannot do this, he must explain in what sense he uses the old ones.

These pigeon-holes are not for imaginative minds; and all such classifications, which form the stock in

trade of so many critics, are of recent origin, and a
not very creditable origin at that. One should recon-
ceive the states of mind and the tones of feeling that
lie behind these labels. Every real writer partakes of
the nature of all these categories and is partly romantic, partly naturalistic, classical, humanistic and all
the rest.

In view of all these notes, I have sometimes wondered if Allston really had a position at all. How did
he judge authors? Did he merely feel about them
as William Morris felt, as he rubbed with both hands
the part of his waistcoat that covered the seat of his
diaphragm?—"I always know when a thing is really
good by its making me feel warm across here."

Now, it was one of Allston's notions that we only
understand ourselves when we find that others mis-
understand us; and he might never have been driven
to define himself if other critics had not attacked
him. One of these critics accused him of a "soft
Emersonian idealism" that kept him from grappling
with his subjects. Others said that he had retired from
the field of contemporary letters and had become a
"scholarly story-teller." He had become a back number, he was out of touch with life, he had withdrawn
from the "arena," and several friends and well-
wishers favoured him with dire warnings,—unless
he kept his former self ever in his mind's eye, he was
sailing straight for the demnition bowwows. He recognized in all this grains of what might perhaps be
true, and he wondered if he was really going to the
devil: for he was an idealist, certainly, and his recent subjects were largely historical, and, as for his
being a back number, that was all too likely. All

American writers were back numbers after their reputations were five years old. But had he indeed gone
back on himself? Had he not always been an idealist? And, if he wrote of the past instead of the present, did this mean that he was not writing in the
present tense? As for the warning that he ought to
watch his steps, he felt that he could parry this, at
least; and he could not consider the notion that he
ought to watch his *former* steps,— he felt, in regard
to worshipping his own dead self, as he felt about
other forms of ancestor-worship. For the rest, he
said:

> I have no choice whatever in the matter of my
> thoughts. I think what my constitution obliges me
> to think,—in other words, what I *do* think, what
> comes up from inside and forms itself in words with-
> out any interposition of my will. How absurd to tell
> me then what I *ought* to think, or that I should think
> as I thought when I was thirty! As well tell me that
> I ought to have wings, or blond hair, or green eyes,
> or that I should be four or seven feet tall. And yet
> these well-wishers pride themselves on their percep-
> tion, their knowledge of psychoanalysis and all the
> rest.

Allston was the victim of his own self-determination.
His mind could not escape from its own skin. He felt
that he had evolved from his own past and could
have had no other evolution, that his present and his
past were all of a piece, and that, however his emphasis had changed for the moment, the original
germ of his mind had remained unaltered. As for the
"arena," whatever arena he was in he had never been
out of; or, rather, if he had withdrawn for a moment,

and taken up "scholarly story-telling," it was to return again with heavier ammunition. No, he had not
gone back on himself, although he was grateful to
these critics for obliging him to reckon with this
question; and, if he seemed to be out of the fight, it
was merely because these other critics had never
really shared his point of view. They had seemed to
share it because in former days he was more concerned with negation than with affirmation. As long
as he had attacked society, they had gone along with
him, for their mood was chiefly negative all the time,
but when he rallied to the defence of whatever was
good in society they said he was a traitor to himself
and them. Actually, his point of view had remained
the same both in defence and in attack. His negations
and affirmations had the same root; and they disliked
this root and would not have accepted it in him if he
had not shared some of their negations. This root was
idealism, which they could not stomach because they
were fatalistic in spiritual matters; and they accused
him of being "soft" because they believed that they
were "hard,"—there they were certain that they had
him. There was the crux of the matter, indeed; and
Allston felt that if he met them there he would be
able to go on his way serenely. It was the Marxist
critics who were most sure that they had him, and
most of the others who attacked him were touched
with the Marxist philosophy. (The others were
mostly muddled Marxists, who lacked the force to
see their philosophy through.) They did not respect
him because he believed in free will; and, while they
did not respect him, they could not forgive him. This
was because, when he wrote about literature, he

would not admit that its core was economic. The idea
of the autonomy of literature they could not abide.
This was the bull that Allston had to take by the
horns, and he proceeded to take it in the following
note:

> My communist friend accuses me of a "soft Emer-
> sonian idealism." It amuses me to be regarded as soft
> because I am a free-willer and not a materialistic de-
> terminist. I say that our Marxists are soft, softer
> than the Vicar of Bray, who, having no mental stabil-
> ity, at least turned his own mind. They let their
> Marxist party turn their minds for them. Emerson's
> soft idealism was also John Brown's. It has been the
> motive-power of all the potent American movements;
> and, let me add, or, rather, let me begin by saying, it
> has been the motive-power of most of the potent
> American writers. It has been and it will be to the end
> of the chapter.

Now, Allston was aware of most of the current
objections to what is called idealism and what is
called romanticism. (For, although he deplored the
abuse of these terms, and sometimes even deplored
their use, he found that, after all, he was driven to
use them.*) These attitudes, he knew, had lent them-

---

* An English writer, named below, defending the use of the word
"romantic," defines it, somewhat loosely, yet in a manner that Allston
might have accepted: " 'Romantic' and 'classical' are, indeed, so valuable
because they are indicative of the main tendencies in every personal
experience. In ourselves we feel both the duty of obedience to tradition
and the urge for individual assertion; the spirit which affirms and the
spirit which denies; the simultaneous need for conformity and non-
conformity . . . The romantic is in general the rebel, the individualist,
the liberal, the protestant. The classicist is the authoritarian, the tra-
ditionalist, the conservative, the catholic. The division enters every de-
partment of life. So Æschylus is classical and Euripides romantic; Julius
Cæsar romantic and Marcus Brutus classical; Saint Bernard of Clairvaux
classical and Peter Abélard romantic; Michael Angelo romantic and
Leonardo da Vinci classical; Ignatius Loyola classical and Martin Luther

selves to many abuses, a vague and spurious eloquence, a wilful self-aggrandizement, a greedy self-
blinding in emotion or sensation that evaded any sort
of objective control. There were many living romantic minds that had not won their own security,—they
had inherited their basis: and there were others who
had triumphed, but triumphed over what? Had they
ever encountered the obstacles that foundered others?
Had they undergone the conditions that made their
age an inferno for others? In short, if they talked of
courage, love, mercy, honour, faith in life, had they
earned the right to speak of these large matters? It
was certainly true that these were the matters of
which great writers had always written and, as Allston was convinced, would always write; but he
agreed that no one was entitled to write of these matters unless he knew whereof he spoke. Was he himself entitled to speak of them? Had he lived enough
himself to use these great words not in vain? I can
only say that he used them in good faith. Idealism,
romanticism, in the name of which he used these
words, were banners of the faith that he followed as
a critic. How far he had the right to bear them was
not to be judged by his professions,—it could only be
judged by the body of his work as a critic; and he

romantic; Shakespeare romantic and Dante classical; Wellington classical
and Nelson romantic; Disraeli romantic and Gladstone classical; Cézanne
classical and Van Gogh romantic; D. H. Lawrence romantic and James
Joyce classical.

"To these dangerous generalizations I will add one more. The *great*
romantic is usually superior in achievement and influence to the great
classicist; he has the superabundant vitality which can both create and
rebel and he has the more profound vision. But minor classicists, even
at their worst, are saved by that very Form which the individualist
overthrows from the pointless inanity into which minor romantics de-
generate."—Hugh Ross Williamson, *The Poetry of T. S. Eliot.*

felt it was not for him to determine just how far he
was whole-souled,—this was for others to determine
if they wished to do so. For the rest, he claimed the
immunity of other professors of other faiths: the un-
worthiness of ministers has never been regarded as a
judgment on the worthiness of the faith in question.

So it seemed to Allston that his personal qualifica-
tions had nothing whatever to do with the faith he
practised. The only proper question was whether the
faith was true or not; and, inasmuch as the great
themes *were* courage, mercy, love and honour, he had
no doubt of the truth of the faith that expressed them.
Nor could he see any reason why this faith should
be judged by its weakest manifestations, even if they
were most evident in the age he lived in. Idealists
were often vague, just as romantics were often
greedy; and their attitudes were often easy for the
fatuous and the feeble. Was idealism therefore necessarily vague? Was romanticism inevitably greedy?
Why should idealists be wilful? And why should
romantics evade objective control? And why should
either be "divorced from reality"? The fact that they
often were was beside the question; and Allston,
whose critical faculties were certainly awake, said
that the proof of the pudding was in the eating. As I
have observed, he did not like theories, and I shall
cite few more of his, leaving the rest of his proof to
his practice at large. But I must add one word or two.
He said that all the great writers were contemporary
writers, they were all living in his mind, and he
judged his actual contemporaries in relation to the
rest; and he added that, as an idealist, he spoke for
the history of literature, as in calling himself a ro-

mantic he spoke for American literature. (For were
not modern Americans writers, whatever their professions to the contrary, mostly romantic in grain?
Who had ever been more romantic than Scott Fitz-
gerald or Thomas Wolfe? Was not Faulkner's cyn-
icism highly romantic? Was not Dos Passos a secret
romantic reacting against himself, as one saw from all
his early books,—*One Man's Initiation,* for example,
—not to speak of Dos Passos's recent hero, Glenn
Spotswood? Then there was Hart Crane, with his broken romantic bridge to the future, and there was E. E.
Cummings, with his "shining things," and there was
Ernest Hemingway, with his matadors,*—and Allston said that *A Farewell to Arms* was much the same
tale as *Evangeline,* granting the difference of feeling
between the two epochs. Were they not similar stories
of true love lost? And what could be more romantic
than the American feeling for "Europe," whether
the Europe of Paris or the Europe of Moscow?)
Idealism was the dominant tendency in all literature,
he said,— it was the warp of literature in all ages and
peoples; as the peculiar idealism of the romantic
type was the dominant strain in American literature.
This was the warp, and it must have been close to
reality or it could not have been so. As for the further question of wilfulness, this could be settled in a
phrase. All the greatest writers, whatever they were,
romantic, idealistic, whatever one called them, and
whether in this country or in the world at large, had
harmonized their wills with the nature of things; or

* Allston compared Hemingway with Gabriele D'Annunzio, who told
Mrs. Winthrop Chanler that he "hunted for the sake of extreme sensa-
tions, and because he saw death lurking for him under every obstacle."
(Mrs. Chanler, *Roman Spring.*)

at least they had recognized the nature of things,—
whether they called it God or the All or Nature,—
as something to which they owed allegiance. "In Thy
will is our peace" had been their motto.

What, then, was reality if it was not the nature of
things, and how, except through idealism, could one
know it? If there was a Something that determined
one's *modus vivendi,* could anything, as reality, be
comparable with it? Yet how could one approach it
except by way of ideas and concepts?—it was nothing that one could handle, touch or taste. And how
could one approach it save through the health, which
placed a man in harmony with the nature of things?
Only through health, the health of the psyche, could
one find oneself by losing oneself,—only by the measure of health could one know sickness,—and one
could achieve health only by the ways of health, the
ways of courage, justice, love and mercy. These were
the ways of the healthy psyche; and they followed
the biological grain. For it was by means of these
ways that the race had risen; and therefore whatever
followed this grain was true for human beings, as
whatever controverted it was in some way false.
Great literature favoured the "life-drive," as the psy-
choanalysts called it; and whatever favoured the
"death-drive" was necessarily secondary. This was
the basis of Allston's faith, and he took for his criterion,—which served him as well as another for
American letters,—a passage from Walt Whitman's
essay on Poe: "I wanted, and still want for poetry,
the clear sun shining, the fresh air blowing, the
strength and power of health, not of delirium, even
amid the stormiest passions,—with always the back-

ground of the eternal moralities." He had never found any reason to feel that this was not an adequate touchstone by which to measure American literature. The reader will admit that Allston is entitled to offer his proofs for this position, and I shall proceed to marshal them in the chapters that follow. He believed that certain elements in men are constant. He believed that the constancy of these elements results in standards; and he believed, as a third note, that, inasmuch as these standards exist, they presuppose the objectivity of literary truth. When I turn from his theory as a critic to his practice as a critic, I shall attempt to explain what he meant by these statements. Let me conclude this chapter with a single remark:

Literature has been out on a branch. We must return to the trunk.

CHAPTER XVI

CRITICISM: PRACTICE

ALLSTON observes that Sainte-Beuve, in his essay on Leopardi (*Portraits contemporains, IV*), apologizes for writing of a foreign author, persuaded as he is *"que la critique littéraire n'a toute sa valeur et son originalité que lorsqu'elle s'applique à des sujets dont on possède de près et de longue main le fond, les alentours et toutes les circonstances,"*— "literary criticism has its full worth and originality only when it applies itself to subjects of which it possesses, through immediate contact and from a long way back, the source, the surrounding facts and all the circumstances." Certainly, Sainte-Beuve had written of many foreign authors, with surpassing grace and understanding, and yet it seemed to Allston that he stated a principle here to which a critic might well give heed in his practice. He said that the poet Yeats had the same thought when he wrote, "One can only reach out to the universe with a gloved hand,— that hand is one's nation, the only thing that one knows even a little about."

This was a principle that Allston followed in all his work. He wrote, I might say, exclusively of American subjects; for, although he had written of foreign subjects, he had begun with American sub-

jects,—and how could he ever cease to be interested in
them? He had accepted the principle after the fact,
for his practice was based upon interest and interest
alone; and he felt that he could not exhaust this interest. The only thing that worried him was whether
he could ever get to the bottom of his subjects.

Such was the basis of Allston's practice, but before
I proceed with this subject I should like to mention
a general point regarding American literature. Allston was sometimes annoyed by the ignorance of Europeans concerning the writers of his country. He
quoted Carlyle on the state of German literature before the Napoleonic wars, which exactly paralleled
this situation: "During the greater part of the last
century, the Germans, in our intellectual survey of
the world, were quietly omitted; a vague contemp-
tuous ignorance prevailed respecting them; it was a
Cimmerian land, where, if a few sparks did glim-
mer, it was but so as to testify their own existence, too
feebly to enlighten *us*. The Germans passed for ap-
prentices in all provinces of art; and many foreign
craftsmen scarcely allowed them so much." Allston
pointed the parallel with this remark:

> There is a sounding-board behind European writ-
> ers that carries their voices across the ocean, while
> American writers, facing the other way, face a keen
> east wind.

But, in general, I think he felt this was good for our
writers. He valued a long obscurity, as giving writers
a chance to prove themselves, and he said, "We'll be
discovered soon enough." He liked a story that
Brandes told about a Danish author who called upon

Sainte-Beuve and reproached him because he knew
so little about the Danes. Sainte-Beuve laid his head
a little on one side and replied with roguish imperti-
nence, *"Eh bien, faites quelque chose! on parlera de
vous."* Brandes delighted in this, and so did Allston.
Just *do something,* and the rest will follow,—if you
are doing something good. Allston knew that Americans were doing many good things; but could they
ever be good enough? It became instantly evident,
after the conquests of Hitler, that America was soon
to have a place of power; and it would need much to
sustain this power. Could there be a better reason for
raking American literature fore and aft?

Thus everything convinced Allston that to write
about American literature was his special privilege
and obligation; but I must add that, although he
wrote of American authors, he was also interested in
authors and literature as such. He believed in tradition, as I shall explain, and, behind the American
tradition, the human tradition, in the light of which
he saw his American subjects. He differed sharply
with T. S. Eliot in the matter of this human tradition, as I shall have to show in a later chapter, discussing his general view of literature; but I am con
cerned at the moment with his practice as a critic,
and, first of all, his motive in criticism. Why did he
write criticism? Did he hope to reform his world?
Did he hope to improve or redeem the writers? Was
he concerned, essentially, with consequences? I said
in my opening chapter that he was not, although he
believed that criticism has consequences. He ampli-
fies this question in one of his notes:

I write criticism as Plutarch says he wrote his
Lives, with the same motives and the same objective.
He wrote to repel from his own spirit the worthless,
evil or ignoble feelings aroused by the enforced associations of everyday life. Plutarch's aim, in short,
was to enlarge his own spirit, not to awaken his readers, in the first instance; and he succeeded in awak-
ening his readers because he fulfilled this proper
aim. By acting first upon himself, enlarging his own
spirit, he was enabled to enter the spirit of his
heroes. How else could he have conveyed the feeling of their largeness?

This is also the meaning of Goethe's saying, "I
have, in my trade as a writer, never asked myself,
How shall I be of service to the world at large? All
I have ever done was with the view of making myself better and more full of insight, of increasing the
content of my own personality; and then only of giving utterance to what I recognized as the good and
the true."

Allston did not write, then, for the sake of improving
other writers, or to win a hearing for them. He wrote
to establish the principles by which writers should
write, or, rather, by which they should live, by seeking to establish these principles in his own life. That
this was a vain task, he was well aware, for how could
he ever touch the garment of truth? But for what else
could he strive in his life as a critic? Was any other
task worth striving for? He knew that only in so far
as he approached the garment of truth could his
criticism have any value whatever. Its "consequences"
would otherwise remain as sterile as its *fond*. As for
his view of writers in general, it was determined by

this,—since he could not hope to possess the truth, it was always likely that they possessed it. He seems to have had this in mind in the following note:

> I have an instinctive will to believe that all writers are virtuous men. Below the level where I agree or disagree with writers, I like and respect them all because they are writers.

He felt that writers generally had a feeling for truth, which he was able to share only at moments. But, in a less expansive mood, he adds:

> Of course, there are rhinoceros writers, wart-hog writers, copperhead writers. There are literary Hitlers and Mussolinis. There are writers like those animated blood-puddings who rule the German nation and stick one another with "putsches" and "purges." Do I like these writers, or only as I like a large Texas rattlesnake in August? Would I perhaps like to kill them? According to Hemingway, who likes killing even more than I do, we can only kill what we love. I am inclined to love Hemingway, though I do not wish to kill him, but I cannot always share his catholic tastes; and I do not doubt that he loves the hyenas whose bowels so amuse him when he shoots them out. Still, perhaps I might love them too, as much as Hemingway loves them; and no doubt this is the way I love these writers.

Allston was not sure, then, whether he loved all writers or not, but he felt sure that writers are highly important; and this thought lay behind his criticism. He felt it was the first law for critics to take them with the utmost seriousness. On this point he writes as follows:

Dr. Alexis Carrel says that what the world needs is a "high council of doctors" to rule it for its good. So H. G. Wells has always said that the world should be ruled by engineers, and all the West Point men feel that the world should be ruled by a General Staff. I know I have a tendency to feel that the world should be ruled by writers; but, though Goethe was a good administrator, I do not forget Frederick the Great's remark that the worst thing he could do to punish a province was to sentence it to be governed by men of letters. No, let writers rule by writing, as they do rule, even at present; for "imagination governs mankind," as a practical man, Napoleon, said,—and who rules the imagination more than writers? I say they rule even at present, and I might say especially at present, when, as Yeats said,—in a different sense from mine, no doubt,—

> The best lack all conviction, while the worst
> Are full of passionate intensity.

Thus Allston felt there were goats among writers, or, rather, wolves among the sheep,—though I must defer this also to another chapter. What he would have said was that, inasmuch as writers rule, it is of the first importance that they should rule wisely; and in so far as criticism in its way rules writers, it is important that criticism should itself be wise. To be wise, it must have principles and be governed by them; and how could it have principles unless it accepted the source of principles? As truth was the only source, there was only one way for criticism, to profess the existence of truth and strive to embrace it. That truth existed, Allston never doubted,—had not all the sages of all the races and all the ages agreed on certain root ideas? And was not truth the measure of literature also? Allston quoted Hume, in his *Standard of Taste:* "Among a thousand different opinions that men may have on the same subject, there is but one just and true, and the only difficulty is to ascertain and fix it." That critics often achieved this was obvious also,—did they not often "hit the nail on the head"? Whenever a critic did this, every qualified reader perceived it; and did this not mean that something existed between the critic and the reader that could only be described as the sense of truth? Allston settled the point for himself by asking a further question, "When we call a person perceptive, what does the perception imply?" But he had already settled the question in two of his experiences, which he relates as follows:

J. asked me to read through his six volumes of poems, and select those which I thought most suitable for a collected volume. There were about eight hundred poems, and I reduced them to about five hundred. Then I found that I had chosen the same five hundred that he had selected with the same end in view. We differed in regard only to about five or six poems.

On the second occasion, he had agreed to make selections from a long unpublished journal:

Much struck, as I select these passages, by the feeling that I am not doing the selecting but that the passages select themselves, and that any other competent editor would select and reject the same passages that I do. It is just as it was when I selected what seemed to be J.'s best poems and found that his choice agreed in almost every case with mine. This

repeated experience indicates a number of things,—
for one, that such a thing as taste exists, in the sense
of a virtually absolute standard, *in minds properly
qualified,* for long experience in discrimination has
led in my case to this result. Ten years ago, I was not
nearly so confident. I used to waver in my judgment,
feeling that my judgment was personal, and that it
should not be personal,—not feeling at all, as I do
now, that some impersonal standard, call it reality,
call it truth, was literally operating in me. This points
to the validity of a principle of authority in matters
of taste, an authority that is not mine but that I
merely represent and that is obviously inherent in the
nature of things. What, then, becomes of impres-
sionism and all subjective critical modes in so far as
concerns the determination of value?

This journal, when it is printed, will have selected
itself, with scarcely any interposition of my personal
preferences; for I have the strongest feeling that any
qualified person who had read the whole journal
would say that my selection was the right one. My
only concern was to give the "best," and the best
declared itself through me. I feel that I am selecting "with authority," and that "I" am not the selec-
tor. I deduce from this the existence of truth, in the
literary mode, and the possibility of attaining it in
practice.

Allston would have said, I think, that the whole
practice of criticism consisted in this simple double
law, to profess the existence of truth and strive to embrace it. To repeat what I said in the previous chapter,—he believed that certain elements in men are
constant; he believed that the constancy of these
elements results in standards; and he believed that,

inasmuch as these standards exist, they presuppose
the objectivity of literary truth. (For is not human
nature constant? Is not this the joy of the saints
and the despair of the reformers? Is not the world
still full of Herods and Hamlets, of Iphigeneias,
Ophelias, Robin Hoods and Falstaffs? Would people so persist in reading the classics if they did not
find themselves reflected there?) He felt this was all
in the nature of things, as,—to refer again to the
previous chapter,—he felt that health, and health
alone, the ways, that is, of the healthy psyche, placed
a man in harmony with the nature of things. I shall
have more to say of this presently. Meanwhile, he remarks, in regard to standards:

Why this mourning over the loss of standards?
Standards are reborn every moment, whenever a
healthy mind finds itself.

And again:

People keep repeating, There are no standards any
longer, there is nothing one can hold to or believe
in. This is a lie, and every time it is uttered we ought
to nail it. Standards are inherent in the constant facts
of human nature, and I see that even Japanese poli-
ticians have taken to quoting Confucius. They pay
this tribute to the reality of truth, whether they
practise it or not.

So it is with writers. They fly off the handle. They
divagate from the nature of things. But when they
grow up, if they grow up, they return to the nature
of things. What do we mean when we say that a
writer *finds himself* if we do not mean that he finds
himself in harmony with the nature of things? That
is maturity, when a writer outgrows his eccentric ego

and speaks the universal language. At that point his
mind unites with ours.

Consider, again, the question of style. People say
there are no standards of style any longer. But I
repeat that good writers always exemplify standards,
and that readers always recognize them. The main
line always continues. As Southey says in one of his
letters, "There is, as you must have heard Wordsworth point out, a language of pure, intelligible English, which was spoken in Chaucer's time, and is spoken
in ours; equally understood then and now, and of
which the Bible is the written and permanent standard, as it has undoubtedly been the great means of
preserving it." This is just as true in 1940 as it was a
century ago.

Allston was aware, of course, how far novelists and
poets were sometimes obliged to deviate from the
standard language. This language, he said, following
Dr. Johnson, "never becomes obsolete," and he further quoted Johnson: "There is in every nation . . .
a certain mode of phraseology so consonant to the
analogy and principles of its respective language as
to remain settled and unaltered. This style is to be
sought in the common intercourse of life among those
who speak only to be understood, without ambition
of elegance. The polite are always catching modish
innovations, and the learned forsake the vulgar, when
the vulgar is right; but there is a conversation above
grossness and below refinement, where propriety re-
sides." He knew that novelists and poets must also
seek "strangeness," and he knew there were times,
like the last quarter-century, when they were driven
into anarchism, when the "roof of heaven" had to be

broken for all manner of new forms. There were times when the standard stank in one's nostrils, when it had to be abandoned, or partially abandoned, so that it might recover its normal lustre. Yet the standard always returned, with reborn freshness, as men always recovered their feeling for courage and honour; and it interested Allston to see how contemporary writers, those who deviated from the standard style, were apt, from time to time, to return to this style, as baseball-players return to home-base. So, for example, Dos Passos, after writing his *U. S. A.,* wrote another novel in the orthodox manner; and Gertrude Stein also returned to "intelligible English." Just so the painter Picasso liked these lucid intervals, and, as if to prove to himself that he could still do so, occasionally struck a note reminiscent of Poussin. Did not these illustrations prove the rule?

In Allston's theory and practice, then, there was little new and little his own. He wished this to be as little as it might be, for he regarded the personal as merely eccentric: it was a derogation of the nature of things. This, perhaps, is the leading thought behind the following scattered notes, with which I conclude this chapter on his criticism:

Make no generalizations in regard to American literature that cannot be exposed to the light of universal literature.

The only "Americanism" that is worth pursuing for literature is a by-product of the process by which genuine men living in this country genuine lives are genuinely expressing their convictions and conceptions.

In criticism, no faint praise. Take from the author everything that is not his by right, take it as a surgeon takes away every last cell of morbid tissue, with a strict and relentless knife; then cauterize the wound and help the victim to his feet again and send him away with both hands filled with flowers.

An author whose tissue is so morbid that he cannot survive the ordeal should not be subjected to it. He should be allowed to die in peace.

Criticism exists to determine values, to cherish them, define them and maintain them. That is the reason why criticism is central in civilization. Our criticism is too high-pitched. It is always in the position of Philip drunk, who cannot stay drunk forever and is always waking up with a morning headache. Its midnight enthusiasms look very bleak and drear in the rays of another sunrise, bleaker than they ought to be or would be if they were midday enthusiasms, or judgments formed in dark and cloudy weather. This high pitch does not pay. What caused the prodigious success of *The Education of Henry Adams?* As much as anything else, its tone of understatement. This ingrained New England tone, applied to our history, in a world that was no longer used to hearing from New England, caused a sensation in contrast to the hullabaloo of the criticism to which the public is accustomed.

Good as our best reviewers are, and they are very good in comparison with the reviewers of twenty years ago,—I do not say fifty, for that is another matter,—they are still strangely the reverse of learned. When they are not too eager to score, to strike while the iron is hot, they show a shocking lack of general reading. The field of their consciousness and reference is infinitesimally narrow. The same fixed names occur again and again in everything they write of current books, a few conscientious references to Aristotle, or some other classic author who happens to be in vogue, because some French or English author has brought him to their attention, a little patter of popular names,—especially John Donne's, —and Flaubert at the end of every vista. This literary cosmogony that begins with Flaubert is a very singular thing. Still, it is better than the cosmogony of twenty years ago, which often began with Oscar Wilde. But what a descent in learning from the days of George Ripley, who wrote about books in *The Tribune* in the days of our grandsires.

It is true that in readability our reviewing has improved. Many of the reviews in the weeklies are remarkably fine. But most of the reviewers sail without a keel. As they seem to be able to hold in their minds only a handful of recent discoveries, they are constantly discovering for themselves things that other people have always known; and then most of their movements are herd-movements, like those of the rest of the population. They are always "going over in a body" to some new major prophet, who may indeed be a major prophet, Freud, Marx, Spengler or Pareto. The shortness of their memories is only matched by the facility of their transformations. Thus, at the present time, a few old fogies still speak up for Shaw and Wells, who represent the past before the deluge. But Shaw and Wells were talked about to death; and I foresee that, in another five years, Eliot and Joyce will not have where to lay their heads. If one runs through a bound volume of one of the weeklies, one learns what mutability means in a world that has lost its memory.

It is right that living authors should fill the foreground of a reviewer's mind, and perhaps the mind of a critic. But if one reads these reviews five years later, one is surprised to find how remote they seem. This is because the subjects have not been related to the general stream of critical tradition. The authors have not been read as wholes or brought into connection with other wholes. The reviewers have lived so much in the present that they have not even seen the present, and, having no sense of the past, they have no sense of the future.

One can sum up in a phrase the weakness of our reviewers, and of our critics in general. They can only parry direct attacks. They cannot stand up against flank attacks, still less attacks from the rear.

The Function of Criticism. "The rocky, dry, fallow ground says, 'I can produce nothing, nothing will grow; yet I see the sun and feel the rain as much as you do.'—'Aye,' replies the corn-field, 'but they have plucked away my stones and turned up my surface and let in the water-courses; and now the sun and the air, the heat and the snow all serve me.' "—Emerson's Journals.

No one is fit to judge a book until he has rounded Cape Horn in a sailing vessel, until he has bumped into two or three icebergs, until he has been lost in the sands of the desert, until he has spent a few years in the House of the Dead.

In view of the mistakes he is always making, a critic should wear sackcloth as his everyday garment.

"I have planted, Apollos watered; but God gave the increase."

CHAPTER XVII

LITERATURE TODAY

"WITH what high hopes the twentieth century opened!" Allston says of the years during which he had come of age. "How exciting was the vista of the future that had dominated the world since the 'Rights of Man'! One has only to reread the early books of H. G. Wells, who followed Whitman, Ruskin and William Morris, to see how exciting was this vista. Why did the first world-war destroy it? Because it revealed that the depths of man were not what we had supposed them. These depths are more evil than we thought, but they are also better; and, in any case, life is illusory unless we live in the depths. We must re-create this vista of the future. Meanwhile, this is the time to think of the present, of the values that should be in the present in order to make the world worth fighting for. Living in the future, in Wells's way, in a world of 'acceleration,' took away all the depth from life. The way to build for the future is to build for the present."

Perhaps I can best approach Allston's view of literature by dwelling on this subject for a moment; and, since he has referred to Wells, let me quote him on Wells again, in conjunction with another modern author:

In *The Future in America,* H. G. Wells remarked: "I am curiously not interested in things, and curiously interested in the consequences of things." This reminds me of the remark of the great George Brandes, to which I have already referred,—the romantic mind asks for the significance of things, while the modern mind asks for their causes. I draw from these two phrases a general deduction. As between Wells and Brandes, the modern mind cares only for causes and consequences, not for things themselves and the significance of things. The latter concern only the "romantic mind."

Well, then, I say we must restore the romantic mind, if this is its definition. We must restore the sense of things, the sense of their significance, along with their consequences and their causes. If things have no "significance," things are hollow; and, if things are hollow, are not their causes and consequences hollow also?

Allston applied this to his own profession. What, he asked, is literature? Is it hollow? The literature of our time might be hollow; he did not say it was, but perhaps it might be,—one might entertain the proposition; but this would not mean that literature itself is hollow. In fact, it is not hollow,—all critics agreed in this; and he therefore asked, What is its significance? He was delighted to learn from such an eminent critic as Brandes that his desire to ask this question proved he was "romantic." He knew he was romantic, and he rejoiced in being so, for it showed that he had a centrally American mind; and that literature is very significant he never doubted. Thus he remarks in one of his notes:

"In literature alone," said Leopardi, "the regen-

eration of our country can have a substantial beginning." This, I believe, is true; and, in any case,
whether it is true or not, every real writer writes as
if it were true.

Here, verily, he might have added, is the mouth
speaking great things. What could be said for such
an exalted claim? If Allston was romantic, he was
realistic also, and he knew that he lived among men
who were born in Missouri. He was aware of the
prejudice against the romantic view of things,—had
he not in his own youth reacted against it? And was
not this claim romantic in the highest degree? Allston replied that Leopardi was a man of parts. He
was a man of intelligence and a man of genius (Allston knew him best in the dialogues and essays) ; and,
if Leopardi made this statement, he must have had
some sensible reason for it.

Now, I see that I must explain a little the growth
of Allston's point of view, for, although he was born
romantic and so remained, he had reacted earlier
against this position. He had been offended by the
fatuous talk about "high ideals" that governed the
general mind when he was a boy; and, as a young
man, in his first critical essays, he had attacked the
romantic American classics. He had been struck by
the train of abuses that followed in their wake, and,
in order to assail the results, he assailed the causes,—
in so far as these were literary causes. He had ridiculed Emerson, Longfellow, Whittier and Bryant,
as the young Frenchmen ridiculed Victor Hugo, as
they ridiculed Tennyson in England; nor did he regret this, although he regretted now and then that
he had not really read these poets first. He had not

really read them, for he was too impatient with them, but it would not have changed his feeling if he had read them,—they stood for "high ideals," and that was enough. This was because the abuses that lay behind the "high ideals" were more actual to him than the ideals themselves. He saw the ideals as veils that covered the abuses. Had not Ibsen disillusioned all the young with the humbug and the fraud of the respectable classes, who intrigued for power and sweated the poor, while they concealed their own sins and hushed up their scandals? The young people took for their motto Bernard Shaw's phrase, "Our whole bourgeois society rests upon a soil teeming with the pestilence of lies;" and Allston was in sharp reaction against the business world about him, as I have suggested in a previous chapter. At no time, early or late, could he make his peace with this business world; and yet this business world, in his earlier days, had marched or professed to march under Emerson's banner. It quoted Emerson on wealth, Emerson on self-reliance, and it quoted the other poets when they suited its fancy; and Allston not unnaturally felt that the "high ideals" and the low abuses were faces of the same almighty dollar. It was true that one side of the dollar had a certain vague charm that the other lacked; but the point was that he did not like the dollar. He crumpled it up and tossed it out of the window.

In all this, Allston was much like most of his friends and coevals, who were more and more preoccupied with these abuses. They might have grown up in happy households, but they adopted the mood of their time, as sensitive young people usually do;

for is it not true that the young are the children of
their friends more than they are the children of their
fathers and mothers? Besides, there were many who
had not grown up in happy households,—their families also lived in the frame of their time, and this
was a bad time for human values. All the young people were rebels against a materialistic world, which
pretended to be moral, ideal and loving, when it was
largely loveless and often base; and they felt it was
a swindle, and, since it professed to be honest and
real, they felt that all it professed was a swindle also.
How could the trustful trust trust? How could the
affectionate believe in affection? Morality and ideals
were a stench in the nostrils!—and the more the
young and the sensitive were affectionate and trustful, the more they turned against their affection and
trust. They did not wish to believe in things, they did
not wish to love things; they cultivated suspicion,
distrust and hatred, because they wished to be honest
themselves and save a part of their self-respect,—
only on these terms could they survive. No doubt,
they knew there was something real in trust, in love,
in ideals, in affection; but they had to throw over the
cargo to save the ship. So they felt, in any case, and
that was the important point, for their poems, their
novels and their plays expressed these feelings. Allston scarcely shared these feelings, but he knew how
most of his friends felt, and it seemed to him that he
understood the feelings; and he knew that if he did
not share them it was because of his good luck,—although, for the matter of that, *was* he so lucky? He
might have been lucky as a man and unlucky as a
writer; for the minds that were perfectly focussed

during this time were those that most fully shared
these feelings. The intensest minds of the time shared
all these feelings, and is not the lucky writer the perfectly focussed? He had been focussed in earlier
days, and he hoped that he might be focussed later;
but he felt that his mind was in abeyance. He could
only wait and watch and look for a turn of the tide
that would bring his forces into play again.

So Allston watched these dominant minds, these
minds that were perfectly focussed and that were giving literature its new direction. For, while there
were admirable writers who did not share their negative feelings, it was these who gave the time its peculiar stamp; and the first world-war had intensified
their negative feelings. The young and sensitive
minds that grew up in the shadow of the war were
still more disillusioned, for the peace was a greater
failure than the war had been. They felt they had
been betrayed, and, as evil triumphed, they came to
feel that nothing else was real; and the writers grew
still more cynical, hard-boiled, hard-bitten. They
followed Mencken when he spoke of the universal
"boobery," they quoted T. S. Eliot on the "myth of
human goodness;" and it seemed as if the most
powerful writers, from James Joyce to Hemingway,
from Eugene O'Neill and Theodore Dreiser to Eliot
of *The Waste Land* were bent on proving that life is a
dark little pocket. Influence goes with intensity.
Whoever possesses intensity is bound to conquer
other minds, whatever the intensity may be, positive
or negative, major or minor, angelic or diabolic, human or inhuman; and the good and the positive
lacked in our time the intensity they have possessed

in ages of faith or in times of great causes. The genius
that was moulding the mind of the present was almost wholly destructive; and even where, as in many
cases, these writers were fighting for social justice,
they pictured life as hardly worth the trouble. It
seemed to them vain, sordid, ugly, the plaything, in
Theodore Dreiser's phrase, of "idle rocking forces"
or currents of material interest. What did Joyce's
Ulysses say if not that life is a bad joke? What did
the novelists say if not that nothing good exists, that
only the ugly is real, the perverted, the distorted?
Faulkner and Dos Passos seemed to delight in kicking their world to pieces, as if civilization were all a
pretence and everything noble a humbug. For Robinson Jeffers, the human heart was vile and humanity
was "the mould to break away from." Ezra Pound's
Odyssey touched at every known shore and found no
men who had not been turned into swine; and the
heroes of most of the others were gunmen or moral
cripples, human jelly-fish or hobbledehoys. In the
testimony of most of these writers, life was ugly and
men were base, and there was next to nothing to be
done about it; and in fact they had turned literature
into a sort of wailing wall from which nothing rose
but the sound of lamentations and curses. They made
the present contemptible and the future impossible.
Moreover, there were teachers and psychologists who
backed them up. Allston marvelled over two statements of a certain well-known psychologist: 1, Men
have always known that the romantic picture of love
is false: 2, That which portrays the neurotic and defeated in human nature is closer to truth than that
which pictures the aspirations of men. Love is a lie,

in short, and the only realities are defeat and failure. This mood of incredulity, this mood of despair had penetrated millions of minds, and one found it in the most unexpected places. There were people, educated people, who really thought that Plutarch's heroes were humbugs, that Plutarch was pulling the wool over the eyes of his readers when he pretended that heroes had ever existed. For these people, and they were many, all the closets were full of skeletons, and for them even Diogenes was optimistic. What a gullible fellow Diogenes was,—imagine wasting one's time, going about with a lantern, looking for an honest man, as if such a thing were to be conceived of! Allston recalled a talk with a famous professor about O'Neill's *Mourning Becomes Electra*. This man said that O'Neill had given the only true picture of New England, the New England not only of the present but of the past,—that Cambridge and Concord a hundred years ago were just like this household in the play, whited sepulchres, full of dead men's bones. The writers who had presented a different picture were simply hypocrites and liars. So far had this iron of incredulity entered into the modern soul.

Now, Allston observed this with growing doubts of another kind. He knew that modern society had called for exposure, and he knew that the influence of these writers was partly good. If the young were so wary now of hypocrisy and humbug, was it not thanks to this exposure? And was it not good to be exacting, was it not good to demand the real? And had not the optimistic picture of our life that prevailed in the last generation inevitably led to this reaction?

That picture had been too good to be true, and, as
Howells could scarcely bear to look at the ugly
things in life, the ugly things had become an obsession with the novelists who followed. A similar reaction took place in the sphere of language. The ob-
scenity and profanity of many of our writers was as
childish as the prudery of Howells; but Howells was
prudish, and much of his generation was prudish,
and this was bound to lead to what might be called
an inverted prudery. Just so, we had had our "de-
bunking" biographies, in reaction against the writers
who had drawn the veil over the faults of their
heroes. Yes, all this was called for, and much of it
was valuable; but how far could truth be fulfilled in
terms of *reaction?*—and were not most American
writers *reacting against something* far more than they
were *acting in favour of anything?* They were in reaction against restrictions, against conventions,
against business or Puritanism or the towns they were
born in, against civilization or against the middle
class, against codes, courts and sheriffs and the ways
of the tribe, against man, reason, conscience and law,
against hand-me-on ideas, against "feeling," love and
eloquence, against false culture and against real culture, against their romantic predecessors or against
their own romanticism, against America, with Eliot
and Pound, or against the "cheerfulness, optimism
and hopefulness of the nineteenth century," although
cheerfulness and hopefulness represent strength. To
assume a positive attitude, one had to be against some
things; but was not this positive attitude the only
mature one? To be always in reaction was juvenile or
adolescent; and was not the mature view the view of

the whole that lies below and above and beyond reactions? How many writers were living freely in the
world of true values, in which they clearly knew
what they were *for?* Had not the pendulum swung
too far in all this modern "realism"? Had it not
swung beyond the truth? How much of this realism,
indeed, was real? One error that an optimist made
destroyed his whole case, while a pessimist could get
away with murder. Could a critic regard this as right
or truthful?

Such were a few of the questions that Allston asked
himself, and he wondered why other critics did not
discuss them. Regarding this he says:

> Most of our critical writing deals with technical
> questions, and technical novelty, as it seems to me, is
> almost the only virtue it demands or praises. Not
> whether a writer contributes to life, but whether he
> excels in some new trick is the question that is usu-
> ally asked. It is their formal originality that has
> given prestige to writers like Joyce, Eliot and Ezra
> Pound; and perhaps this is natural in an age of tech-
> nics. But how can we ignore the larger questions in-
> volved in this drift of the modern mind? Obviously,
> it represents the "death-drive," as certain psycholo-
> gists call it, the will to die that is said to exist side by
> side in our minds with the will to live. Defeat and
> unhappiness can reach a point where we accept them
> and embrace them and rejoice in our enervation and
> disintegration. And, whether we rejoice in it or not,
> this literature is disintegrating. "All that is ugly,"
> Nietzsche said, "weakens and afflicts man. It reminds
> him of deterioration, of danger and of impotence.
> He actually suffers loss of power by it. The effect of
> ugliness," Nietzsche continues, "can be measured by

the dynamometer. Whenever man is depressed, he has a sense of the proximity of something ugly. His sense of power, his will to power, his courage, his pride,—they decrease with the ugly, they increase with the beautiful." (And I further agree with Nietzsche that literature is not important unless it is a "stimulus to life." *) That is what I mean by suggesting that all these writers represent the death-drive; and if, with their technical virtues, they destroy our faith, our will to make the world worth living in, we cannot let their influence go unchallenged. Is this the kind of literature that Leopardi had in mind when he said it could regenerate a country? Is it not rather the kind that Chekhov spoke of, when he said of the writers of his time, "Lift the robe of our muse and you will find within an empty void"? Chekhov continues, in one of his letters, "Let me remind you that the writers who, we say, are for all time, or are simply good, and who intoxicate us, have one common and very important characteristic. They are going toward something and are summoning you toward it too, and you feel, not with your mind, but with your whole being, that they have some object . . . The best of them are realists and paint life as it is, but, through every line's being soaked in the consciousness of an object, you feel, besides life as it is, the life which ought to be, and that captivates you. And we? We paint life as it is, but beyond that—nothing at all. We have neither immediate nor remote aims, and in our soul there is a great empty space."

This, Allston felt, was the dominant note of our epoch, although, to be sure, we had writers who con-

* Allston had come slowly to this position. In one of his earlier note-books I find this sentence: "I can make my peace with any view of the world that is held by the master of a good style."

veyed quite another impression. Many of these were
clearly affirmers of life. All manner of writers were
living in the world, and if, confining oneself to
America, one thought of talent, and even genius, the
present seemed to him beyond all question one of the
brilliant epochs. In literary capacity, in vigour of
style, in the number of our novelists, poets and critics, we were obviously in the midst of a revival; and
he was only quoting foreign writers, English, Irish,
French, Scandinavian, Russian, when he said that
never before, outside this country, wherever books
were read, had American writers been so influential.
But there were few of these writers who clearly felt
what ought to be and for whom life was noble and
important. In Frost, Sandburg, Lewis Mumford, to
mention three of these, one found a courageous confidence in human nature, an abounding faith in the
will, a sense of the heroic in the human adventure,
good will, the leaven of existence. All fine things
seemed possible as one read these writers; and, as he
thought of them, Allston recalled another remark of
John Butler Yeats. The old man had spoken of a
friend of his in Dublin, a judge who had retired
from the bench. When someone asked this judge
what remained in his mind, what had most deeply
impressed him, during his fifty years in the criminal
courts, his answer was "The goodness of human nature." The grand old Yeats, who also loved his species, quoted this with a smile of agreement, for, although he did not take an easy view of life, he felt
that a seasoned magistrate knew whereof he spoke.
Allston never forgot this, and, the more he thought
it over, the more he agreed with Yeats and this Dub-

lin friend. Was the goodness of human nature a
"myth" or a fact? Regarded as hypotheses, was not
the one as real as the other?—and which, in actuality,
was closer to the real? Like many modern readers,
Allston felt that *War and Peace* was the greatest of
all novels, and a passage in this novel especially impressed him because of the thoughts to which it led.
Let me quote this passage: "On the 12th of June the
forces of Western Europe crossed the frontier, and
the war began, that is, an event took place opposed to
human reason and all human nature. Millions of
men perpetrated against one another so great a mass
of crime,—fraud, swindling, robbery, forgery, issue
of counterfeit money, plunder, incendiarism, murder,—that the annals of all the criminal courts of the
world could not muster such a sum of wickedness in
whole centuries, though the men who committed those
deeds did not at that time look on them as crimes."
Now, here was a true picture that was repeating itself in our time, a sufficiently tragic picture of human affairs; and Allston asked, Well, then, why did
Tolstoy, drawing this picture, say it was "opposed to
human reason and all human nature"? Because its
historical context proved it to be so. The age that
preceded Napoleon was evil enough; so was the age
that followed down to our time. But in neither of
these ages did the "millions of men" perpetrate this
mass of crime. They recognized that crimes are
crimes, they recognized the criminal courts, and, in
fact, these millions were relatively decent and peace-
ful. If they had not been so, if the good had not outweighed the evil, how could society have outlived
such a cataclysm? And, if society outlived it, does

this not prove how large is the fund of human goodness? And society has outlived all cataclysms. Human nature buoyantly rectifies itself, and that is why
Tolstoy said of such events that they are "opposed to
human nature." If men were not preponderantly good
they could not survive. But how can one see this
unless one sees the historical contexts of these cata-
clysmic moments, unless one has a historical conception and *idea?* Unless one has an *idea* of human nature, one cannot see the facts in their true relation;
and Allston applied this to the writers he spoke of.
Life was ugly and men were base, but his own friends
were not base nor were their lives ugly; and how
much did he really know about other people? And
what would become of life if one saw it only as contemptible? What would become of the world if one
saw its future as impossible? The *idea* of the world
was more deserving. The idea of the future was not
impossible, and even the idea of the present merited
respect. Human nature, as an idea, if not in actuality,
—and Allston admired this also,—was certainly
noble; and it was, at least, the best we had. Well, then,
were not ideas to be cultivated? Allston's mind had
gradually come full circle. He remained a realist, for
he liked to keep his feet on the ground, but he realized
that he was an idealist also. He had always been a
latent idealist, but his mind had largely remained in
abeyance while all these writers were kicking their
world to pieces. But now, as he saw that his own mind
had clarified, he felt that the time had come to assert
his idealism. The world was another Humpty-
Dumpty, and no one denied it had had a great fall.
But was it not imperative to put the world together

again, since human beings had to go on living? The
realists who were nothing but realists denied that this
was possible; but such a denial as this was impossible also. The world *had* to be put together, and the
only way to do it was to see it again,—and see life,—
in the light of ideas.

So Allston returned to these negative writers in the
light of the positive writers who stood for health,
will, courage. In the minds of the positive writers
the idea was always dominant, they instinctively saw
the context of historial events, and they believed in
man, in the destiny of humankind, because through
this faith alone the race had endured. Allston was
convinced that literature must contain this germ of
faith, if it was to carry out its function, and that the
greatest literature had always done so. This mood
was the warp of literature, as the rest was the woof
(not that one did not need this woof,—how else could
one have any fabric?) ; and Allston felt that writers
were certain to return to it, as water always rises to
the level of its source. But this was not the mood of
the last two decades, and it seemed as if these writers
had lost the day; for even those who cared for justice wrote as men without hope. They reverted to in-
fantilism and primitivism, and they could not contain their contempt for society and man. Allston
brooded over this. He had known many writers, and
they were almost invariably scrupulous men, lovers of
their kind, compassionate, intuitive and full of good
will for other people. They were, of all men, those
who naturally loved life most; and obviously, as a
class, they were disappointed. Was this not because
they lacked the sense of the idea, which enables one

to see facts in their true relation? All they could see
was the present débâcle of man, the impotence of human beings confronted with the powers of evil that
bragged and bullied their way towards the rule of
the world.

Now, the writers in question, possessing their feelings, could only have written as they had. Allston did
not quarrel with them for this; he did not quarrel
with them for being sincere. But was it not *immature,*
he said, to throw up the sponge of life as they did?
Was it not immature to "break away" from the mould
of life and seek for death, or the primitive, or a
nihilist Nirvana? Was it not immature to whine, with
Eliot and Pound, about the "pure" past and the "vulgar" present? Was it not immature to throw oneself
under the car of Juggernaut in sheer desperation of
the world one lived in? Or to say that the world was
a jungle and leave it at that? Who were these writers
to say that life was vile? Were they superior to life or
unequal to it? Allston felt they were immature, and
he felt that writers must break with them and intro-
duce another attitude; and, while things were not to
be judged by their consequences, he was interested
in the consequences of these negative feelings because
of the light they threw on the feelings themselves. And
where had they led our literature and even our life?
Had not these writers poisoned the minds of their
readers?—and how could a world that was sapped
by these negative feelings resist the triumphant advance of the powers of evil? France, sapped by negativism, had gone down before Hitler; and Allston
had eagerly watched the defiance of England. The
English writers of the post-war years had shared the

negativism of American writers, and he said to himself, If these English writers really express the English people, England will go down before Hitler also. But England did not go down,—whatever the outcome might yet be, the English had proved that these writers had never expressed them. The English behaved in the fashion that Tennyson pictured, with Dickens, Wordsworth, Milton and so many others. Milton was still living at this hour, in spite of all the sneers of Eliot and Pound; and, as Allston observed this, a light began to break in his mind. The people had proved to be more mature than the writers. And might this not prove to be true in America also? Had these writers expressed the country, as literature had once expressed it, in *Walden* and Emerson's essays, in *Uncle Tom's Cabin* and *Leaves of Grass?* If they had not expressed it, this was reassuring, while it meant that writers had not been performing their function; and this left the function still to be performed, as it had been performed in earlier epochs. Allston, pursuing this train of thought, asked himself a leading question, which he proceeded to answer in the following note:

Is there any one respect in which the literature of our time,—the literature that dates from the first world-war,—differs from the literature of previous ages, and I would say most, if not all, of these ages? I mean the literature of this period exclusively, for I omit from consideration Frost, Sandburg and various others whose work began before the first world-war. I think it has one trait, and one that is striking, in a perspective now of twenty-five years; and this is that writers have ceased to be *voices of the people.*

In the Victorian age, as in previous ages, writers were voices of the people. Tennyson was a voice of the people in England, Victor Hugo was a voice of the people in France, and we in America had Emerson, Walt Whitman and others. What was true of the poets was true of the novelists also. Tolstoy, Dickens, Manzoni, Björnson were all voices of the people. These writers were all great literary artists as well as popular voices, and it was in this double character that they differed from the writers of our time; for, while it is true that we still have writers who are popular voices, they are seldom literary artists, while our literary artists are seldom popular voices. This is a large generalization, and, like every rule, it admits of exceptions; but is it not self-evident when one says further that our literary art, as such, is "highbrow"? Preponderantly, our literature of the last quarter-century has been the expression of self-conscious intellectuals who do not even wish to be voices of the people. Some of these writers have laboured *for* the people; they have fought valiant fights for social justice. But their perceptions have not been *of* the people. They have ill-expressed the hearts of people. Some, again, have passed through this "highbrow" phase and wish, without surrendering their literary standards, to make themselves voices of the people. The tide in American literature is already turning, and one seems to foresee in the future a high literary art that will be an expression of the people. But, regarding the quarter-century of which I am speaking, it is certainly true that this time has produced few writers who were both literary artists and voices of the people.

This is a way of saying that the literary mind of our time is sick. It has lost its roots in the soil of

mankind, although it possesses a certain energy. I
think it has great energy, which makes the phenome-
non all the more glaring. In other words, our literature is *off-centre;* for when great literary artists are
not voices of the people, as all the greatest *writers*
have been, are we not driven to feel that they are
off-centre?—which leads one to the further question,
What centre are they off? In other words, What is
centrality? Do not the people possess centrality, and
is this not the reason why we feel that writers should
be voices of the people? These writers say that the
people *did* possess it in the days *when* the writers expressed the people: they possessed certain postulates
which they held in common, postulates regarding the
aim and the meaning of life. But these writers say
that the people no longer possess it, no longer possess
these postulates held in common,—which gives them
their excuse for ignoring the people. So they actually
rejoice in being off-centre. But have not these writers
misprized the people? Are not the people central all
the time? Evidently, England is sounder than its writers, and I feel sure that America is sounder also.

So far Allston pondered this question, wondering
what the upshot was. He had been one of the "intellectuals" ever since he began to write, he had been
at odds with the "people;" but it seemed to him now
that the intellectuals had got themselves out on a
branch, as he put it, and that somehow or other they
had to get back to the trunk. They had cut themselves
off from mankind and formed a circle of their own
that was wholly out of relation to the springs of life.
They had broken their organic bonds with family
life, the community, nature, and they wrote in a
private language of personal friends; they felt noth-

ing but contempt for the primary realities, which they had ceased to feel and completely ignored, and human wisdom played no part in the system of aesthetics that characterized their artificial world. They lived with their fixed ideas in a vacuum; they were the victims of inbreeding, poisoning one another with their despair, and poisoning society also; * and they had come to represent the suicide of the human spirit of which Europe was the monstrous illustration. Were they not really unequal to life instead of being superior to it, as they proclaimed on all occasions? And was this not the reason why they had withdrawn from life into a self-protecting coterie? Well, could literature of their kind "regenerate" a country? Allston remembered how Dostoievsky had rebuked the Russian intellectuals,—he had told the intelligentsia

* How far writers and intellectuals influence the mind of a country is a purely practical question, Allston said. It is a point of common sense, outside the purview of criticism, and one that any shrewd observer can settle. Thus Allston quoted the Viennese journalist, William S. Schlamm, in his book, *This Second War of Independence:* "Within every society, be it ever so democratic, there is a relatively small group of intellectuals who give that society its tone and character. What one thousand professors, writers, bishops think, write, preach, is handed on by three hundred thousand teachers, journalists and ministers to the 130,000,000 Americans, and forms the consciousness of the entire nation. The process is as inconspicuous as it is overpowering. Just cut these thousand key intellectuals out of the national body politic and the nation will, within a few years, have a completely changed complexion. The circulation of an author's book is unimportant (not for him, of course, or for his publisher), for its effectiveness depends not on the number but on the social importance of its readers; a book which has made an impression on 3000 teachers and 2000 journalists alters the essence of our national being more appreciatively and enduringly than a novel which is read by two million housewives. Ninety-nine and nine-tenths per cent of the American people have never held a work by John Dewey in their hands, but all Americans have, in some degree, been educated by him, simply because the thoughts of this great pedagogue have activized the transmission belts of our educational apparatus . . . Though its mass may be relatively insignificant, the catalytic agent will basically alter the larger chemical process."

Allston said that Balzac made this point in nine words,—"the hundred persons who tell France what to think."

to *humble themselves;* and he felt that the time had come for him to break with the intellectuals, to scramble off the branch and return to the trunk. Writers had lost a sense of the distinction between primary literature and coterie-literature,—was it not time to make this distinction clear? And. since one had to find it, what was the trunk?

CHAPTER XVIII

WHAT IS PRIMARY LITERATURE?

"WHAT is primary literature?" Allston asks. "When I speak of the branch, what do I mean by the trunk?" He never attempted, so far as I know, to wrestle with this question, though I doubt if the question was ever long out of his mind. In earlier chapters I have quoted a few of his remarks that seem to be suggestions of a definition; and perhaps by reassembling these and adding other observations I may find the centre of his thought. Primary literature somehow follows the biological grain, he says; it favours what psychologists call the "life-drive;" it is a force of regeneration that in some way conduces to race-survival, on what might be further called the best possible terms. I think this is the heart of Allston's notion. The great themes, he adds, are those by virtue of which the race has risen, courage, justice, mercy, honour, love.

Now, certainly these are large assertions, though if Allston had been systematic he might have made some effort to vindicate them. There are various classical treatises upon which he might have drawn; but Allston was not skillful in expository writing. He was impatient, as I have said, his mind leaped from point to point, he could not develop an argument or a train of thought. He could only enforce his intuitions by summoning other intuitions; but is not feeling, after all, the way of truth in literature? Allston's ideas were harmonious with some of the great definitions of literature. There were two such definitions that especially pleased him, one by Walter Pater, which I have already quoted, the other, more prophetic, by Maxim Gorky. Allston liked to contemplate extremes and try to fill, imaginatively, the space between them; and he could think of no two modern authors who appeared to have less in common than Pater and Gorky. Yet regarding the nature of primary literature both had spoken to the same point, or in terms that were easily reconciled in the space between them; and Allston neither felt nor wished to feel that he was adding anything to their testimony. He could only hope to corroborate these noble expressions. Thus Pater observed, in *Appreciations,* "It is on the quality of the matter it informs or controls, its compass, its variety, its alliance to great ends, or the depth of the note of revolt, or the largeness of hope in it, that the greatness of literary art depends, as *The Divine Comedy, Paradise Lost, Les Misérables,* the English Bible are great art." From this Allston passed to Gorky, in one of his manifestoes, "Literature, the living and imaged history of the exploits and errors, of the excellencies and failures of our forbears, possessing the mighty power of influencing the organization of thought, of refining the crudity of the instincts, educating the will, must finally fulfill her planetary role,—the role of the power which most firmly and most intimately unites the peoples by the sense of their sufferings and long-

ings, by the sense of the community of their desire
for the happiness of a life that is beautiful and free."
Allston felt that somewhere in the space between
these definitions there was room for all his own remarks,—that great literature favours the "life-drive,"
that it is somehow regenerative, that it expresses the
states of mind by which the race has risen. What else
did Pater mean when he spoke of its "compass,"
when he spoke of its "alliance to great ends, or the
depth of the note of revolt, or the largeness of hope
in it"? And what else did Gorky mean by its "planetary role"? Well, then, if this was true, what were
great writers? Tolstoy called them the "high priests
and leaders of evolution, the real sovereigns who
rule, not by force of guns and armies, but by moral
authority." Was Tolstoy mistaken, or was he right?

Tolstoy was only repeating what great writers had
always said, and myriads of human beings had accepted their words; and a point in the life of our
epoch that interested Allston was that writers had
wholly ceased to speak so. They never spoke of the
power of poets to create new worlds and destroy the
old, as the proud poets of other years had spoken. It
almost seemed as if the idea of greatness had vanished
over-night in the human mind,—what writer save
Thomas Mann was occupied with it? The Goethe-
intoxicated Mann was all but unique in maintaining
this principal note of the great tradition. American
writers had altogether lost it. For instance, there was
Pearsall Smith's *Milton and His Modern Critics.*
This writer set out to defend Milton against a group
of modern critics who are always "looking for fleas in
the lion's mane," to quote a phrase of Elie Faure; but

he uttered only a line to suggest the real case for this
greatest of poets and passed it over at once for his
"verbal music." He spoke of "the shining truth that
any supreme work of art is always, or almost always,
the product of a great imagination, the echo of a
lofty mind, of a personality or soul possessing some
kind of greatness." One might have supposed that,
in a defence of Milton, here was the place to pause
and ponder. But no, this incorrigible amateur was
only concerned with the "wonder-working" sounds
of the noble poet. He even suggested that style alone
survives, that "every burning question burns itself
out" and "we come to read the most earnest prophets
for their style." Allston would have said, no doubt,
that he could think of a few questions which had not
burned themselves out in five thousand years; and I
wonder what he would have said of one of Pearsall
Smith's quotations from a living English critic, F. L.
Lucas: "Such is the common lot of preachers and
moralists. It has happened to Ecclesiastes and Isaiah
and Plato . . . It is simply that men's feelings about
beauty are more vital than their theories about good."
What, Allston might have asked, has happened to
Ecclesiastes? What sorry fate has befallen Isaiah and
Plato? They have failed to impress Mr. Lucas, they
are only words to Mr. Smith, but various humbler
souls here and there have been known to find something in Isaiah; and Allston would not have accepted
the notion that men's "feelings" about beauty are
more vital than their "theories" about good. (Just
what were Isaiah's "theories"? he might also have
asked.) Allston was the last man to belittle the virtues
of style and manner, and he felt that a great style

was the visible garment of an inward matter and substance that were equally great. He agreed with Matthew Arnold that the "two superiorities" are "in steadfast proportion one to the other;" but he had his own opinion of those who could see only one of these "accents," for whom only the manner existed and not the substance, not the "great imagination," not the "lofty mind," not the "soul possessing some kind of greatness." And were not Messrs. Lucas and Smith types of the moment? The humble souls who found something in Isaiah besides a little verbal beauty were not expressed in modern criticism; yet even in the mind of Pater, the lover of beauty, the beautiful was second to the good. With what were Pater's "great ends" allied? The "depth of the note of revolt" and the "largeness of hope." And what was the "planetary role" that Gorky spoke of? Could "wonder-working" sounds comprise this role? *What was the nature of great literature few discussed at the moment,** although T. S. Eliot, who seldom or never discussed it, admitted that it was something more than "art." In *Essays Ancient and Modern,* he said, "The 'greatness' of literature cannot be determined solely by literary standards;" and he remarked again, in a note in his study of Dante, "Both in creation and enjoyment much always enters which is, from the point of view of 'art,' irrelevant." Could its aim then be merely to "amuse," as Mr. Eliot said in his book on Dryden, even if this amusement was entirely "proper"? Eliot had spoken of his own work

---

* Ezra Pound, in *How to Read,* offers the following definition: "Great literature is simply language charged with meaning to the utmost possible degree." Obviously, great literature is nothing of the kind. It is language charged with *great* meaning, which is quite another matter.

as a "superior amusement," however he might later have regretted the phrase, and he said that Dryden's age was peculiarly happy because people had not enquired what poetry was *for*. But this was what men *had* enquired in times that were greater than Dryden's; and they replied in the manner of Tolstoy and Milton. They sometimes spoke of hungry sheep, they often spoke of the bread of life, and they asked the poets and the prophets to give it to them.

That a great writer is a great man writing, not a mere artificer or master of words,—was not this the fact that our time had forgotten? * And what, by the common report of humanity, is a great man writing? One who embodies something great, something that enriches life, something that enhances life, something that makes it higher or wider or deeper. A great man writing is one who bespeaks the collective life of the people, of his group, of his nation, of all mankind. The greatest are those who speak for all mankind; and every great man writing knows what men and women are and what they have it in them to become, —through him humanity breathes and thinks and sings. He shares the traits of others in larger measure. That men should have life and have it more abundantly, this is the general aim of great men writing, of Erasmus, Dickens, Rabelais, Dostoievsky, of Goethe, Ibsen, Whitman, whomsoever one chooses.

* "One of the great defects of our critical vocabulary," Mr. Pearsall Smith remarks, "is the lack of a neutral, non-derogatory name for these great artificers, these artists who derive their inspiration more from the formal than the emotional aspects of their art, and who are more interested in the masterly control of their material than in the expression of their own feelings, or the prophetic aspects of their calling."

Well, if this name does not exist, it is because "artificer" is an adequate name; and if, as Mr. Smith says, the name is derogatory, it is because of a general feeling that the fact merits this connotation.

They differ in their emphases, they differ in their
outlooks, but in one way or another they vindicate
the statements of Gorky and Pater, as Tolstoy vindicated them in *What is Art?* Allston was aware of the
limitations of Tolstoy's taste, of the false simplifications to which he was prone and which led him to
condemn his own novels; but, in the matter of literature, how could one question the underlying truth of
Tolstoy's thesis? As the Greeks considered art good
only when it served goodness, so Tolstoy said that
the purpose of literature was to advance the life of
humanity. That literature was a transmission of feeling which the writer had experienced, that it united
humanity by transmitting this feeling, that it was a
means of union, joining men together for the "progress towards well-being" of mankind, such was Tolstoy's view,—and who could deny it? It transmitted
the highest and best feelings to which men have risen,
and it rendered accessible to men of later times all
that had been experienced by their best and foremost
predecessors. Such, from Tolstoy's point of view, was
the nature of universal literature, and who could question it or doubt it? Was not this self-evident? So it
seemed to Allston, and he would not have dwelt upon
the point if it had not vanished from modern criticism. For the emphasis of modern criticism was
wholly on "form," which caused it to ignore many
great writers. Now, form is a word that aestheticians
like to play with. Its primary meaning is quite clear,
but modern critics do not like clearness, and they
have developed, Allston said, an obscure metaphysical jargon that covers their own pretentious vague-
ness. One has only to utter the word "form," in the

literary circles of the moment, for good sense to retire from the field in confusion. In a metaphysical
sense, no doubt, the soul has form, which is reflected
in one's writing; but this is by no means identical
with aesthetic form, which many great writers have
almost wholly lacked. There have been great writers
who were scarcely "artists" at all, who have been
"mere fluid puddings," in the matter of composition,
—this was Henry James's phrase for Tolstoy. Was
not Victor Hugo such? Were not Rabelais and Whitman? It was not the shape but the yeast that made
them great. It was the "great imagination," it was the
"lofty mind," it was the "soul possessing some sort of
greatness." It was the "depth of the note of revolt,"
it was the "largeness of hope" in them that gave them
their "planetary role,"—how else in a world so
crowded could they have survived? For they have
not survived by virtue of the critics, but because they
have expressed what humanity needed for its own
survival on the best possible terms. Why have certain
authors weathered every change of fashion, considering what a gauntlet they have had to run, what tests
they have had to meet in order to survive? They have
survived because they have spoken to the constant
mind of man; for, if this mind had not been constant,
how could it have remained so faithful to them?

To think of literature as merely literary, as something that was derived from literature, struck Allston
as utterly frivolous. He certainly enjoyed, no one more
so, the play of the critical mind; but not to see vital
necessity as the governing law of literature seemed
to him the utmost of critical blindness. Writers, to be
sure, drew strength from writers, but they drew most

of their strength from something else, a consciousness
of human needs and longings; and their ultimate
value was to be determined by the measure in which
they responded to these longings and needs. One did
not always have to say this. In times when it was understood, one might affirm the fact by implication;
but the great critics had affirmed it, either by statement or implication,—human values underlay their
literary values. But was this the time merely to imply
it, when one saw literary values floating in a void?
Had not the time come to restate it? Mr. Eliot,
in his way, recognized that this time had come; but
his "well turned compliments to religion," as Mr.
E. M. Forster called them, struck Allston as inade-
quate and meagre. At best, he had seen these values
in sectarian terms and not at all in terms that were
broadly human; for how many of the great writers
would have survived if they had had to fit his bed of
Procrustes? Mr. Eliot's judgment of writers according to their "orthodoxy" was a matter of straining at
gnats and swallowing camels; and this, in fact, was
the nature of his critical procedure. He had denied
the primary in the interest of the secondary: was it
not by this means that he had effected a "transvalua-
tion of English literature," to quote the phrase of one
who admitted this claim? Milton, he said, was "un-
satisfactory," *Hamlet* was an "artistic failure,"
Goethe, in philosophy and poetry, merely "dabbled,"
and "made no great success of either," Emerson was
no "real observer of the moral life," Emerson's
essays were an "encumbrance," Byron was "uninter-
esting," Shelley and Keats were overrated, the genius
of Dickens was "decadent," and so on and so on.

Meanwhile, Dryden, the "great master of contempt,"
was virtually more important than any of these.*
Dryden, in any case, with his "art of making the
small great," was one whom Eliot admired beyond
these others,—by virtue of affinity, perhaps; and
Eliot made even Dryden smaller than he was, as one
saw by comparing Lowell's magnanimous essay on
Dryden with his treatment of this poet. While, at this
Eliotizing of history, all the mazed world stood by
hushed, Ezra Pound too rearranged the classics. He
admitted Confucius and Homer and two or three
dozen other authors (who did not include Thucy-
dides, the "journalist") ; and, "without the slightest
compunction," he "chucked out" Pindar. There was
room in Mr. Pound's list for Rimbaud † and Corbière, but he had not troubled to chuck out the
others : he found them unworthy even of a gesture of
contempt. Allston said these statements were "interesting but tough," as Huck Finn remarked of *Pil-
grim's Progress;* and equally interesting were the
statements of Mr. Ivor Winters, who had taken heart
from the boldness of Eliot and Pound. Mr. Ivor
Winters had run through American literature, in
which he had unearthed surprising facts, as that
Emerson was a "fraud at the core," Melville's *Omoo*

---

* Eliot fails to quote one of Dryden's phrases that might be applied
to himself: "They who would combat general authority with particular
opinion must first establish themselves a reputation of understanding
better than other men." Except in the little school that follows him,
general authority, in every case, has overriden these particular opinions.

† I find in one of Allston's journals the following comment on Arthur
Rimbaud, which strikes me as intemperate, to say the least:

"This little neurasthenic wretch 'destroyed' justice, history, republics
and peoples. *A bas! Assez! Périssez! Passez!* Was not that cute for
seventeen?

"I say *assez* Rimbaud. Like John Randolph's dead mackerel in the
moonlight, he shines and he stinks."

and *Typee* were trifles, Poe was a "bad writer, exceptionally bad," and *The House of the Seven Gables,* like *Hamlet,* was a "failure." Now, if ever acts of genius were performed in America, they were these writings, precisely; and Allston could only say, reading Mr. Winters, "His bread is my cake, and vice versa." But could one "transvalue" literature in this fashion? Beyond the exhibition of one's own folly, could one accomplish anything by such a procedure? "For the law of the gods," Allston said, "they have set up their own traditions;" or, if not the law of the gods, the traditions of men. No doubt, it was wholesome to challenge tradition, and perhaps by over-emphasizing aesthetic standards these critics had served a useful purpose.* But was their "hard bright precision" worth so much?—and were they not floating in a void? Luckily for them, these critics reached only a handful of readers, among whom they could say what they chose,—they ran small risk of exposure to the light of truth; yet how strange, in

* But what were even their aesthetic standards? What, at least, were Ezra Pound's? Allston was amused by one of Mr. Pound's characteristic statements in *The ABC of Reading:* "I took my critical life in my hand, some years ago, when I suggested that Catullus was in some ways a better writer than Sappho, not in melopœia, but for economy of words. I don't in the least know whether this is true. One should start with an open mind." And evidently so end also, Allston said; for, aside from the insolubility of the question involved,—and was this not insoluble and therefore fruitless?—the portentous tone of the statement was only equalled by the utter lack of conviction with which it was made.

Allston remembered how, as a child, he had pondered over a statement in Ruskin's *Mornings in Florence.* It concerned a sculptured pillow on a tomb in Santa Croce. Ruskin insisted that the tassels of this pillow were incomparably finer than the tassels of a similar pillow on a neighbouring tomb. Allston, who took Ruskin hard, spent an hour comparing these tassels, and with all the good will in the world he could see no slightest difference between them. Would he have seen this difference thirty years later? He had often asked himself this question, but he remembered that Ruskin, more than once, strained at imaginary gnats. However, this was an unusual procedure with Ruskin, while it was the rule with Ezra Pound.

another decade, it was sure to seem that a few little
men in any circle could have got away with all these
murders. Were they not, in regard to all these
writers, in the position of Henry James, who said
that Tolstoy and Dostoievsky did "not *do* to read any
longer"? They did not do to read because they lacked
James's neatness in the sphere of aesthetics; and yet,
in James's own phrase, the "quantity of presenting
their genius launches them in" precisely rendered
this neatness impossible to them.* Well, if one had
to make a choice, which should one prefer, the neatness or the quantity of genius? Humanity chose to
accept the genius, with as much form as it could get,
and, if need were, to sacrifice the form in favour of
the genius. It was something quite beyond aesthetics
that caused one to read Dostoievsky and Tolstoy and
all these other great writers whom the critics
"chucked out;" and these critics had given a sorry
account of themselves by ignoring what humanity
needed and intended to have.

So rose in Allston's mind the question of tradition,
which Mr. Eliot especially took under his wing. In
one of his essays, Mr. Eliot had given a good account
of tradition. "The historical sense," he said, "com-
pels a man to write not merely with his own genera-

---

* In expounding his doctrine that "the novel" is to be judged by its
"oneness," James admitted that Tolstoy and Balzac could never have
followed his method: "The promiscuous shiftings of standpoint and centre
of Tolstoy and Balzac for instance . . . are the inevitable result of the
quantity of presenting their genius launches them in . . . With the com-
plexity they pile up they *can* get no clearness without trying again and
again for new centres."—Letter to Mrs. Humphry Ward, 1899.
Allston wondered why this passage, so obviously true, had not at-
tracted more attention. Did it not invalidate the *general* authority of
James's writings on the art of fiction? It showed why James's theories
are good for Jamesian novels only, or novels of a similar tenuity and
paucity of subject-matter.

tion in his bones, but with a feeling that the whole
of the literature of Europe from Homer and within
it the whole of the literature of his own country has
a simultaneous existence and composes a simultaneous
order." With this historical sense, precisely, Allston
wrote himself, and he admired Eliot's definition: the
literature of his own country, the literature of Europe, the literature of all mankind, he said, composed
for him a "simultaneous order,"—with the life of
mankind, of Europe, of his country behind it. In
theory, therefore, he agreed with Eliot, although
Eliot seldom spoke of the life of mankind; and he
sometimes wondered what Eliot's "own country"
was,—it certainly was not America, and was it England? Was not Eliot's vague tradition a Latin tradition? However this might be, and however they
agreed in theory, in practice Allston and Eliot were
worlds apart. Defining his traditionalism, Eliot
quoted a phrase of Remy de Gourmont: "To erect
into laws one's personal impressions, this is the great
effort of a man if he is sincere." This was the rule that
Eliot followed in practice. He had erected into laws
his personal impressions; he had made up a tradition to suit himself,—and was not tradition really
necessitated? For what had one's personal impressions to do with tradition?—and what was a man who
erected his impressions into laws? Was not such a
man more truly a destroyer of tradition? Tradition
is the sum of all that humankind has kept alive for its
own advancement and perfection; it is that which
unites mankind in its common struggle and gives it
stability and direction. But Eliot had no wish to unite
mankind except on his own peculiar sectarian terms;

and he had gone far to repudiate the common tradition in favour of his personal impressions and his personal choices. He had plucked out the plums that pleased himself, implying that the rest of the pudding was not worth eating; and was the pudding his to pluck from? Was it not rather, in truth, humanity's pudding?—and was he not like any other Little Jack Horner? Like Henry James, for instance, who thought the plum of *The Awkward Age* was better than *War and Peace* and *The Brothers Karamazov?* Little Jack Horners always prefer the particular plums that please themselves, and they regard these plums as the big plums; they even insist that their plums are big, for, if these turned out to be little, what light might this not throw on their own dimensions? Meantime, they forget that they are in a corner, while the centre of the room is occupied by someone else. But the someone in the centre sits in the place of humanity, and he has the final word. Eliot's tradition, Allston said, was no real tradition. It was a phantasmal tradition merely, and this phantasmal tradition was a dog in the manger. It would not eat the corn and it blocked the doorway, so that no other creature could get at it and eat it.

Now, Allston had taken tradition for granted ever since he was a boy. He had never thought of explaining or defending it, for the sense of the past was instinctive in him as well as the sense of the future. But his gorge had slowly risen as he saw this false traditionalism assuming such authority in the world of letters, and at last he felt constrained to say with Campanella:

Do thou, with heart fervent and proudly mild,
Make war upon these fraud-engendering schools.

Tradition results from vital necessity, he repeated
more than once. One cannot make up a tradition, as
Eliot does, by leaving out the beef and potatoes that
constitute the meal in favour of the sweets and con-
diments that please one's palate; and to take this tradition for "orthodoxy" is to block the door indeed.
There was James Joyce, the sick Irish Jesuit, whom
Eliot described as orthodox,* and who had done more
than Eliot to destroy tradition. Had he not, in
Ulysses, in his *Oxen of the Sun,* run through the
whole of English literature, depreciating with his
parodies its greatest authors, deforming every one of
them, Gibbon, Burke, Goldsmith, Lamb, De Quincey, Dickens, Ruskin, Newman, Bunyan, Burns and
a dozen others? What fools he made them seem, as
he filled his travesties of their styles with trivial and
salacious implications!—and all for the glorification
of James Joyce. For what a big boy he must be to
have put all these authors in their places! The past
in all of Joyce's work went out in a bad smell, while
Joyce settled down complacently in his "snot-green"
world; and yet Joyce was represented as defending
tradition! Out upon this nonsense, Allston said. He
admitted that all this de-romanticizing had a minor
function, which one might compare to the insulin

---

*A sample of what Eliot calls Joyce's orthodoxy: "Greater love than
this no man hath that a man lay down his wife for his friend. Go thou
and do likewise." As Eliot says, "The spirit killeth, but the letter giveth
life." So also in *Finnegans Wake* occurs the phrase "Lead kindly foul!"
This is intended to leave a drop of acid on everyone's associations with
Newman's hymn. And what in the hymn deserves this retribution?

treatment for schizophrenia. Its object was to rub down the mental grooves formed by conventional habits, restoring the mind to the primitive for a fresh start. But suppose the patient did not react? Suppose the treatment did not succeed? And was not humanity rather an important patient? Besides, in literature one had to remember the standard of health, and Joyce was not at all concerned with this. His falsification of tradition had well-nigh wiped tradition out in minds that were already divorced from tradition: and it seemed to Allston that to reaffirm the true tradition was an indispensable task of the contemporary critic.

Thus Allston returned to Eliot's definition, which Eliot failed to sustain: the literature of his own country, the literature of Europe, the literature of all mankind, he said, composed for him a simultaneous order,—with the life of mankind, of Europe, of his country behind it. He began at home, with his own country, as the door through which to approach the rest; and he said it was time to restore the American classics, retaining the critical spirit, subjecting them to the proper tests, but accepting them, where one could, with one's whole heart.* For what was more important than a sense of one's group-history, if only as a means of entering other groups? What could be more tonic, if only as a means of understanding the

* Allston liked to repeat a remark of Sainte-Beuve, uttered in conversation with Matthew Arnold. When Arnold said that Lamartine was not an important writer, Sainte-Beuve replied, "But he is important *for us.*" Allston applied this to certain standard American writers. Aside from the few American classics who were important for everybody, there were half a dozen, not otherwise important, who were important *for us.* Among these he might have included Whittier, as the folk-poet of *Snow-Bound* and also by virtue of his passion for freedom.

life of the rest of mankind? It seemed to Allston
highly important that we should possess an American
memory, and this had driven him into historical
writing. What could contribute more to the stiffening
of American writers, promoting their maturity and
health, giving them the sense of a group to which
they are responsible, affording them stability and
purpose? Yes, the sense of the past behind them is
the tap-root of American writers, the sense of the
achievements of their group; and, behind this, they
must have a sense of the life and achievements of all
mankind, a sense of the collective effort of the human
race. What else could so contribute to knit them together, to give them a line of direction for the future
of the race? Such was tradition, Allston repeated,
the great sustainer of primary literature, the sum of
the literary wisdom which the race has kept, the em-
bodiment of those traits which humanity needs for
its survival and perfection.

CHAPTER XIX

COTERIE-LITERATURE

SO MUCH for Allston's view of tradition, which, conceived in these terms, implies that human-kind is marching forward. It implies what Tolstoy called a "progress towards well-being," a struggle on the part of humanity for advancement and perfection. I have explained in a previous chapter why Allston believed in this advance, which justified his latent optimism; and this was precisely what Eliot and Joyce denied. They were so far in reaction against the idea of human progress, or the somewhat mechanical "progress" of the last age, that they denied all progress whatsoever. Joyce, by implication, had shown the movement of English literature, the record of the moving English mind, as rather advancing backward than advancing forward; and Eliot not only spoke of the "myth of human goodness," but he disparaged "revolution." The beliefs of Shelley excited his "abhorrence," he decried the American Revolution and the French Revolution, and he spoke of humanitarianism as "improving nothing." ("Has it really improved nothing?" Allston said. "The future lives on its hopes.") And in this both Joyce and Eliot spoke for the mood of the post-world-war years; they expressed a very large segment of the modern mind. From this mind had vanished, along with the

notion of greatness, the idea of the "march of humanity," which Tolstoy took for granted; and no sooner
had Spengler ceased to be fashionable than people
began to talk about Vico, with his fatalistic theory of
the "law of cycles." (Brooks Adams's "law of civilization and decay" was a much-discussed American ver-
sion of this law of Vico.) Many held the view that
man had steadily deteriorated since the Middle Ages;
others agreed with Nietzsche's idea of "eternal recur-
rence." Whether they saw history as simply a movement down-hill, or whether they saw man as a squirrel
in a cage, solemnly going round in circles, they had
lost all faith in human progress.

Now, primary literature, Allston said, presupposed
this faith in progress, which was the inevitable off-
shoot of a prior faith, the faith in human nature and
human goodness; and he said that even in those who
denied the reality of progress there was still something that believed in progress. Did not these writers
think of themselves as a "vanguard"?—and what did
this conception of a vanguard imply? Joyce referred
to Ireland as "the most belated nation in Europe."
Belated, Allston asked, in relation to what? Others,
again, who denied evolution, spoke of the "evolution
of the novel," which had reached its grand climax
in *Finnegans Wake;* and, as Allston put it, evolution
for evolution, which of these two was the more incred-
ible? Did there exist such a thing as "the" novel to
evolve? Was there one peculiar form that constituted
the ideal novel, the laws of which had gradually
revealed themselves, so that the perfect novel could
at last be written? Or were there not rather countless types of possible novels, as numerous and as vari-

ous as the minds that write them? * So even those who denied progress believed in some kind of progress, which might be far less plausible than the other kind; † and most of them saw themselves as the acme of progress, as heirs of all the ages and summits of time. Thus Ezra Pound had no doubt that he was an advance on Pindar, and Eliot was quite sure that in moral perception he had left the encumbering Emerson far behind. They never expressed these beliefs, but they certainly implied them. They implied a general denial of progress; and why did they deny this, aside from the fact that they did not see it? Because to have admitted it would have been to see that they are not primary themselves. If there was no progress, there was nothing to prevent them from taking their personal bent for the primary thing. They cut away the standard by which they could be measured as the minor poets and novelists they assuredly are.

These writers, then, were secondary, as Allston was obliged to say, however they might have dominated the modern horizon; and he described their work as coterie-literature, to distinguish it from primary literature. He greatly admired Edmund Wilson's account of these writers in *Axel's Castle,—*

* On this subject D. H. Lawrence uttered the last word in one of his letters: "Tell Arnold Bennett that all rules of construction hold good only for novels which are copies of other novels. A book which is not a copy of other books has its own construction, and what he calls faults, he being an old imitator, I call characteristics."

† So also John Crowe Ransom, who is not noticeably concerned with progress, believes in the progress of criticism. Thus he says of R. P. Blackmur: "Intelligent readers when they make acquaintance with him will know that they read what could not possibly have been written earlier than a few years ago . . . Critical writing like this is done in our time. In depth and precision at once it is beyond all earlier criticism in our language. It is a new criticism."

Proust, Paul Valéry and Gertrude Stein, along with
Eliot and Joyce; and he said that Edmund Wilson,
who partially agreed with him, had given him plenty
of ammunition with which to defend his point of
view. These writers defined themselves as coterie-
writers, and they represented the "death-drive" more
than the "life-drive;" and their influence, he said,
had to be cleared out of the way in order that primary
literature might be reinstated. For had not this influence affected the whole of modern literature, led
the dance in poetry, magnetized the novelists and
overborne the world of criticism? And were these
writers really a vanguard, or were they not rather
retrograde? Did they not represent a "cultural lag"?
Were they not a "dead hand," the dead hand of the
fin de siècle, which had prolonged its grasp for forty
years? Was not James Joyce, for one, the ash of a
burnt-out cigar, were they not all of them ashes of the
eighteen-nineties, aside from the one matter of tech-
nique? And had they really possessed the "sense of
their age," to which they were always laying claim?
Or were they merely bats, as Allston said, that had
flown in the twilight between the wars? This question
of the "sense of one's age" interested Allston deeply,
for he agreed that all great writers possessed it; but
just what was the "sense of one's age"?—who was to
define it?—had these writers offered a convincing
definition? Here again Allston turned to Tolstoy,
for, having rediscovered him at fifty, he could not
contain his joy in this great man. "In every period
of history," Tolstoy said, "and in every human society, there exists an understanding of the meaning
of life which represents the highest level to which

men of that society have attained,—an understanding
defining the highest good at which that society aims."
Tolstoy called this the religious perception of the
time, and in our time, he said, this consists in ac-
knowledging that the aim of life is the union of mankind. Moreover, he said, true literature transmits
sound feeling, and sound feeling can only exist in a
man who is living on all his sides the life that is
natural to mankind. Such, according to Tolstoy, is
the "sense of one's age," and who, by this definition,
may be said to possess it? Those who live most fully
the primary life of their age. The great Romantic
poets lived this. They were humanitarians and liber-
ators because humanitarianism and freedom were the
prime notes of their age, and the poets fully shared
these sentiments. The great nineteenth-century critics
lived this. Ruskin, Renan, Taine, Sainte-Beuve and
Arnold were concerned with human destiny and the
purpose of life because these concerns were the prime
notes of their age, and they lived on all sides the life
that is natural to mankind. How was it, on the other
hand, with these coterie-writers? Eliot said that
Baudelaire, and not the more characteristic Romantics,—not Victor Hugo, for example,—possessed in
his time the sense of the age, because he was *not* concerned with humanitarianism and freedom, because
he did *not* find progress interesting; and Eliot maintained that the coterie-writers possessed the sense of
our time, although they lived in no way the life that
is natural to mankind. They lived, and they rather
gloried in living, in "silence, exile and cunning," detached from the life of mankind, which they scorned
and condemned. But then how could they possess the

sense of their age? And was there any proof that they possessed it in the fact that younger writers said they possessed it? Was not the blind worship of prestige a curse of our age, an age that is sadly confused in the matter of values? Young writers always follow the leader, and the leaders are the intensest minds who happen to be dominant at the moment; but that certain minds are dominant does not mean that these are the minds which possess the sense of their age. They may be only the most articulate; and Allston felt that these coterie-writers did not possess the sense of their age, for they denied the sense of *all* ages. (Except those ages of decline, the Alexandrian age, for instance, that have had no counter-currents of thought, such as mark the present age. These ages of decline were passive ages, whereas the present age is an age of struggle.) They certainly possessed the sense of a decade or two, a decade of defeat and disappointment; but was this sense properly the sense of the age? Was it not a mere continuation of the sense of the eighteen-nineties, at a time when the human mind was exhausted and weary and could not reassert itself? And was there not current some other "understanding of the meaning of life"? The coterie-writers and their camp-followers had had things much their own way; but in this age, as in every other, there was an "understanding defining the highest good" at which society aims, and this aim was still the "union of mankind." Had not American writers recently proved it? Were not virtually all these writers on the "left,"—the side of the "union of mankind"? In this age, as in the last age, the central minds, Allston said, were those who continued to pursue this aim,—they had never ceased to pursue and express it. The others had been poisoned by their coterie-leaders.

But I am anticipating. Allston said that these coterie-writers, whining over the beautiful past, had expressed no present whatsoever; or, rather, they had expressed only a moment in which they had caught humanity napping. And they had passed for primary when they denied, when they presented as nugatory the primary in all things! (Yet were not some of them beautiful writers? Allston gladly admitted this. He enjoyed their artistry as much as any man living.) Was not their famous Symbolism a deliberate exodus from the primary? It represented, beginning with Poe, a cultural secession from the common interests of mankind, which had always been the primary concern of writers; and thus, precisely thus, the "decadence" began, of which these coterie-writers were the continuation. Primary literature always expressed "the feeling of the people in the language of scholars," and the Symbolists turned away from this in order to pursue aesthetic concerns alone. They isolated their symbols from the common concerns of humanity, of which the great symbols had been expressions,—the Cross, Jove's thunderbolt and the doves of Venus,—and used them to express a private language, which might have been a kind of baby-talk. For only a few initiates could know the meaning of their symbols, which were, in short, mere personal hieroglyphics. There have always been coterie-writers, and they have always used this language. Some of the minor Elizabethans used it, but so was not Shakespeare written; and all the mental habits of these coterie-writers were in harmony with this. There was Mallarmé, who lived on the "confines of poetry," ignoring the centre of poetry, which he left to the tradesmen; he withdrew from the centre of poetry, which he thought of as arithmetic, in contrast to the algebra which he hoped to attain. Rimbaud aimed at "monstrosity of soul,"—he would not use the language of the "human pigs,"—and there was the naughty brat Laforgue, who stuck out his tongue at all things human. One and all, these poets played with symbols, as they might have played with marbles or behind the barn. They founded a school on a sonnet assigning different colours to the vowels, and Mallarmé wrote verses for ladies' fans,—there was a fine revenge on the Romantic poets who had stood for the liberation of mankind. That a great poet is a great soul with something great to say,—for any such notion as this they had nothing but scorn; and, while they contributed something to the study of form, they reduced the dimensions of literature to the area of a school-yard. Children always have secret words for their infantile concerns, and the Symbolists played at literature in little groups like children. Was not this well-known in their day? *Ce sont des enfants qui se sucent le pouce,*—they are children sucking their thumbs, Renan said; and did this not fairly describe them?

Such were the forbears, then, of the coterie-writers who have dominated our literature for a decade or two; and can we not say of them, with Santayana, "Nothing is so poor and melancholy as art that is interested in itself and not in its subject"? The Symbolists doubted, said André Gide, whether life was worth living; and they scarcely even believed in literature. How far had Rimbaud believed in it when he not only gave it up but also later expressed his hopes for his son, that he might become "a famous engineer, powerful and rich through science"? So Eliot wonders now and then if there is any use in writing, and Paul Valéry says that "reading and writing . . . still bore me a little." What concerns Valéry is "the form,—the *matter* is of small importance,"— only the method interests him, not the subject; and his hero, Monsieur Teste, is a symbol of the human consciousness isolated from "all the opinions . . . that spring from the common life." He adds that "enthusiasm is not an artist's state of mind," a view that Eliot reflects again and again. A poem, both aver, is "something *constructed*," an "intricate intellectual problem," successfully solved. Well, said Allston, which is right, Eliot or Socrates, who expressed the Greek view of this matter? "All that can be produced by art," Socrates observed, "vanishes before the offspring of mania." Mania, possession, or, if one likes, enthusiasm, that was the state of mind of the classical artist, which Eliot apparently does not wish to be. The classical artist was possessed, and what possessed him was the *matter,* and he strove to construct the poem *after this fact.* Those for whom construction comes before the matter are those who have not the matter in them, and those who repudiate "mania" in the interest of deliberation are those who know not mania and cannot command it. And is one, indeed, a poet at all if one lacks both matter and mania? Or is one a clever artificer merely? Let those who condemn the Romantics question themselves.

They scorn the Romantics for their "vague" expressions of "vague" sentiments, and there have been Romantics who are rightly so scorned. But there are other Romantics who have expressed magnificent sentiments, and who have expressed them fitly,—because they have had the mania and the matter.

Here was the heart of Allston's case against these coterie-writers, who doubt the value of life and of literature also. They doubt the value of life because they have so little of it, and they doubt the value of literature because it is an expression of life. Valéry feels that literature may well be on its way out. He feels it is already obsolescent, as if men could cease to be men and could cease to speak!—and Valéry is the poet who prefers to contemplate women asleep because sleep is a kind of death *plus précieuse que la vie*. And there was the spoiled child Proust, a beautiful writer,—was not death to him better than life, or could he have endured life without sickness? He chose the cell of the invalid, in which he could picture the world as sick, as sad, vain, useless and putrescent; and he pictured romantic love as impossible nonsense. (Pray, what, said Allston, made Proust an authority on love?) What was Proust's sickness if not an excuse for dropping out of the common life, to which he was not superior but unequal?—and all these writers made of their helpless and supine state a virtue which they proclaimed to the world of letters. They all resigned life and made a virtue of it, although they valued so little what they resigned; and it is only the measure in which one values things that gives one's resignation its degree of virtue. A profound self-pity, the offspring of weakness, lay be-

hind these attitudes, which were anti-literary as well
as anti-vital; and it was only a step from these writers
to the Dadaists, whose campaign was directed *against*
literature. It was only a step to Gertrude Stein, who
tried to empty literature of emotional content, or, one
might say, literary content, of all except its verbal
and rhythmical content. She could not *command*
emotional content, and all the rest of her theory was
a rationalization. Why was her *Three Lives* so good?
Because she really cared for the people she wrote of;
she threw herself sympathetically into the infantile
minds of her German servant-girls and her Negress.
In short, when she wrote *Three Lives,* she had the
mania and the matter, while later the infantile became fixed in herself because her imagination was
unpeopled (or peopled only by the most vacuous
types). She lived in France, among strangers, with
whom she had no vital connections, and her feeling
for human nature became abstract; and it was then
that she began to follow the abstract painters,—out of
her exigency she made a virtue. Did not her autobiography show how narrow was the range of her
sympathies and interests? To empty painting of literary content was the great effort of Braque and
Picasso, and perhaps they were justified as painters,
though Picasso, in his "Guernica," brought the literary content back when the man within the painter
was moved for once. But to empty literature of literary
content is to achieve the absurd, although Gertrude
Stein carried the day with many, thanks to her high
hand and her sangfroid: one can only say that no
one would have wished to do so who had not been
pushed into a corner, who had possessed the content

that literature expresses. She conceived the notion
that words can be used as colours are used, divorced
from their associations and their function, although
this is quite alien to the nature of words, which are
not what they "say," as colours are, but what they
"mean," as our memories tell us. To use them as colour
and sound alone is not to communicate as with colour
or sound,—it is to utter gibberish by definition; and
no one would dream of playing with language as a
baby-language who had any sense of the life that language conveys. Literary content, Allston said, is the
result of responsible living, in a world with which
one has real connections; and Gertrude Stein was infantile, like many of these other coterie-writers, who
have spent their lives in countries not their own. They
were mostly out of touch with the primary realities,
for they had no real connection with the world they
lived in; and their only responsibility was to their
art, which thus, by the nature of things, became a
game. Moreover, they were victims of their own personalities, which were floating in a void; and hence
the air of the mystagogue that enveloped them all.
Omne ignotum pro magnifico,—they were international mystagogues, concerned, above everything else,
for their own prestige; * for, as maladjusted persons,

---

* Regarding this concern for their prestige, Allston quotes Carl van
Vechten, who says in his introduction to *Three Lives,* referring to Gertrude Stein: "When some incident inimical to comfort occurs in a hostelry
where she and Alice Toklas may be stopping for the night, it is Alice's
habit to make her complaint to the manager in terms of a set formula,
'La Baronne n'est pas satisfaite!'" This, said Allston, brings the house
to book. Just so Henry James, in the middle of the world-war, insisted
on getting the Prime Minister to sponsor his naturalization. Any other
Englishman would have served as well. But no, James would have the
Prime Minister, if he had to stop the Battle of Flanders to get him.
Modesty is a virtue these persons can seldom afford. Their self-assertion
requires corroboration.

they were insecure, and, being insecure, they developed a morbid will to power. Lacking all that makes for content, they said that literature should not have content, or, at least, that the only essential matter is form; and they ridiculed half the great writers for the best of reasons. These writers, truthfully seen, would have overwhelmed them.*

Thus, in the hands of the coterie-writers, literature became a game, an intellectual pastime for dilettanti; for, serious as they may be as artists, what are they as human beings? Does not the word dilettante well become them? Their only care is to be good writers, and one respects them for this, but this, in literature,

---

* I find among Allston's papers this further note on Gertrude Stein: "Most of her American satellites were young Middle Westerners who were outwardly defiant in their posture but inwardly full of 'fear and trembling,' as Glenway Wescott puts it. It must have been a joy to them to find in Paris, whither they had fled from their prairie homes, the mature Gertrudian bosom, much like that of their far-away prairie mothers, but of a most gratifying sophistication. Miss Stein gave them back their nursery-rhymes, and they had fine babbling times together."

I also find this note on Ford Madox Ford: "In 1925, when Ford was in New York, he called me on the telephone and asked me to have lunch with him. I was most flattered and grateful, and Ford was such a kind and good-natured man that no one could have helped liking him. I had known his books from of old. I had read his Pre-Raphaelite memories when I was a boy, and no writer was too young or too raw to attract his fatherly interest, his truly astonishing flair for the art of writing. But his mind was like a Roquefort cheese, so ripe that it was palpably falling to pieces, and I do not think he was a good mental diet for the young Western boys, fresh from the prairie, who came under his influence in Paris. Sensitive young men are apt to be unstable, and they seldom achieve stability unless they have seen it in their elders. Ford was an uprooted creature who, from his earliest days, had feasted upon whatever was exotic in late Victorian England; and then, as a half-German, who changed his name during the war, he was half an alien in his country. He propagated a notion of literature to which the prairie boys were too much disposed already, having come from a part of America where the roots of life were indigestible, as Sinclair Lewis's *Main Street* had seemed to show. Ford and Gertrude Stein, playing into the hands of Joyce, Eliot and Pound, provided a diet of nightingales' tongues for boys who knew nothing of beef and potatoes; and the maternal Miss Stein and the fatherly Ford appealed to their filial instincts also,—which made the authority of these writers all the more compelling."

is the affair of Cæsar; for is it not more important
that the man behind the writer should live in such a
fashion that he has something to say? Living the
lives of dilettanti, and therefore having little to say,
they talk of the "mechanics of good writing" as if
this were the sole concern of writers; and thus they
resemble the modern "masses," as Ortega y Gasset
describes them, who make games and sports their
central interest. This is indeed the sole concern of
the school of coterie-critics that has risen in our university world. These critics, many of them Southerners, reacting against Southern ways,—the extremely personal nature of the Southern mind, the
Southern sentimentality and so on,—have been
drawn, as a natural consequence, to the world of ab-
straction; and, having small love of literature,—for
they really prefer mechanics and science,—they have
swarmed all over the field of American letters. Assuming that they are literary critics, they are more
like entomologists or geometricians; yet they have
largely preempted the sphere of university critical
study with what John Crowe Ransom calls the "new
criticism." Mr. Ransom makes interesting claims for
this new criticism, which is practised, he says, by
"many distinguished critics," whose guardian angel
is Eliot and whose John the Baptist is I. A. Richards,
a neurological psychologist who lives in England.
Still according to Mr. Ransom, this criticism "in
depth and precision is beyond all earlier criticism
in our language;" it is "patient and consecutive" as
nothing has ever been before, and it abounds in
"amazing passages." It is, in fact, "unprecedented"
and has produced a "sort of hero" in an eminent

practitioner who shall be nameless; and, while R. P. Blackmur especially excels in depth and precision, there is also Cleanth Brooks, who, as Mr. Ransom says, "prefers poetry to science because he judges that poetry is capable of the nicer structures." Then there is Ivor Winters, with his "skill in analyzing structures,"—Winters is "the critic who is best at pouncing upon the structure of a poem." Finally, among various others, there is Mr. Ransom, who hopes to see an "ontological critic." (He thought for a time that he had found one in a certain Chicago scientist; but no, this gentleman would not do, nor would another professor who was collecting the work-sheets of poets so that young student-poets might see the "actual process of perfecting poems by revision.") All these achievements of the new criticism are indeed unprecedented, Allston said, and no one can deny that serious thinking about poetry, serious from any point of view, may well have a good effect on poets. But is this really "criticism" or "literary"? Is it not mechanical or scientific? This consciousness of what Ransom calls "methodological standards" may well amuse the "undergraduate thinkers" whom Ransom and his colleagues have in mind. It may even serve to educate them, if they are thinkers to be educated. But in what fashion will it educate them? This was the question that Allston was constrained to ask; and he felt that it would ruin them as writers, by making them over-intellectual and over-conscious, although it might serve them as chemists or engineers.* In

---

* Allston liked to quote the phrase of Anatole France, in *The Garden of Epicurus:* "Poets must not be too keen to argue about the laws of their art; when they lose their innocence their charm goes with it, and like fish out of water they flounder helplessly in the arid regions of theory."

fact, he felt certain that students who were really
thinkers and who underwent this discipline would
probably end as chemists or engineers; and, if this
was the upshot of the new criticism, what did it suggest in regard to its essence? What was to be said
of critics like Cleanth Brooks, who,—and the phrase
describes them all,—"prefers poetry to science *because* he judges that poetry is capable of the nicer
structures"? Do not these critics deceive themselves?
Very few great poems have as nice a structure as the
greatest bridge, and moreover there is this difference
between them,—if the structure of a bridge is not
nice, the bridge is worth a great deal less than
nothing, for not only will the bridge collapse but
people will be drowned, while a "poem" like *Hamlet*
can be, as Eliot says, a "failure," because it is not like
a bridge, and yet remain one of the world's great
poems. A critic who prefers poetry to science for this
reason only, or chiefly, is therefore one who really
prefers science; and this is undoubtedly the truth
about all these critics. They have made literature a
training-ground for science, as science, in the last few
decades, has been a training-ground for literature.

So, Allston said, the "new criticism" was not really
criticism; and, as it evaded the whole world of
values, which is justly the concern of criticism, it lay
outside the field of literature. It was properly a discipline in the field of science. What could be said
for its values? Ivor Winters, who "pounced upon the
structure of a poem," did not know genius when he
saw it, for had he not also pounced upon the greatest
works of American genius in order to signalize them
as "bad" or "failures"? And could one trust the judg-

ment of any of these critics, who took in one another's washing, while they proclaimed that many of the greatest writers are too dirty to be washed at all? * They found Byron and Browning too "crude" to be thought of, while they quoted one another on every page.† (Good heavens, said Allston, if Browning is crude, what must Homer be?) They had no comparative sense of the minor and the major, and, pursuing the "study of metres . . . with extreme precision," they had no literary feeling whatsoever. Their ignorance matched their pretentiousness, for they were pretentious beyond all bearing,‡ and they went round and round in a little circle of references, sneeringly resisting everything else, in a way that revealed too clearly how little they had read. They were pretentious because they were not on firm

---

* They took in one another's washing, but did they really believe in one another? Did they even believe in their guardian angel? Allston quoted Mr. Ransom's remark about T. S. Eliot: "As for the comparative intelligence of Eliot beside Dryden or Johnson, or other famous critics in our language, I think surely he does not yield to any of them; he is 'closer' and more patient than the two mentioned. It is likely that we have had no better critic than Eliot . . ." "This is a large claim," Allston said; "but is Mr. Ransom sure of his ground? When, from the general, he comes to the particular, he says that *The Metaphysical Poets* is Eliot's 'most famous and valuable essay.' Then he comes to the heart of this essay and continues as follows: 'I must add that, having worked to the best of my ability to find the thing Eliot refers to in the 17th century poets, and failed, I incline to think there was nothing of the kind there.' In short, Mr. Ransom, having found Eliot better than Dryden and Johnson, ends by finding Eliot himself a mare's-nest. This suggests to me that, before one seeks the 'ontological,' one should make sure that one has the logical first."

† "Eliot may very well talk about the modern crudeness of Browning's 'feeling' though he could talk as easily about the crudeness of Browning's imagination or perception."—John Crowe Ransom, Essay on Eliot.

‡ "Winters admires Baudelaire as the author of poems the best of which are probably 'superior to any French verse of the nineteenth century' with the exception of two poems by Corbière."—John Crowe Ransom, Essay on Ivor Winters. Has Mr. Winters read every poem of the nineteenth century? And on whose authority are "two poems by Corbière" better than all of Victor Hugo?

ground, but their pretentiousness carried the day with others, who were too immature to judge pretensions and for whom they closed the door on the world's great writers (always excepting Donne and Dante); and they had established an Eliot club in every university, like the Browning clubs of yesteryear. The Browning clubs served a noble purpose. They were a focus for earnest souls who deeply believed in spiritual things but who could no longer accept the teachings of the Church; while for souls who were less earnest they served another purpose,—they exercised one's ingenuity, like detective stories and crossword-puzzles. Was not this essentially the purpose of the Eliot clubs? They provided a learned game for students to play; and the metaphysical poets were good for this because they were closest to chess and to crossword-puzzles. Because they were ambiguous and obscure, they lent themselves ideally to just this end; and Allston said that it must be fun for an "undergraduate thinker" to feel that he was a "lay aesthetician." (This was another of Mr. Ransom's phrases.) What could be more amusing than to look at a poem with reference to its "tenor" and its "texture," exploring the "private character of the detail items"? * To follow the "private history of an item" might indeed be tamer than looking for a bloody finger-print; but it was more suitable for students,— it was less like a mystery-story and more like chess.

* For the study of a poem Mr. Ransom suggests this procedure: "I think we must waive the psychological magic involved in the act of feeling our thought in honour of something much tamer and more credible: the procedure of suspending the course of the main thought while we explore the private character of the detail items. We stop following the main thought, and take off in a general direction, as we follow the private history of an item; then we come back to the main thought."

The procedure had its dignity, perhaps; but why should mature readers be interested in the speculations of "advanced university students specializing in poetry"? Could they have anything to say to people who have lived?—and what was one to think, in fact, of this professorial attitude that has impinged so heavily on the world of letters? Allston knew many professors, who varied as much as other men; he knew at least a dozen who had touched the depths and heights of life and who regarded literature with reference to them. But, with his distrust of theory, he deprecated these other professors, who theorized, as he said, *in vacuo.* It was not only that they wrote exclusively in relation to pupils, but that they wrote of literature without reference to feeling; and this was because they did not possess feeling, however they explained the matter otherwise. Did they not express the "grey plaster temperament,"—William James's phrase for the "Ph.D.'s,"—or the "graduate-school mentality," as Newton Arvin called it, which had no visible relation to the world of men? They were certainly "patient," Allston said. They had the patience of coral-insects, but these at least build a useful reef, while they would be better employed in collecting the insects; for the reef of poetry disappeared under the hands of their patience and nothing remained but analyses and classifications. What became of the music-makers, the builders of cities and movers of men? What became of literature in the path of these critics? They left not a rack of it behind them.

CHAPTER XX

WHAT A SET!

NOW, Allston was aware that these coterie-writers were only one group of modern writers. Luckily, there were other writers who represented primary literature, and some of them represented it to the finest effect; but the Symbolists and their heirs and assigns possessed a special prestige that made them really formidable dogs in the manger. Their endless talk of technical matters closed the minds of younger writers to the substance and purpose of true writing, and Allston felt it was time to bring them to book. He did not undervalue technical matters,— I sometimes felt that he was an artist himself; * but, regarding all these coterie-writers, he said, "What a set!"—as Arnold said of Leigh Hunt and his circle. What a set, to have hypnotized our modern world,— for these prestidigitators were spell-binders. They possessed the "prestige" the meaning of which is illusion or glamour, a word that also means to blindfold or dazzle. It means enchantment or deception, and these writers have enchanted our age; and Allston, freely granting that some of them are men of

---

* "All this technical talk is vulgar," Allston says in one of his journals. "It concerns what Henry James called the 'secrets of the kitchen,' and in the kitchen it has dignity, but it should not be obtruded at the dinner-table. *Ars est celare artem.* Artists give results, and only results, if they are really proud."

genius, asked what other age had been enchanted by men of less intrinsic merit. For they were devoid of spirituality, which they possessed in appearance only. Allston said he preferred the scepticism of the Epicurean to what he called the epicurism of a professed devotion. Renan, he said, avowed that he was a dilettante, and he justified his position on the ground of aesthetics. But Eliot avowed a position that only religious feeling could justify, and this appeared nowhere in his writings.

So Allston dwelt on this question of prestige, the sorcery of our age, and he asked, What real merits can withstand it?

It finds (he says) an unparalleled field for expansion in an age that has known so few standards; and, if I resent these prestidigitators, it is largely on behalf of those who are younger than myself. When I think what one's years of reading mean in youth, when I think of the great books that came my way because the air of my youth was saturated with them, how easy it was for me to find Tolstoy, Emerson, Ibsen and Ruskin, men with great horizons, who had known great draughts of experience, who did not find life too hot or too cold,—like these little shivering aesthetes,—men who had endured great ordeals, men who had penetrated to the depths and heights and whose influence was tonic and expanding,—then I feel a blind rage on behalf of younger sensitive minds who have had no other pabulum than these one-eyed writers, sickly adolescents, self-centred and neurotic, inexperienced persons, divorced from the soil, divorced from their country, often, and from parenthood and love, ignorant of the general life, with no horizon beyond their noses or the spiritual slums in

which they live. They are besotted egoists, one and
all, stewing in their vanity, throwing dust in the eyes
of their readers, mystagogues and swindlers. When I
think how easily the eyes of youth are dazzled, then
I understand Jeremiah, who cursed the false prophets. Better one chapter of Victor Hugo, with even his
prodigious conceit, than all these paltry poets of a
cheap despair.

Allston spoke often in this vein; * and was it not a
curious thing that writers of this calibre had been
taken for great? What a descent from the nineteenth-
century writers they despised, who had spoken out of
the heart of the human race!—who had been clear
and direct because their feelings were clear and deep
and who fought for the welfare of men because they
loved men. They had believed in themselves and
their work, whereas these coterie-writers really believed in themselves as artificers only; and these
writers dwelt on death because they knew not life,
and, having no sense of the heights, they dwelt in the
abyss. They revived the metaphysical poets not because these poets were great but because they were
acid like themselves, and they returned to the primitive not because it was primary, but because they
could not rise to true civilization. They had all the
excuses, and they made the most of these excuses,—
modern relativity, the mechanization of modern life,
the triumph of contemporary science and a dozen
others. These were indeed excuses, which they exploited all too fully; but they did not alter the fact

* Perhaps I might say here that I heartily sympathized with Allston.
Often, when I heard him say these things, I remembered Goethe's
observation, "My beliefs become indefinitely more certain to me when
I find that another shares them."

that emotional rightness and fullness are the essential things in literature and that great writers are those who possess them. Great writers are creators who create in the teeth of all excuses, and those who *must* are those who *can,*—had not creators always found a way? Allston had something to say on this subject to which I shall return. Meanwhile, a few further remarks on the coterie-writers.

Here it must be said that he sometimes uttered half-thoughts, thoughts that were ill-considered, impatient and hasty. Here is one, for example:

> Why this morbid suspicion of the popular? Why do they see it as a menace? Because the popular, as we know it, is a vulgarization of the primary, and it has the primary in it, which they have not.

This is rather more than half true. So is the longer reflection that follows, in which he considers the proposition that to understand is to forgive. He knew that a critic was obliged to understand things, or try to understand them, whether he liked them or not. But he said that to understand should not be to forgive, or, rather, that, understanding the criminal, one should not forgive the crime. He consistently applied this in literary matters. But there were times when he was impatient and did not wish to understand:

> The spread of science has made us feel that we ought to be "broad-minded" and strive to understand every point of view, however it may repel our natural tastes. It is more important that we should maintain the right of our natural tastes, at whatever cost in "narrow-mindedness." There are large areas of mod-

ern speculation, of thought, feeling and writing, in which the proper response is to say nothing but to kick one's foot, as Dr. Johnson did, against the first object that comes in one's way. Kicking one's foot is an eloquent statement that may have a world of thought behind it. Every man of good sense knows when not to argue and has his mind made up on a thousand matters that are not discussible for him. In fact, without a closed mind one cannot have an open mind. One becomes a house without doors or windows, and I should not call that an open house.

There are intellectual "monsters" which, to see, is presently to pity and then embrace. If we embrace these monsters, we assume their point of view; and, in that case, what becomes of our own? A critic should be able to assume all points of view *dramatically*, as a playwright assumes the views of his characters; but he must remain the author of his own "piece." Our natural perceptions were not given us for nothing, and we should maintain them against all comers.

So, with his feeling about the coterie-writers, who had got their readers into a "dark little pocket," whose influence was triumphant and triumphant for evil, he liked to bait and challenge them on all occasions. I choose these remarks almost at random,—he might have called them "arrows of the chase," directed at some of the foibles of the writers in question. In several cases he withholds the name of the writer he has in mind, in the spirit of the following observations:

It is my practice not to mention in print the names of writers of this calibre. Nature intended them for private life.

There are writers who, as writers, ought to die, and the only way to contribute to this end is not to mention them.

In other notes the reader may recognize a well-known writer:

She ought to be given a hearing, she should have the benefit of the doubt, etc. But she is given a hearing, she has the benefit of the doubt. Tolerance ceases to be a virtue when the benefit of the doubt is habitually given, except to those who have no new tricks.

They leave the life out of art. The only possible next step is to leave the life out of life.

Verlaine's well-known remark, *Tout le reste est littérature,* long since became a peripheral observation. To leave out of literature all the rest *besides* the rest is the ultimate achievement of the modern mind.

Whatever sneers, whenever it sneers, is antipathetic to me.

Eliot insists upon metaphysics as giving depth to literature, and he tries to persuade us that literature which is not metaphysical is shallow. But the real depths are vital depths, emotional depths. There he is shallow indeed, where the simplest ballad-poet may be profound.

> "So much they scorn the crowd, that if the throng
> By chance go right, they purposely go wrong."
> —Pope, *Essay on Man.*

I still quote Tolstoy: "It has come finally to this: that not only is haziness, mysteriousness, obscurity and exclusiveness elevated to the rank of a merit and a condition of poetic art, but even incorrectness, indefiniteness and lack of eloquence are held in esteem. . . The direction art has taken may be compared to placing on a large circle other circles, smaller and smaller, until a cone is formed, the apex of which is no longer a circle at all. That is what has happened to the art of our times. . . Manufactured counterfeits of art in which borrowing, imitating, effects and inter-estingness replace the contagion of feeling."

I resent the space that mountebanks occupy in the public mind, for they occupy most of the space which the public mind can spare for art and letters.

I call a mountebank every writer who exploits his personality, or suffers his personality to be exploited, either in his actual person or by cultivating his man-nerisms. The real writers have always rather culti-vated the commonplace and have even done their best to abolish themselves. If, after this, they survive and have something to say, then and only then do they count for literature.

The mountebanks thrive on the modesty of those who know better but who cannot feel that their opin-ion matters. Everyone's opinion matters who has a feeling for truth.

These tiresome cosmopolitan gangs make a Grant Wood farmer's wife look like Jerusalem Delivered.

An effect of cosmopolitanism,—it makes fashion the lawgiver. Deracinated people have no standards aside from the standard of fashion, for they are out of touch with the bases of life. They have few or no ties that create responsibility and give one a scale for measuring values. Fashion is the only law for all these floating people. Besides, as the aesthetic of social re-lations, fashion is attractive to artists, and all the more to artists who are also floating. This infects artists with a fear of fashion. One saw this fear of fashion even in the poet Yeats, whose anthology of modern English poetry was almost ruined by it. He included many bad poems that were not at all to his taste because of his respect for literary fashion.

With regard to Gertrude Stein's theory that words can be used independently of their associations, it is to be said that a word is nothing but the sum of its associations. Then how could this theory have gained adherents? Only because the society for which Gertrude Stein writes has no associations in common. The uprooted world of cosmopolitan urban people can meet only on the plane of abstractions. They have nothing in common of the past, and in fact they are usually anxious to forget their past. Abstract art is the peculiar art of these people, and now abstract writing.

All these writers depend on immediate returns. They have to keep their goods in the shop-window. They have to cash their drafts at once, for fashion allows only short credits. The real writers are like real swells who can afford to be simple and to disregard the times.

An essay by our well-known expatriate poet, who, so far as this country is concerned, is living in the days of Grover Cleveland. It would be different if these people had left the country for convenience. But they have left it in a pet, and this has the effect of "freezing" their American assets. They are stone cold about the country and imagine that the country is as cold as themselves. That it is living and growing they cannot imagine. So they continue to indulge us with these prehistoric gibes, the detritus of a slang that was current in Silurian ages. These people are geological specimens. They should be gathered together and put under glass, along with the fossil ferns and the petrified banyans.

Of course, it means nothing to them that, so far as this country goes, they are living in the days of Grover Cleveland. They took it for granted that America was "provincial" and that the only real movement was the movement of the centre,—that is, the movement of London and Paris. It did not occur to them that the centre might shift, as it has been steadily shifting since the first world-war. It is London and Paris that have become provincial, while New York more and more becomes the centre; and no one is more pathetically out on a branch than these Americans who have misprized their country. If they had put first things first and grounded themselves in solid values, they would not have found themselves so stranded. Those who put first things first are always central and do not have to seek the centre, while those who seek the centre as a primary object are in a fair way to lose it. And then they are literally nowhere.

Cosmopolitanism in literature is an external substitute for universality. No cosmopolitan writer is ever read very long outside his own language, while the local writer who has universalized himself on his own acres passes muster in all languages. Hawthorne's German translator told him that the Germans took *The House of the Seven Gables* for a purely German book, instantly applicable to German conditions, German pride of family and all the rest.

CHAPTER XXI

NATIONALISM AND REGIONALISM

SO MUCH for these international mystagogues, as Allston also called the coterie-writers. But, in attacking the cosmopolitan, I am sure that, beyond a point, he was not defending nationalism. He knew that too much nationalism was as bad as too little. His sympathies were international. He hoped to see the time when all the national sovereignties would yield before a planetary political system; and he was culturally international,—he loved a variegated world,—the more it was diversified, the better. But what made real diversification was the strength of the component parts, the density of the groups that were interrelated; and therefore, up to a certain point, Allston rejoiced in nationalism. He liked Ibsen's saying, "Culture is unthinkable apart from national life." Could there be any real culture that was not the culture of primary things? And could there be a culture of primary things that was not the expression of some group-life? Only through the group, by means of ties and loyalties, could one apprehend primary things; and consequently men were better citizens of the world if they were also, and first, citizens of their country. And writers were extensions of men.

Here, then, was Allston's case for literary nation-alism. What was the "fluid" which, as Victor Hugo said, should run between the writer and his readers, the living stream from which both draw strength? What but the sense of a shared experience, a common fund of understanding, a fund of sufferings and longings realized in common? When this was raised to the level of universality, one had the primary literature of all nations and peoples, the matrix of the literature of all mankind; and when it was less than universal it still possessed the poignancy of all that is radically human. But cosmopolitan literature, deprived of this fluid, expressed the experience of phantoms rather than men,—it was the literature of "hollow men," who had lost their organic bonds with their group and with nature. These men were artificial in their isolation, their work was of the "mind," not of the "bone;" and, whatever their integrity as artists, they had no tap-root in the general soil of mankind. They were incomplete as men because they had broken with their group-life, because they had ignored their "societal instinct," as D. H. Lawrence called it, in favour of some personal taste, some personal whim or bitterness, some personal ideal of "silence, exile and cunning." That they had taken their groups so lightly, quarrelled with them on personal grounds, as one saw in the case of Eliot, Joyce and Pound, already indicated a certain weakness; for the societal instinct is atrophied already in those for whom the group is more trivial than the ego. Eliot had felt this: he had done his best, like Henry James, to identify himself with another country,—but his attachment to England had remained synthetic.

(And consequently was he not himself the "hollow
man," the image in which he conceived his fellow-
creatures?) D. H. Lawrence felt it and said the final
word about it, although he had felt obliged to break
with his group. (Because, from his point of view,
which was personal also, society smothered the natural life of men.) Lawrence felt what others did not
feel who took their groups lightly and gloried in
their deracination. "What ails me," he said, "is the
absolute frustration of my primeval societal instinct
. . . I think societal instinct much deeper than sex
instinct—and societal repression much more devas-
tating . . . I am infinitely hurt by being thus torn off
from the body of mankind." There was the whole
story, and, from Allston's point of view, those who
took lightly their "societal repression" were somehow
essentially shallow.

This explains, I think, Allston's view of the cosmopolitan; and let me recall here his feeling about
expatriation, which I have explained in a previous
chapter. The upshot of this, as regards Americans,
was that one should "root oneself,"—*Enracinez! enracinez!* as André Gide exclaimed. Allston was by no
means addressing all Americans, as I have already indicated,—the self-possessed require no exhortations,
neither do they need rules or laws; but perhaps he
was exhorting himself a little. He talked so much
about expatriation! He seemed unable to forget it!
He struck me as distinctly morbid here, and I wondered if he was reacting against his own early tendencies. Born in a suburb, he had no deep local attachments, and many years had passed before he
learned to love his country. He had been drawn to

Europe over-much; and, besides, he had seen Americans who were deeply planted, after a few years abroad, unable to take root again at home. Had not Hawthorne and Lowell, after writing deep American things, reverted to the European homeland? Had not William James always said that he had to thin his blood again in order to live here happily after living in Europe? Mark Twain had grown to prefer Europe, while others, like Thoreau, feared to jeopardize their local attachments. Had not Thoreau refused to go abroad, feeling that he might be alienated from his native woods and pastures? Allston had felt for a long time that he must cling to America to preserve his personality from disintegration, and this had become in a way an obsession with him. For expatriation, he seemed to feel, leads to irresponsibility: one ceases to be responsible in terms of one's own society, and one fails to become responsible in terms of any other society. But he saw that this menace had passed with the new generation. The "European career" had ceased to attract the younger people, for whom Europe had destroyed its own spell; and the coming-of-age of America for them was real. They had inherited a feeling for the country that many had not shared in Allston's youth; and they felt they belonged to a continent, with multifarious strivings behind them, multifarious failures and struggles and triumphs. Elements of many kinds had formed this continental feeling, the motor-car that opened up the nation, biographies, histories and novels published in thousands and numbers of other causes that were deeper than these; and the feeling of the national destiny possessed men's minds again, as in the epoch

after the Revolution. The cause of the national sentiment had been vindicated beyond all doubt; and Allston rejoiced in the rise of the regional feeling. This
was quite different from the "local colour" movement that had swept over the country in the days of
Howells. The movement of Bret Harte and others
was superficial beside this,—it was concerned with
pointing out the "differences" of local life, the elements of oddity and quaintness in the local scene (not
that it did not sometimes achieve much more) ; while
the new regional movement was not concerned with
local differences as a prime object of contemplation.
It sprang from a self-identification with the local
group to which one belonged, the group in which
one's roots were most firmly embedded; and the rationale of the movement was that, because of this,
one might so best achieve the universal. Of recent
novelists, Dreiser, Lewis, Hemingway, Wolfe and
Dos Passos had ranged over the nation and beyond;
but there were others,—there were more, because the
nation was so complex,—for whom the local group
had proved a boon. Steinbeck's California, Faulkner's Mississippi, Farrell's Chicago Irish and the
Georgia of Caldwell had served in every case as an
admirable focus. (And even, as regards the others,
had not Dreiser gained from having an original base
in Chicago, Lewis in "Gopher Prairie" and Wolfe
in Asheville?) None of these novelists was concerned
with the glorification of a region; nor did they point
out the differences of their regions from others. They
used the group not as a fetish but merely as a means
by which to seek the universal. The group was a more
immediate extension of themselves.

Now, Allston, who had no local attachments, could not share this regional feeling, though he felt that for him, as a critic, it did not matter. He was detached from all regions, and he hugged the feeling of his detachment. He hugged the feeling, wherever he went, in Boston, in the South, that he was an outsider; and he said that in a sense, indeed, one must be an outsider in order to be an artist of any sort. One had to be outside the social complex, and, being an artist, in fact, one was outside,—which explained why artists are always *inside,* why nobody can keep them out, why they are always received and everywhere honoured. (For everybody knows that, if one is a real artist, one is not a "social menace." One doesn't wish to marry their daughters, one doesn't wish to belong to their clubs; and therefore all mankind says to the artist, "Come in, come in, my darling child.") Allston felt that, as a critic, he could not be too far outside; and might this not be true of novelists also? As artists, they had to be outside the social complex, and even to be outside the *feeling* of a region made no appreciable difference in numbers of cases. Had Hemingway or Dos Passos suffered by it? Even for other writers Allston felt that regionalism was not the last word in literary truth. How far could it be a resource without being a fetish? William McFee had said to him once, "There is too much regionalism here. American literature is all regionalism, and what the country needs is a Kipling to unite it." Well, by all means, Allston replied, let us have a Kipling. Let us have another Walt Whitman. But why not regionalism also? The size and the chaos of the country necessitate it; and there is a difference between the regional social complex and the regional feeling. One can be outside the one and gain from the other. This was especially true, thought Allston, because of the dominance of New York, so different from the capitals of other countries. The universal that springs from the national too often takes the New York colour and does not represent the country, as the "national" of other countries represents them. New York is an exotic city that has always mirrored London and Paris; it has not mirrored America as London and Paris have always mirrored France and England. Now that the influence of London and Paris has been removed, New York should grow to represent the country; but meanwhile it is detached from the primary life of the country, and to get in touch with this one has to leave it. Our regional movement expresses this fact, and it flourishes because to react against New York is a means of getting in touch with the universal.

So Allston, although he could not share it, rejoiced in the growth of the regional feeling. For many it was obviously the line of growth. It was a way of building up the continental consciousness by leavening all the regions with self-understanding. (And all the racial groups as well.) Besides, did not living in cities impoverish minds? Did it not divorce them from worthy subject-matter, which is always a by-product of organic living? To get in touch with the common life, with small-town life and rural life, was certainly to grow closer to the elemental. Allston especially valued this tendency because he had heard in his childhood so many words of the order of "rube" and "hayseed." He had heard these words on every hand, in school, in the streets, in the theatre, and he felt they expressed what Americans wished *not* to be; and hence, he said, the general divorce from all that spoke of the elemental. To get in touch with the elemental, to get in touch with the common life,—what could be more important in a time like ours when fashion ran all the other way? Literary fashion had been set by writers who were at odds with their homelands; and the time had come to seek one's home-base if one wished to take the game away from these. So Allston was happy to see young writers returning to the regions which they had once regarded as God-forsaken. Greenwich Village had swarmed with exiles from the South and West who could scarcely bear to think of their far-away homes; and they were streaming homeward now, settling in the remotest regions, determined to find them interesting or make them so. And what was certain to result from this recent movement? In another generation would not all the States possess their own traditions and centres of culture?—and what a synthesis would follow that! One saw the results in several States already, in Iowa, South Dakota, Kansas, Missouri. The regional feeling united the artists and the people as they had been united in New England; and a situation was rising there in which the writer could be at one with the general mind he shared and, sharing, expressed. There lay the hope of major literature, foreshadowed and even achieved at moments in the Western folk-poets, Sandburg, Lindsay and Masters. Allston had observed in several cases the effect of New York on Western writers. He had seen their real natures emerging when they were at home, and he had seen them disoriented by the life of the city. He had seen Mary Austin, for instance, both in New York and California, where she was a different woman. In New York she had had a chip on her shoulder, she was uneasy, vain and strained, while among her own people in the West she expanded and blossomed. She was at home with her own depths, as when she had written her fine books there; she was natural, sympathetic, large and wise. The same thing had happened with Hart Crane, as Philip Horton showed in his life of this poet. At home, in the West, in his father's inn, a striking change came over Crane, and the strained, egotistical, violent man became the natural human being.* Other things being equal,—and they were not equal with Crane,— did this not show the value of being *at home?*

Let me pass, without apology, to a few notes on regionalism. I begin with two or three brief statements:

> In a regional area one can find everything if one has had a taste of the world and if one has developed a sense of proportion. If, moreover, it is the area of one's deepest feeling, there is nothing like having one's vital connections concentrated within it. Ex-

---

* "It was little short of amazing that, having drunk to such habitual excess in New York, he was able to maintain almost complete abstinence for three months without evidently suffering any strain or reaction. This would seem to confirm the interpretation that his use of alcohol, together with its correlative defiance and violent egotism, was part of a complex mechanism of self-defence. In New York, in Paris, and presently in Mexico,—in short, wherever he felt exposed to the abysmal insecurity and suspicions of the world,—he needed the license of intoxication to override his fears and assert himself against the encroachments of doubt. But in the inn at Chagrin Falls where he was surrounded with simple people who, knowing little of his life in New York and caring less, still accorded him full measure of spontaneous affection for his human qualities, there was no necessity for such devices."—*Hart Crane,* by Philip Horton.

cept in the case of the strongest talents, the attempt to embrace the whole country tends to make one's emotional life sketchy, thin and vague.

What an odd notion that one cannot make a Kansas garage a focus of universal intuitions.

In California I used to feel "so far away." Now I should ask, Far away from what?

It is the rule that writers flourish best in the oldest part of any country. So New England will never be deserted, nor will the South be. Just so, regionalism flourishes best,—other things being equal,—in the oldest part of the given region.

The notes that follow are allied with these. Regionalism required one to reckon with one's native town, and Allston had grown up at a time when most Americans seemed to feel that their native towns were peculiarly damned. "A young woman tells me," he says somewhere, "that she was born in Reading, Pennsylvania, and this is one of the facts of her life she is 'trying to live down.' How often I have heard some such remark. My generation will be remembered as the one in which everyone hated, often without visible reason, the town in which he was born. Have I not myself shared this feeling? Most of us felt that our towns were peculiarly damned. There was no one there to talk to, nobody to understand us! Was not this the general feeling twenty-five years ago? I cannot count the number of my friends who complained of the human 'sinks' and 'dumps' in which their lines were cast." Well, how had various great writers felt about their towns abroad? How had it been in the Europe that Americans envied?

Allston had heard perhaps too many of these complaints at home, for he seems to have taken pleasure in assembling foreign witnesses. He noted that Stendhal was bored in Rome, in 1831, "for lack of the opportunity to exchange ideas with anyone;" and he thus continues:

> Does history repeat itself? Hear the words of Leopardi on his native town: "As to Recanati," he writes to one of his friends, "I answer that I will leave it, escape from it, hurry away from it, as soon as ever I can. But when can I? That is what I cannot tell you. Meanwhile, be assured that my intention is not to stay here, where I see no one beyond our household, and where I should die of frenzy, of life-weariness, of hypochondria, if one could die of these ills . . . It is all very well to say, Plutarch and Alfieri loved Chæronea and Asti. Loved them and left them. In this fashion I also will love my native place when I am far away from it. Here literature is a word unknown. The names of Parini, Alfieri, Monti, and of Tasso and Ariosto, and all the others, need a commentary." Are these the words of an Italian poet? Or of one of our own poets of the present time regarding the Gopher Prairies of their childhood?

On the margin of the journal containing this, Allston has pencilled a note:

> Out of the frying-pan, into the fire. See also what Flaubert says of Paris, and what our friends say of New York: "Do you know in this Paris, which is so great, one single house in which literature is talked about? And when it is incidentally approached it is always in its subordinate and exterior aspects, the question of success, morality, utility, etc. It seems to

me that I am becoming a fossil, a being without any relation to the creation that surrounds me."

Allston adds: "These parallels settle no questions, but it relieves the sting of one's feeling about one's native town to find that Flaubert felt the same way in Paris."

I continue with a note that is somehow related:

Reading Halvdan Koht's *Life of Ibsen,* greatly struck, as many times before, by the parallel between the Norwegian literary movement and the century-old American effort to create an independent literature (now undoubtedly achieved). In the West, where they are starting all over again, where each of the newer States is having its coming-of-age, they should forget London and Paris and study these parallel national and regional movements, Ibsen's Norway, Dostoievsky's Russia and the Irish revival. Ibsen's milieu constantly suggests America,—the white clapboard wooden houses, the small-town society and the ethical centre of the Norwegian mind. I have only to close my eyes, while reading him, to feel that I am living in Salem or Portsmouth, or, as often, in some Main Street of the Middle West. There is no literary life like Ibsen's for showing a Western writer how to observe his world, and how to universalize himself,—for Ibsen's mind was formed in the stress of Norway before he went abroad. Our Western writers make a mistake when they saturate their minds with the "mysteries of Paris." They should study Ibsen's struggle against the aestheticism of which, as an artist, he felt the pull, while knowing it was opposed to his natural genius.

We have everything to learn from the Norwegians, who are so closely related to us. It took a Norwegian

writer, Ole Rölvaag, to understand what, in human
terms, was the real meaning of pioneering. It took
another Norwegian, Thorstein Veblen, to explain
this in economic terms.

I pass to a longer entry in Allston's journals:

A letter from L., who lives in Tennessee. He says
they have in M. a few cultivated people, who know
what is going on in literature and art, but they are off
the main highways of travel and very little comes to
them in the way of music, lectures and plays.

When I think of this vast country and these remote cities, with a few enlightened people here and
there, struggling to keep their minds alive, it seems
to me very pathetic. What poverty of opportunity,
and, in another sense, what wealth,—if one can maintain one's health of mind. These great towns were
not built with culture in view, or with any thought of
the sensitive minds of the later generations that have
risen in them. They were founded, as all towns have
been founded, since the dawn of history, by aggres-
sive, objective-minded men who were seeking an out-
let for their primitive forces; and everywhere strength
in time has given birth to sweetness, *ex forte dulci-
tudo,* the honey in the jaws of the lion. The intro-
verted poetic types have appeared and demanded
their place in the sun, and often, with some wealth
behind them, they have seen the world and known
men and cities before they have returned to the native
scene that always, whether we like it or not, controls
the deep source of our being. There is not an American town of consequence, however far-flung or abandoned, that does not contain a handful of persons
who, in their personal organization, their culture and
fineness of spirit, are the equals of anyone living.

There are flowers of all history in all these towns, as in the provincial towns of the old world,—in Parma, Lübeck, Cracow, Bergen, Sligo,—aristocrats of the mind, gentle souls, if any such exist on the planet.

One of the singular facts of American life, a result of the way in which the country was settled, is that the individual has evolved far beyond the society in which he lives. This is the case everywhere with the man of genius, but in America it is the case with the ordinary man of culture. With a little means, with native capacity, the individual of any race can place himself abreast of the first in the world; but it requires centuries of collective effort to produce a community of culture. Thus, while the man of genius is always a sport, whether in London or Paris, whether in Sioux City or Lincoln, Nebraska, with us the sensitive man that abounds in every third or fourth generation is also a sport in the same degree. His individual traits are as highly developed as the individual traits of similar men in the most developed communities. But his community is primitive; and thus he finds it as difficult to adapt himself to the ordinary life about him as a genius like Shelley or Poe. He feels that he is the heir of all the ages, and indeed, as a man, he is; but there is no communal life behind him of the sort his imagination demands and to which he almost feels entitled.

This tragedy of the superior type, so common in the undeveloped races, repeats itself every day in our undeveloped country. It is the tragedy of the developed person in the undeveloped environment. No wonder the American fiction of our time is saturated with sadness. Not a day goes by but some young man, in some remote corner of Tennessee, or of Idaho or Kansas, who has read all the poets, wakes up and

asks himself, as he surveys from his bedroom window the litter of wooden tents around his house,
"What am I doing in this galley?" A few years ago,
as a publisher's reader, I ran through a novel every
day that told me what this young man was thinking.
It seemed to me that the West and the South were
filled with young men and women, many of them obviously superior types, intelligent and humane in their
instincts, who could not understand and could scarcely
forgive the fate that had placed them in such surroundings. Just to escape from these towns and tell
the world how ugly, false and brutal they were seemed
to be almost the motive of these writers in living.
They were obsessed with ugly memories, ugly as to
material things and mostly as to spiritual; and I
smiled in their defence when I heard their elders say
they were neurotic. When a whole generation is neurotic, something is to blame; and one has to pursue
that something until one finds it.

I hope I can find it, but let me cut the knot for the
moment and go back to men like L. While they have
not chosen their dwelling-place, everything depends
on their staying there. The motives that underlay the
settlement of these regions could not conduce perhaps to a good immediate future. Granting this, however, as a *fait accompli,* one has to conclude that
these regions can only come right through the local
efforts of the superior types. They are kept there perhaps by necessity, not by choice,—by a family house,
connections, local means of support; and that they
are often unhappy might go without saying if it were
not so evident in their writings. But what is the philosophy of their situation?

Perhaps one might say, in the first place, that too
much freedom of choice is, in itself, not good. I agree

with the Quakers in this. I believe in action, not from conscious choice, but from an inner necessity. It seems to me that all my own fortunate actions have been dictated not so much by my conscious wishes as by a concurrence of other impulsions. It was not so much because I desired to act in such a way as because all the factors of my life, external as well as internal, seemed to say, This is not an arbitrary thing, this is the inevitable thing. When we consult our tastes alone, when we say, for instance, Why not go and live where it would be most pleasant for us to live?— we very often find we have made a mistake; for the inmost constitution of our natures is often at war with our tastes. That is why "going to live in Europe" has so often proved a fallacy, and that is why divorce is so often fallacious. Our constitution does not back up our impulse. Too much necessity crushes us, but the only guide we have is our sense of the *inevitable thing*.

Well, I think that, nine times out of ten, one feels the inevitable in Doudan's saying, *Il faut vivre, combattre et finir avec les siens*,—one must live, struggle and die among one's own. Allowing for all exceptions, this is one of the laws of existence; and what William James said about living in America is also true of our regions,—"Europe has been made what it is by men staying in their homes and fighting stubbornly, generation after generation, for all the beauty, comfort and order that they have got. We must abide and do the same." One may have the sense that one is only a coral-insect, toiling to build a reef; but even a coral-insect is better than one of those butterflies in October, which one sees hovering about the garden, mechanically poised over blossoms they seem to be enjoying, but which actually have no mouths or digestive organs. It is better to be a living fact than an optical illusion, better to be unhappy in Tennessee than a mouthless and meaningless phantom floating about the Riviera.

CHAPTER XXII

BEYOND NATIONALISM

I PASS without apology to another theme that was a favourite of Allston's. He said that the ideal of "sophistication" seemed to lead all others in the American mind, just as, to judge by the magazines, the secret of social elegance outweighed all other secrets in popular interest. Was not this the theme of all our advertising? (And beyond the magazines and the advertising, there was Edith Wharton. What was her touchstone, in *The House of Mirth,* if it was not simply the avoidance of the "dingy"?) Especially where writers were concerned, this struck him as childish. He said that, in regard to all such matters, Coleridge had laid down the law for writers: "The world in which I exist is another world indeed, but not to come."

What Allston deplored was the absence of this "other world," together with the presence of the mundane, in the minds of writers:

> What do I mean by "the world" (he says), when I speak of it as dangerous and hostile, as something to which one owes hostility and disdain? I do not mean necessarily fashion, sexual charm, etc. On the contrary, for enlightened people the world is a joy and a grace. It is only evil when we accept its values

as the ultimate values. For the real illuminati there are other values, and the world itself is a phantasmagoria. They feel as Pierre, in *War and Peace,* felt in the Slobodsky palace: "He suddenly felt that wealth and power and life, all that men build up and guard with such effort, is only worth anything through the joy with which it can all be cast away." That was Tolstoy's feeling from first to last.

The question is not, Do you enjoy the world and all the good things in it?—but, Is there something in the name of which you would throw all these good things to the winds? "All for love, and the world well lost" is the motto of artists and lovers alike. For them the first cockcrow of a faith or a conviction dispels the world as the nothing that it is.

This feeling lies behind all the greatest novels, which, when they deal with the world, are satirical from the outset. How swiftly, in *Smoke,* Turgenev disposes of the world! Balzac is one of several possible exceptions, but usually, in writers, when the world bears down too heavily, when the satirical vein does not run clear, as in Thackeray, Henry James and Proust, one feels the alloy of a base metal. It is not artist's gold, however the alloy is alembicated. If, as many feel, the Russian novel is the greatest of all novels, it is because all the Russian novelists have felt as Tolstoy felt.

He elaborates this point in a further passage:

I cannot call a writer great unless he sees the world as essentially phantasmagorical. For the great writer reality is a drama that he views from the outside, as the Lord and the Heavenly Host view the drama of Faust. So it was, for instance, in the mind of Cervantes, and Dickens had the writer's attitude towards the intrinsically mundane, which takes the world's values as the ultimate values. Of all the parts of reality, he saw the mundane as more grotesque even than the obviously grotesque, because, representing more power, under the sway of a false belief, it inevitably represented more distortion.

For this reason, if, among the parts of reality, some are more appealing to the writer than others, it is apt to be those that represent the least power, from the mundane point of view. For they evoke in the writer compassion, the response that is most natural to him. One feels an artistic rectitude in Dostoievsky's pity for the poor and the humble, as in Chekhov, Swift and Victor Hugo, which one does not feel in the furtive admiration of the worldly-successful in Thackeray and Henry James (full as James was of compassion for the *fashionable poor*). It appears that Dickens will outlive Thackeray, a much more accomplished writer, for some such reason.

Most of our living American novelists feel in this matter as I feel,—Ellen Glasgow, Steinbeck, Dos Passos, Hemingway, Farrell and Wolfe. They describe the irregularities of the so-called upper classes with an irony they never exhibit in the case of the dispossessed. They are consistently against the exploiter and against the selfishness of powerful persons. There are fifty reasons why they should be so, and, being so, they are artistically right.

Moreover, among painters, why are some peculiarly writers' painters?—Blake, Daumier, Hogarth, Goya, El Greco. Partly because of their compassion for the poor and the humble, because of their disdain of the mundane, their feeling, often intense, for the "other world." For some such reason, John Sloan is an American writers' painter; while Ryder, who

lived wholly in the other world, is our writers' painter
above all others.

The paragraphs that follow further explain Allston's
feeling:

The devotees of Henry James have been driven to
find for his later books a *raison d'être* outside the
aesthetic field, and they have discovered that he was
the "satirist of a greedy parasite class." There is a
will to believe. The satirist existed in James, but how
much is left of the satirist when one places in the bal-
ance the idolatrous admiration of more than half the
things he satirized? If the abuses of the world had
had only Henry Jameses to struggle against, where
would the world be now? It would still be hankering
after the old regime that Alfred the Great abolished.

James had enough perception of evil to wish to
satirize it, but he was confused by his admiration for
the objects of his satire. He retained his instinctive
awe of the forms of power that filled the horizon of
his adolescence and that never lost their glamour for
him,—there was in his soul too much of the butler,
guarding the sacrosanct household. In short, he never
grew up. Howells, less great as an artist, a writer of
less intensity, was more mature as a man. His point
of view, as it slowly developed, was that of the great
writers. That it did not develop enough is another
question.

I dwell on this matter of "the world" because it
indicates Allston's approach to more than one problem of life and letters. Thus he returns to the ideal
of "sophistication" which I have just mentioned:

Sophistication, as the word is used, is a state of
mind which consists in knowing too much and at the

same time knowing too little,—too much of the pe-
riphery of life, too little of the core and centre. It
expresses itself in a language of insinuation and is,
for the rest, a sort of cosmetic equivalent of wisdom
that is terrifying to the uninitiated. Of all the ways
in which the art of "putting it over" manifests itself
among our countrypeople, this is the most tragic; for
it prevents the instructed from learning anything
really important, and meanwhile it sets up a barrier
between simple folk and those who should be vehicles
of knowledge. To what is this unhappy condition
due? Partly to the extreme ingenuousness of so much
of our population, which gives rise to a constant
temptation to impose upon them; partly to the rarity
of the fully conscious, which tends to give these latter
an excessive conceit of themselves and of the importance of their "awareness;" partly again to the fact
that those who are conscious have owed their en-
lightenment too much to European associations. This
has destroyed their sense of obligation to their own
people; and it has also filled them with a light so
unrelated to their own experience as to be a mere
phosphorescence ("luminosity without combustion").
All this has happened before and elsewhere,—in Russia, for example, where Dostoievsky was always trying to humble the intellectuals. It happens with every
people that has failed to generate a conscious, characteristic life of its own. The intellectuals seek their
nourishment where they can, the result being that
they are improperly nourished and despise their own
flesh and blood as well.

As opposed to this ideal, Allston continues,—

We should speak less of sophistication and much
more of innocence, I mean the necessity of innocence

of which D. H. Lawrence spoke: "How to regain
the naive or innocent soul—how to make it the man
within man—your 'societal;' and at the same time
keep the cognitive mode for defences and adjust-
ments and 'work'!" We cannot tell how far we are
capable of this until we have ceased to preach know-
ingness. What painters call the "innocence of the
eye" belongs to the writer too; and how right Amiel
was in requiring naivety of a story-teller, saying,
"The novelist must be ingenuous, at least when his
pen is in his hand." He means the fresh heart that
can be surprised by things, that gift of "looking at
the world with eyes wide open in wonder," as Ortega
y Gasset puts it. All the great writers have had this,
and many of our writers have it, Sherwood Anderson, Saroyan, Thomas Wolfe. This was Whitman's
enormous gift, as it was Tolstoy's also. It is the
spring of all clear perception. Think of Blake's innocence, both of mind and character. The universal
man-of-the-world ideal, which tends to dominate our
modern writers, is altogether foreign to the artist's
nature.

Regarding "the world," he says further:

The world recognizes but one cause as worthy of
man's devotion, the cause that cannot fail, whether it
has man's devotion or not. Let us have nothing but
ideals, but woe to the ideal that is not already thrice
realized and armoured in triple brass.

He adds, a little later, with a resignation of which
I find few traces in his notes:

As truisms need no proofs, so the reigning fact
needs no advocates. It advocates itself twenty-four
hours every day. The intellectual man, if he follows

his instincts, will always throw what weight he has on the side of "lost causes, and forsaken beliefs, and unpopular names, and impossible loyalties."

The little tailor in Grimm got the best of the giants by convincing them that he had killed seven at a stroke. One might suppose from the seriousness with which the mighty organs of popular opinion combat the vicious tendencies of the radical critics, that our great lumbering civilization is as pathetically helpless as these giants. But the fairy-tale in question was a "wish-fulfillment" on the part of its peasant author. In real life, tailors are nothing but tailors, and critics are only critics. Change may come, and revolution, but upon the things that are dear to the world the sun never sets.

In other notes, Allston resumes his usual confidence, attacking the mundane mind and some of its fatuities. These had been especially evident after the first world-war, in the days of the "sun-tanned sophisticates." Many writers then regarded life as cheap and brief, and they placed an exaggerated value on the "civilized" living that concealed the emptiness behind it. I select notes on two of these writers:

There was much that I admired in Thomas Beer, but I think his feeling for values was decidedly shaky. In *The Mauve Decade,* he said that the "titaness," the rampageous female Philistine of the eighteen-nineties, was a natural outgrowth of *Little Women*. This is a *non sequitur*. Louisa Alcott's mind was like good bread; it was the staff of life; and the direct heirs of the Alcott doctrine are really the salt of the earth. The distortions of the distorted types were

produced by a thousand intermediate factors that
Thomas Beer left out of account.

By the same token, he called Emerson's funeral
"preposterous," apparently because Miss Alcott made
a lyre of jonquils to be placed on the grave. But what
would Thomas Beer have preferred in the way of a
village funeral? After all, we have to be buried, and
a few flowers do no harm. And babies and little girls
must have their bread and milk. Or did Thomas Beer
suppose that they ought to have champagne? A satirist who attacks the primary simplicities cannot get
very far; and it is surely an impotent form of wit
that tries to displace the normal. When the normal is
laughed out of court, wit has no relief. The function
of wit is the reverse of this. It is to displace the abnormal by giving the normal unexpected value. Anything else makes very tiresome reading.

In another note he speaks of Arnold Bennett and
one of Bennett's characteristic phrases,—"The subtle
ether which the truly civilized diner demands:"

These "civilized diners,"—how much we hear
about them! Why do I dislike this current popular
use of the harmless word "civilized," in the sense of
savoir vivre? It is not because I dislike *savoir vivre,*
but because it is used to indicate the *ne plus ultra* of
what one desires from life, and I feel that the *ne
plus ultra* should be something less accessible. Those
for whom *savoir vivre* is a desideratum to this extent must have had little experience of this state of
being; and this, no doubt, explains the use of the
term "civilized." It is a phrase that has only come
into use at a time when large areas of the population are in process of rising socially and when that
which is taken for granted on the upper levels has

become an attainable object for those who have been below. The newly arrived exaggerate its value. After five thousand years of civilization, one must be very unexacting to preen oneself on an art that so many have inherited, as they have inherited their hands and feet.

Regarding this passion for the "civilized," Miss Willa Cather says shrewdly, in her story, *Paul's Case:* "Perhaps it was because, in Paul's world, the natural nearly always wore the guise of ugliness, that a certain element of artificiality seemed to him necessary in beauty. Perhaps it was because his experience of life elsewhere was so full of Sabbath-school picnics, petty economies, wholesale advice as to how to succeed in life, and the unescapable odours of cooking, that he found this existence so alluring, these smartly-clad men and women so attractive."

This explains the "civilized diners," Bennett and his American companions. And how many other things it also explains in the literature of the moment! One should regard them as pathetic, and I do indeed so regard them. But to this I must add a further word. Worldly people who are also wise have always known what place in the scheme of things their worldly accomplishments rightly occupy. They have worn their hair-shirts, like Philip the Second. They have offered their libations to the gods, for they know on what tenuous terms their good fortune exists. They have recognized, in other words, other values than their own, though they may not live by these values. If one must have worldly people, I prefer those who are well-seasoned. But I have small interest in worldly people, even from the point of view of manners. There are unworldly people who do everything better.

He adds:

> I often enjoy men of the world, but the men I love are men of the over-world.

He returns to the word "civilized" in another note:

> A "civilized book for civilized readers." This phrase is so tiresome because it insists on a value that mature readers take for granted. It is an outgrowth of the constant preoccupation of reviewers with "uncivilized" books and people. A critic should project his civilization into his hypothetical audience, taking it for granted that they are like himself. By this means only can he become an agent of civilization.

Elsewhere he says of Arnold Bennett:

> I do not like Arnold Bennett's brutal avidity for material things. I like it still less because many of my fellow-Americans share it. It leads to many foolish notions. Thus, for instance, Bennett said, and how many of my countrymen agree: "Nothing is more likely to foster the production of first-rate artists than the existence of a vast machinery for winning money and glory."
>
> Arnold Bennett was speaking of the theatre, and of this remark I can only say, with the movie-director, "Of course, it isn't stupendous; it is only colossal on a small scale." The Vieux Colombier Theatre, the Abbey Theatre players and the Moscow Art players,—by far the three best I have seen,— prove just the opposite.

In the brief notes that follow, Allston refers to other "illusions of the sophisticated:"

> *A well-connected man.* I once knew a man, well-connected in New York, who bore the name of a

great Spanish painter. I asked him if he was related to the Spanish painter. "O yes," he said, "he was a distant cousin, but he belonged to the peasant branch of the family."

People who have not hearts to be hurt should always be treated to plain words. A detached, harsh or ironical tone is the only one to adopt in the presence of the arrogant and brutal, and of the shrewdly worldly. Persons of these types deserve all our missionary efforts in the language they understand.

"Arrogance is worse than a hundred concubines," as Erasmus heard Dean Colet say to his clergy.

All the empires fall through arrogance. Contempt is the principle of all disunion.

The empires all end like the Duke of Alva, who was so weakened at seventy that he was forced to sustain himself on milk, which he drank from a woman's breast.

I believe in force, but only against the strong; irony, but against the arrogant.

Soften the callosities; but, if the creature is a pachyderm, do not spare the whips and scorpions.

By what process of association I scarcely know, the following note seems to me also germane. Allston was spending some weeks at Saint Augustine:

Saw, many times, two large sharks sedately sailing along under their dorsal fins close inshore at Anastasia Island.

Is it possible that sharks and rattlesnakes have nightmares in their sleep, in which they have to feel they are something else, and then wake up again to the delicious realization that they still have their jaws and rattles?

CHAPTER XXIII

NOTES ON STYLE

LET me assemble a few of Allston's notes on literary style and method. I shall not organize them closely, but one who reads between the lines will feel, I think, a certain continuity in them. I begin with a passage describing what Allston meant by the phrase *great writing:*

> Great prose like Bach's music, in texture closely woven, subdued like the early Gobelin tapestries, no emphasis, no climaxes, no beginnings or endings, merely resumptions and transitions, a mind so sustained that there is no effort in starting and every casual utterance is equally great.

> Knowing such work, how can one fail to demand it, how can one fail to grieve that one does not possess it?

> Certainly I like "direct writing," and the contemporary writers who developed this style performed a valuable function. They were reacting against the indirectness of their weak predecessors. But I think direct writing has fulfilled its purpose; and I feel as B. Z. felt when he turned against "direct painting," which conveyed a mere "emotional reaction." He had been reading a German book on the technical methods of the old masters, and he was surprised to discover that Rubens painted even more rapidly, that he could finish a picture in a day or two, by building up his work on a

basis of under-painting. So, as against direct writing, I believe in the study of syntax, the feeling for etymology and all the rest, which give such solidity, density and depth of tone to the old masters of literature. And why should one have to choose between depth and directness?

But of course depth presupposes another mode of feeling. One has to be a Bach before one can write in the manner of Bach. Depth of style can only spring from a deepening of our emotional life. That is what I really demand and look for.

In short, what concerned Allston was a change in the life behind writing, and some of his comments on style referred to this. In the following passage, he attacked one of the popular fallacies that caused the inferiority of so much of our writing:

Americans do indeed like the flat, shallow, pasty product which so very much of our literature is. It is their native element, and they like it, as they like soft drinks and factory-made bread. Intensity, distinction, fire and what I call sincerity, these they do not like and will not have, unless they come with a foreign *cachet*.

To me all this is proof conclusive of the fallacy of the theory that journalism is a good school for writers. It is a universal American belief, and the teachers of composition propagate it. This is the "seeing life" theory, and perhaps the reason why the teachers overvalue it is because they have seen so little of life. However this may be, the belief has prevailed ever since Kipling made it popular, ever since Zola, with his attractive method of getting subjects "up," after the fashion of the reporter, became the god of American realism.

Most of our novelists and playwrights have been, in this sense, followers of Kipling and Zola. And what is the result? An all too general commonness in point of view. Vivid reports, but no distinction of mind, especially no nobility of mind, such as gave to Dostoievsky's *The House of the Dead* a value that the vividest reporting cannot confer on a novel. All the obvious advantages of the journalistic training cannot compensate, in my opinion, for the vulgarizing associations of the journalistic life; and I say this although I know half a dozen journalists who have in no sense been vulgarized. In fiction, as in everything else, nothing matters in the long run but the personal culture of the mind behind it. That is why, although I admire Zola and Dreiser, as men of genius and feeling and as lovers of justice, I still believe that Hawthorne is worth a dozen Dreisers, and Flaubert half a dozen Zolas.

To somewhat the same effect is the following note:

The characteristic American style suggests a plethora of stimulus. It is spiced and "pepped" to a degree that reminds one of the abnormal flush of the consumptive patient. And, in fact, these writers burn themselves out. They write to be overheard in the noise of the subway or to score in a crowded room where everyone is chattering. Their foot is always on the loud pedal, and of course they soon become tiresome. Hence the holocaust of American writers that takes place every few years, when the last "younger generation" is kicked upstairs or out and a new younger generation swarms in at the door.

The style that lasts, the good style that has resources behind it, almost never resorts to the loud pedal. It unconsciously avoids the clever phrase, unless the phrase is more than clever, together with every sort of emphasis, and is therefore never tiresome.

Most of the characteristic modern styles, in music and painting as well as writing, take for granted the "law of acceleration" that Henry Adams described. But to take such laws of the outer world for granted, in the sense of adjusting one's rhythm to them, is to be a goose by definition. As the great composers prevail in the end, over the composers of the moment, in the midst of an accelerated world, so it is with writers. The type of American writers who have prevailed, over and through the "jazz age," are those for whom the age has existed but not the jazz in the age. Those who have accepted the "law of acceleration" have perished by this law. They obeyed the rule of the subway, "Step lively." They who were so afraid to see the door slammed in their faces have seen the door slammed on their backs.

Other notes are more or less connected with this:

In everything that concerns writing, I prefer the low tone, no emphasis, no italics, as few exclamations as possible, understatement, irony and humour as unobtrusive as may be. I like a style that never calls attention to itself. No goods in the shop window. A light that is hid under a bushel. As much dynamite as possible, but packed in a box labelled "harmless." As much "rapture" as may be, but under a sober coat.

Of the praise of neologisms, the promiscuous coining of words, as if it meant initiative and daring, new and fresh life, strength and courage, I say that it more often means laziness and shallowness. The wish to explore and use existing resources is the mark of a sound economy. This habit of easy neologism is all of a piece with our hasty ways in agriculture, our trial marriages and our constant moving. It is a pioneer habit, like the rest.

It is the fashion to decry taste as a superficial thing, but taste is more important than some people think. Many a time I have heard a good reader, one of the sort that writers ought to cherish, say of some author of the moment, "Of course, he has plenty of ideas, but he has such bad taste." In other words, "I cannot and will not read him." If some of our writers were only aware of the handicap under which they labour, they would take this question seriously and try to learn the laws which they offend. We have dozens of talented writers who are wholly in the dark in regard to their failure to receive recognition. They are in the position of the girl of whom the advertisers make so much, who cannot understand why it is that the young men do not flock about her. They are always aggrieved, and they never learn.

We can impugn our friends for every fault, and they will take it good-naturedly. But let us for a moment impugn their taste, and their self-esteem is up in arms. In real life the friends of the girl in the advertisements seldom take her aside and whisper the awful secret in her ear. The advertising men are not so squeamish, nor should criticism be. Our criticism, almost wholly concerned with ideas, and with more technical questions, makes too little of taste. But although, without taste, a writer may win the great public, he will never win the little public that gives the great prizes, but only to those who speak its language.

In the following notes Allston refers to another vulgar error, that of the "unintelligible" writers. He starts with a comment on a well-known author whose style he found extremely irritating:

I am struck by the arrogance of this author. He offers me his book, not personally but through his pub-

lisher, and slaps me in the face for reading it. He is
ill-advised. Authors have often complained of the public, the "many-headed beast," but they have been
shrewd enough to convey to the person who reads
them that he too has suffered from the beast. The
author of this book conveys no such feeling, so flat-
tering to the reader's self-esteem. He remains in a
minority of one, and this is a dangerous position. One
can be a private minority simply by holding one's peace,
but when one becomes a public minority one must have
a caucus and a vote. This author, like every author,
if his ideas are to be considered, depends to some extent on his electors. What does he represent *in them,*
which they can feel sure that he represents? He can
attack the majority as much as he likes, but when he
attacks his own minority the minority in question feels
inclined to vote for someone else.

Great writers are often solitary, but in a different
fashion. They are alone with the Alone. This author
is a minority-party who does not follow the rules of
parties. He is in serious danger of losing the next
election.

In addition to slapping his readers in the face, this
author had not troubled to make himself clear. All
ston was annoyed by this wilful unintelligibility:

The poet Cowper remarked that he could not imagine a man writing without the idea of being read. This
is a point of common sense, and we cannot ignore it in
face of the writers of our day who seem to be so anxious not to communicate their thoughts. In their desire, which is natural enough, not to coöperate with a
vulgarized public, they exclude even the judicious public, to their own great loss. For surely the good will of
the judicious public is one of the prerequisites of good
writing; and a writer who ignores this fact, for what-

ever reason, finds himself, as Melville put it, "bombinating *in vacuo*." So necessary is this coöperation that Vernon Lee well described writing as "the craft of manipulating the contents of the reader's mind."

The good writer of prose stands to his reader in the relation of an interlocutor. He must therefore be a master of the social virtues. The response of the reader completes the work of literary art, and writing loses its sociality, and therewith its completeness, when the writer cannot feel this response from without. It is no accident that the French, the most social of races, are also the greatest masters of prose; and, considering the chaos of our society, it is natural that our writers should be so generally wanting in the social virtues. It is natural that we should lack the serenity and clarity, not to mention the tact, discrimination and grace, with which one becomes endowed only through the habitual presence of exacting but sympathetic listeners. All the more reason then to seek for these listeners and to cultivate the social virtues,—and what can be said for writers who cultivate the opposite and wish, at all costs, to bar us out? And why do they wish it, for that matter? Why do they wish to throw dust in our eyes? Because their personalities are so insufficient that they cannot afford to expose them. If they were intelligible, we should soon see how small they are. "How many authors," said André Gide, "have no personality that would not be lost in the mass of humanity on the day when they consented to use *who's* and *which's* as everybody else does?" These writers are of the kind which, as Gil Blas said, only deceive their own generation. Yet they are permitted to talk one another into fame. They have a way of referring to one another as if not to know of them were to inhabit perpetual night.

Allston continues:

Rhetoric is the social element of style, and this explains why so many young writers abhor it. That rhetoric is humbug is a fixed idea with them, as the omnipresence of humbug is a fixed idea. They regard relative pronouns as capital offenders, *agents provocateurs* and interlopers in their bitter guerrilla warfare with the public mind which they detest. This is one of the new vulgar errors of which the literary mind must rid itself. For a just conception of human nature, and the true relations of sham and reality, one cannot read too often the ancient authors, and one might recommend the same procedure in regard to the question of rhetoric. No one who reads them can hold the puerile notions of rhetoric that prevail in our generation. The ancients would have made short work of the cult of the anti-social that lies behind the cult of mystification and the modern hatred of rhetoric. All the great literary ages have exalted the study of rhetoric.

I add a few scattered notes on style:

For style, I like Nietzsche's saying, "Everything divine runs with light feet."

But I like many styles, including the florid. My friend T., talking on the street-corner, scornfully pointed to the gutter. He said that all the authors of the nineteenth century belonged there. Away with Dickens, George Eliot, Ruskin and De Quincey! Too many flourishes, too many words,—they were all blubber. (Though it goes without saying that he retained the fashionable admiration for Melville, who was perhaps the wordiest of all.) Well, I say that floridity represents emotional fullness, albeit an excess and abuse of fullness; and emotional fullness is a great virtue.

Mannerism is the sign of a second-rate mind; pride in mannerism is the sign of a third-rate mind.

The hideous verb *to contact*. How symptomatic it is that this came into use, that people felt the need of it, in our period of chaos, when so many thousands are lost in the world and seek relationships which they cannot find. *To contact* is the dream of all these beings, who are universally "out of touch." One of the little magazines was called *Contact,* for the same reason and with the same desire.

While Allston was a stickler for American usage in words, he preferred the so-called English spelling, which he followed in his books. On this point he says:

Our standard authors are quite inconsistent in the matter of spelling. In *The Scarlet Letter,*—the second edition, which I have, and which was presumably proofread by Hawthorne himself, no doubt at the post-office, as his custom was,—I find on a single page "neighbour" spelled with a *u* and "honored" spelled without it. Elsewhere in the same volume, "colored" and "favored" are spelled as I write them, while "demeanour" has the *u*. Howells's novels are similarly inconsistent, some adhering to the English spelling, others to the American, as if, between the two, he could never make up his mind. Thus, so far as usage goes, the question remains optional; but I note that, among our living standard authors, Ellen Glasgow, Willa Cather and Robert Frost more or less consistently use the English spelling.

I explain my preference with an illustration. Everyone writes "glamour" even now. Who has ever heard of a "glamor girl"? Why? Because the *u* is part of the glamour. But the word "honour" has glamour also. All good words have glamour for me.

Allston believed that no one should ever publish a book until he has read it aloud to a woman. He was delighted with a letter of Madame Roland, written about 1790, which explained his reason: "Do you know that Massachusetts is a very barbarous name? And that a man of fashion was never known to utter such a word when saying soft things to the fair sex? I have heard of a lady who was so shocked at the sound of Transylvania, which was quite new to her, that she desired the impertinent speaker to leave the room." On this he comments as follows:

> I protest on behalf of Massachusetts, but the principle stands. (And even regarding Massachusetts, the French still have their rights. Léon Bazalgette, who said he could not bear this word, but who was obliged to use it, wrote "Le Mass.") Women are the arbiters of words, and we should listen to them because they live close to the meanings of words. Men become infatuated with words themselves. Women are closer to the general life, the source of good style, while men tend to live the particular life, the source of bad style. So women will never allow you to say "obfuscate" when "bewilder" will do just as well; and they shiver at words like "historicity" and will not be comforted if you use them.
>
> Is not this the reason why French prose is so generally good, and why German prose would be better if the Germans respected women more? The badness of German prose is a judgment on the Germans for their lack of respect for women.

CHAPTER XXIV

A FINAL MISCELLANY

IN THIS chapter I collect a few notes on books and writing, offering them without pretence of order. I begin with a handful of brief remarks:

It is difficult to understand living writers because they are involved in our own problems, which we cannot solve for ourselves.

What we call insincerity is the expression of thoughts that do not go to the bottom of our own minds.

Irony is the mortar with which one fills the space between the partial and the universal.

It is not that the French are not profound, but they all express themselves so well that we are led to take their geese for swans.

Fabre's books on insects,—why are they so fascinating? Because of the ghastly sidelights they throw on human life, the relief into which they cast our own instincts and habits, comparable to that of the theatre.

A generation lasts thirty years, or five, as we say in America. Who form the next generation? Not those who bask complacently in this, although they must have one foot in it in order to make the transition.

"The women lived it, the men wrote about it," Rudolph Ruzicka said of the German romantic movement. This is true of all movements.

One has to be interested in England to enjoy Anthony Trollope, but to enjoy Balzac all one needs is to be interested in life.

"Nowadays everything grows old in a few hours; reputation fades, a work passes away in a moment. Everybody writes; nobody reads seriously." I record this in 1936, but it was written in 1836, just a hundred years ago (by Chateaubriand, in *Sketches of English Literature*).

"Democracy in economics, aristocracy in thought." I like this phrase of A. E. My political creed is based on the assumption that everybody ought to be given a chance. My literary creed is based on the assumption that few will ever take the chance.

Some writers have a tendentious importance that is quite aside from any intrinsic importance. I can think of two living writers, one of whom cannot write and the other has nothing to say, yet who, in the history of our time, will have their place, for they represent tendencies of feeling, characteristic of the time, which the more important writers have not expressed at all.

"*The Genteel Tradition.*" This phrase has had too long a run. It has been stretched in so many directions that it is as useless as an old elastic. One cannot bear too heavily on suggestive phrases, and one grows heartily sick of such phrases as this when they have been used three times. Besides, the writers who use this phrase confound the genteel with the noble. They will be calling Marcus Aurelius genteel next.

Of the ubiquitous "short story" courses in our schools and colleges, there is this to be said, that they tend to destroy the audience of literature. They do so by promoting into "writers," and often opinionative and dogmatic writers, the susceptible but uncreative persons who might otherwise be the best readers.

The psychology of the literary "cult." The devotees of an author,—I mean the kind of author who has devotees, such as Oscar Wilde or Henry James,—differ from those who admire him in the ordinary way. They differ in this, that they always possess the defects of their idol. By means of this idol they worship themselves and find excuses for their own shortcomings.

These two notes refer to the "younger generation:"

A seed-catalogue,—Stumpp and Walter's,—says that if you wish to develop new and beautiful varieties, you must save the weak seedlings. The strongest seedlings are pretty certain to run true to type.

The writers who frighten us most are those who are twenty years younger than we. All our real scares come from the younger writers, not from the older. The younger writers represent the future, and then I suppose one half-consciously feels that one is getting fat and stupid and ought to be sent back to the button-moulder.

For the rest, among writers there are no ages.

(I should add that the phrase, the "younger generation," was one that Allston never used. All generations are alike, he said, when they are "younger," beginning with the one to which he belonged; and all the "older" generations have said the same things about them. What could one add to the comment of Pliny the Younger, when he had become the "older"? —Allston said that it fairly described himself and his friends at twenty-one: "From their cradles they know everything, they understand everything; they have no regard for anybody, pay no attention to anybody and are themselves the only models which they are disposed to follow."—*Letters,* VIII, 23.)

The three following phrases refer to three writers, an Englishman, a Scotchman, an Irishman:

With all that can and will be said of Kipling,—and much will be said, for he was a great writer,—we cannot forget that, in his biblical argot, he invented the thieves' slang of imperialism.

Stevenson always writes as if he were talking with a woman who admires him. It is this that gives him his air of conscious heroism.

A. E. wrote out of the paternal instinct, as Walt Whitman wrote out of the fraternal instinct. All the readers of his prose must have felt that he had somehow lived for them, that he had made himself responsible for their welfare.

Some of these other brief remarks seem to refer to particular writers:

According to Coleridge, it is no decisive mark of genius that a man should write well concerning himself. This cannot be ignored in any discussion of the many autobiographical novelists of our time.

A writer is important not by the amount of territory he enters or claims, but by the amount he colonizes. Tolstoy and Balzac fill all the space they occupy. They do not merely lie, like Milton's Satan, full many a rood prone on the flood.

His nature is so buried under the crust of a journalistic success that he has no strong feelings or discriminations. His swans and his geese are all alike, cooked in the same pot of jokes and money.

His mind is a sort of marsh into which you might sink waist-deep without striking any solid bottom.

His writing always reminds me of a man skating. He seems to be skating all over that beautiful smooth ice, in graceful circles, but never getting anywhere, not even cutting the ice.

This writer reminds me of the Pasha's remark, in Kinglake's *Eothen,* marvelling over the ways of the Europeans, "Whirr! Whirr! All by wheels! Whiz! Whiz! All by steam!"

Here are two notes on Thoreau:

It was easy for Thoreau to like winter. All the winter colours that depress other people, the so-called drab and dreary colours, the browns and iron greys, suggested to him the moral traits that constituted his conception of beauty.

Thoreau has become with time a world-classic. Henry James said of him, echoing Lowell, "He is worse than provincial, he is parochial;" but we have seen his essays paraded before all mankind as the *vade mecum* of Gandhi, the greatest spiritual leader of our time. If there was, however, in Thoreau's nature an element of the really parochial, which still irritates me, was this not the result of an excellent cause? It was due to an over-determination that met the facts of his place and moment. He had to resist the migratory tendencies of other Americans,—the drag westward of the pioneering impulse and the drag towards Europe of the cultivated classes. He knew how hostile these impulses were to the personal growth he lived for; and, feeling this, he could not take Concord for granted. He was driven to insist upon it a little too much.

I pass to a few longer notes:

These novelists are such children. They are story-
tellers, at bottom, whose true place is the nursery;
and, if they depart too far from this primitive function, they may become valuable as something else but
they are not good novelists. I sympathize with Renan's
complaint, "The mistake the novelists make is in thinking that people have the time to read them."

It is true, if we do not read them we do not know
the world we live in, well as we may know life. But
novelists must take their law from the saints and sages,
as Dickens and Thackeray took their law from Carlyle, as Tolstoy took his from the Gospel. When they
become a law unto themselves, as modern novelists
are prone to do, we feel that they do not know their
place.

We have had more than enough of what Wyndham
Lewis called the "cult of the savage and the child."
The cult of *Huckleberry Finn* is the cult of both; yet,
according to Mencken, this is our only classic, and
Hemingway says, "It's the best book we have. All
American writing comes from that."

I think I understand Huck Finn, and I love the
poetry amid which he sits enthroned like an unkempt
cherub on a summer cloud. Moreover, I know how he
feels,—when, for instance, I have been in an air-con-
ditioned library, where I cannot put my feet on the
table, where I cannot smoke or even cough, then I
long for the rags and the salubrious barrel. I resent
this life at "the widow's," where one has to wash and
comb one's hair, all so "cramped up and smothery,"
and I long for the raft, where one feels so comfortable
and so easy and free. I long to light out for the territory, where there are no Aunt Sallies to civilize me;
and I almost understand how Mencken can say that

his discovery of *Huckleberry Finn* was the most stupendous event of his life.

But I reflect that life on the raft would not be so good if someone had not civilized the Mississippi or made it only picturesquely bad. If it had been the resort of savages and panthers only, Huck would not have felt so free and easy. Huck Finn's freedom was only possible because the way had been cleared for him by men who had struggled for his freedom.

Huckleberry Finn is unique as a book of boys, for boys, by a boy. But, if it were our only classic, would it not be sad that a boy should be our Faust and our Don Quixote? Especially when we have had a Leather-Stocking?

Ernest Hemingway. Half of our novelists are boys, determined to remain boys. They will not hear of any other prospect.

Du Maurier's Marty Josselin wrote a story about three naughty boys who "ran away to sea, dog and all; and performed heroic deeds in Central Africa, and grew up there, 'booted and bearded and burnt to a brick,' and never married or fell in love, or stooped to any nonsense of that kind."

This was a little girl's dream in late Victorian times. But this is the dream of real novelists in our generation.

The Primitive. My forbears were savages two thousand years ago. I like to think of their human traits, and I know these were many and charming; and what I most admire in them was their disposition to improve themselves. If they had not improved themselves, they would not have won the admiration of other savages, over whom they sometimes prevailed. They respected this trait in themselves, as I gather from their respect for their chiefs, who had improved themselves the most; and what they most desired was that they should develop, and that their sons should develop beyond them. For scores of generations my forbears strove for these ends, and I do not like to regard them as mistaken or foolish; and this, in regard to the primitive, governs my feeling. The more I admire the primitive, the more I am forced not to believe in the primitive. The primitive itself believes in the developed. In this sense I am primitive also.

What one really admires is the fundamental. This is common to the primitive and the developed, and often the primitive has it where the developed lacks it. But where the developed has it, the developed prevails, for it has its development also.

"Time-provincialism." Half the energy of Americans in the last two generations has been spent in trying to escape from provinciality. They have done their best to ape some dimly conceived aristocracy; they have struggled to place themselves at Matthew Arnold's "centre." But provinciality of place is not the only provinciality. There is also "time-provincialism," in Professor Whitehead's phrase. ("Men can be provincial in time as well as in place.") Those who have jumped out of Mencken's "boobery" have jumped into this frying-pan, and they feel that they are obliged to keep up with some hypothetical "minute," as if to follow the mode were more important than any of the great realities of life and death. Is not this what Ezra Pound means by "awareness-to-the-present"? Authors who are up to the minute, or who represent the last minute, mean much more to them than they mean to me.

In other times people were just as eager to keep up with Dickens and Thackeray, or with Smollett and Sterne. But they also kept up with Don Quixote, the

Bible and Homer. This gave them equipoise and a standard of value; and did they understand their times less well? Of course, they understood their times far better.

How odd it is that people have come to connect the classics with privilege, that the classics are regarded as "snobbish." Max Eastman pretends that because the word "classic" was used by the Romans to mean "classy,"—appertaining to the work of men who were property-owners,—it has not come to mean in two thousand years something wholly different, which alone counts for us. The only book I inherited from one of my grandfathers was a well-conned copy of Plutarch, which he had read as a farmer's boy; and this was rather the rule than the exception in our old American life of the country. Our modern wooden wagon-wheel was invented by a New Jersey farmer, who had found an exact description of it in Homer. It was Thomas Jefferson who recorded this fact, when the invention was claimed for an Englishman, and he proved that it was true. (With equal truth he added that the American farmers were "the only farmers who can read Homer," inasmuch as most European farmers were peasants.)

So the classics will never seem "classy" to me; and democracy in fact was conceived in an aura of the classics, as much in America as in France. The American revolutionists and the French revolutionists met on the common ground of the Greeks and the Romans; and even long years later in France, at the time of the Restoration, it was the liberals and radicals who stood by the classics (just as our Abolitionists stood by them). The royalists were all for liberty in literature, while those who stood for liberty in life upheld the strictest forms in literature. They maintained the classical forms and the classical themes, for the classical themes defended liberty, and the classical forms were the most effective. Was not this what Lucien de Rubempré found when he arrived in Paris?

Sentimental democrats may disregard the classics, but those for whom democracy is based on certain principles will find them where Thomas Paine found them.

Literature, properly speaking, has three dimensions, but, instead of describing these as length, breadth and thickness, I should call them breadth, depth and elevation. Most great writers have had these three dimensions, but few of our modern writers have more than two. Thus Dreiser and O'Neill have breadth and depth, but no elevation. Sinclair Lewis and Mencken have breadth, but no elevation and little depth. Willa Cather has little breadth, but some depth and much elevation. Frost and E. A. Robinson, who are both deep and elevated, have still less breadth than Willa Cather. So it goes. The rarest dimension in our literature at present is elevation, which three generations ago was the chief dimension possessed by several writers. Thus the American mind swings to extremes. The time has come round for elevation, and I hope it will not be abused.

(More or less connected with this, I find another brief note: " 'Stream of consciousness,' yes, but not a mountain stream,—no, a Venetian canal, not without its dead cats and decomposing cabbages. Mountain streams are out of fashion. Nevertheless, they continue to flow.")

We wonder why the lives of the saints are so fabulous, why worthies of the dark ages appear so distorted in history. But what happens in our own en-

lightened age? Wait till you lose by death some
eminent friend, and then go about in the circles he frequented and try to piece together the legend of his
life. You will find that he survives in the minds of his
associates as both a sentimentalist and a cynic, a crim-
son revolutionist and a sky-high tory, a simpleton, a
snob and a bourgeois, a man of bold ideas and a teacher's pet. All these at once, and all revealing what?—
the little serpents and the little doves that every circle
of friends cherishes in its bosom. Rare is the rectitude
of the realistic eye, quite as rare in our age of light as
it was in the ages of darkness. Did we not see Senator
Lodge construct before our eyes the myth of Theodore Roosevelt as the classic statesman, who never
swerved from principle and never acted on any but
second thoughts? One can live in the centre of the
world, in a complicated web of social relations, and
still remain as invisible as a snake in the grass.

I end with one further reflection:

The tough-minded and the tender-minded, as William James put it,—these are the great incompatibles.

I cannot get on with tender-minded people. I like
tender hearts, but I like tough minds, those whom we
used to call hard-headed. The life of the heart thrives
when people are hard-headed, while the tender-
minded play into the hands of the tough in heart.
When people's heads are soft, their hearts grow hard.

It is the tough-minded who achieve the hopes and
aims of the tender in heart.

INDEX